The English Governess
at the Siamese Court

THE SUPREME KING.

THE

ENGLISH GOVERNESS

AT

THE SIAMESE COURT:

BEING

RECOLLECTIONS OF SIX YEARS IN THE ROYAL
PALACE AT BANGKOK.

BY

ANNA HARRIETTE LEONOWENS.

𝔚ith 𝔦llustrations,
FROM PHOTOGRAPHS PRESENTED TO THE AUTHOR BY THE
KING OF SIAM.

OXFORD
UNIVERSITY PRESS

OXFORD
UNIVERSITY PRESS

Oxford   New York

Athens   Auckland   Bangkok   Bogotá   Buenos Aires   Calcutta
Cape Town   Chennai   Dar es Salaam   Delhi   Florence   Hong Kong   Istanbul
Karachi   Kuala Lumpur   Madrid   Melbourne   Mexico City   Mumbai
Nairobi   Paris   São Paulo   Singapore   Taipei   Tokyo   Toronto   Warsaw

and associated companies in
Berlin   Ibadan

First published by Oxford University Press, Inc., 1988

Oxford is a registered trademark of Oxford University Press

ISBN 0-19-588897-9 (Pbk.)

3 5 7 9 10 8 6 4 2

Printed in the United States of America

PREFACE.

HIS Majesty, Somdetch P'hra Paramendr Maha Mongkut, the Supreme King of Siam, having sent to Singapore for an English lady to undertake the education of his children, my friends pointed to me. At first it was with much reluctance that I consented to entertain the project; but, strange as it may seem, the more I reflected upon it the more feasible it appeared, until at length I began to look forward, even with a glow of enthusiasm, toward the new and untried field I was about to enter.

The Siamese Consul at Singapore, Hon. W. Tan Kim-Ching, had written strongly in my favor to the Court of Siam, and in response I received the following letter from the King himself : —

"ENGLISH ERA, 1862, 26th February.
GRAND ROYAL PALACE, BANGKOK.

"To MRS. A. H. LEONOWENS : —

"MADAM: We are in good pleasure, and satisfaction in heart, that you are in willingness to undertake the education of our beloved royal children. And we hope that in doing your education on us and on our children (whom English call inhabitants of benighted land) you will do your best endeavor for knowledge of English language, science, and literature, and not for conversion to Christianity ; as the followers of Buddha are mostly aware of the powerfulness of truth and virtue, as well as the followers of Christ, and are desirous to have facility of English language and literature, more than new religions.

" We beg to invite you to our royal palace to do your best endeavorment upon us and our children. We shall expect to see you here on return of Siamese steamer Chow Phya.

" We have written to Mr. William Adamson, and to our consul at Singapore, to authorize to do best arrangement for you and ourselves.

" Believe me
" Your faithfully,
(Signed) " S. S. P. P. MAHA MONGKUT."

About a week before our departure for Bangkok, the captain and mate of the steamer Rainbow called upon me. One of these gentlemen had for several years served the government of Siam, and they came to warn me of the trials and dangers that must inevitably attend the enterprise in which I was embarking. Though it was now too late to deter me from the undertaking by any arguments addressed to my fears, I can nevertheless never forget the generous impulse of the honest seamen, who said : " Madam, be advised even by strangers, who have proved what sufferings await you, and shake your hands of this mad undertaking." By the next steamer I sailed for the Court of Siam.

In the following pages I have tried to give a full and faithful account of the scenes and the characters that were gradually unfolded to me as I began to understand the language, and by all other means to attain a clearer insight into the secret life of the court. I was thankful to find, even in this citadel of Buddhism, men, and above all women, who were "lovely in their lives;" who, amid infinite difficulties, in the bosom of a most corrupt society, and enslaved to a capricious and often cruel will, yet devoted themselves to an earnest search after truth. On the other hand, I have to confess with sorrow and shame, how far we, with all our boasted enlightenment, fall short, in true nobility and piety, of some of our "benighted" sisters of the East. With many of them, Love, Truth, and Wisdom are not mere synonyms but "living gods," for whom they long with lively ardor, and, when found, embrace with joy.

Those of my readers who may find themselves interested in the wonderful ruins recently discovered in Cambodia are indebted to the earlier travellers, M. Henri Mouhot, Dr. A. Bastian, and the able English photographer, James Thomson, F. R. G. S. L., almost as much as to myself.

To the Hon. George William Curtis of New York, and to all my other true friends, abroad and in America, I feel very grateful.

And finally, I would acknowledge the deep obligation I am under to Dr. J. W. Palmer, whose literary experience and skill have been of so great service to me in revising and preparing my manuscript for the press.

A. H. L.

CONTENTS.

LIST OF ILLUSTRATIONS.

———◆———

MRS. KATHERINE S. COBB.

I HAVE not asked your leave, dear friend, to dedicate to you these pages of my experience in the heart of an Asiatic court; but I know you will indulge me when I tell you that my single object in inscribing your name here is to evince my grateful appreciation of the kindness that led you to urge me to try the resources of your country instead of returning to Siam, and to plead so tenderly in behalf of my children.

I wish the offering were more worthy of your acceptance. But to associate your name with the work your cordial sympathy has fostered, and thus pleasantly to retrace even the saddest of my recollections, amid the happiness that now surrounds me, — a happiness I owe to the generous friendship of noble-hearted American women, — is indeed a privilege and a compensation.

I remain, with true affection, gratitude, and admiration,

Your friend,

A. H. L.

26th July, 1870.

Amarindr Winschsry
Palace Banshon
March 6th 1869

To

Mrs A. H. Leonowens
New York

Dear Madam.

I have great pleasure
in condescending to answer
your sympathising letter
of 25th Nov last wherein the
sorrowful expressions of your
heart in relation to my most
beloved Sovereign Father
in demise which is a venerated
burden and I have till to
this day and ever more. shall

bear this most unexpressible
loss in mind, with the deepest
respect and lamentation,
and resignation to the will
of divine Providence; — are
yᵉ longs for you two to feel,
and share your grief in behalf
The affection you have shor
them your royal pupills, and
the kind remembrances
you have made of them
in your letter, leaves you too
with that respect and love
your are held in ther esteem,
for such disinterestedness
shewn in impart my
knowledge to them diving

your stay here with us.
I had the pleasure also,
to mention you that
our Government in counsel
has elected me to assume
the reins of Government
notwithstanding my
juvenility; and I am
pleased to see the love the
people have, for me, Most
undoubtedly, arising
from the respect and
veneration they have had
for my beloved royal Father
and I hope to render them
prosperity and peace, and
equal measure, they have

enjoyed since the last
reign, in return

May you and your beloved
children be in the peace
of ~~the~~ divine Providence

I beg to remain
Yours Sincerely

Somdetch Phra Paramendr
Maha Chulalonkorn
Klun Chowfa Hua,
Supreme King of Siam
on 114th day of reign

THE ENGLISH GOVERNESS

AT THE SIAMESE COURT.

I.

ON THE THRESHOLD

MARCH 15, 1862. — On board the small Siamese steamer Chow Phya, in the Gulf of Siam.

I rose before the sun, and ran on deck to catch an early glimpse of the strange land we were nearing; and as I peered eagerly, not through mist and haze, but straight into the clear, bright, many-tinted ether, there came the first faint, tremulous blush of dawn, behind her rosy veil; and presently the welcome face shines boldly out, glad, glorious, beautiful, and aureoled with flaming hues of orange, fringed with amber and gold, wherefrom flossy webs of color float wide through the sky, paling as they go. A vision of comfort and gladness, that tropical March morning, genial as a July dawn in my own less ardent clime; but the memory of two round, tender arms, and two little dimpled hands, that so lately had made themselves loving fetters round my neck, in the vain hope of holding mamma fast, blinded my outlook; and as, with a nervous tremor and a rude jerk, we came to anchor there, so with a shock and a tremor I came to my hard realities.

The captain told us we must wait for the afternoon tide to carry us over the bar. I lingered on deck, as long as I could dodge the fiery spears that flashed through our tattered awning, and bear the bustle and the boisterous jests of some circus people, our fellow-passengers, who came by express invitation of the king to astonish and amuse the royal household and the court.

Scarcely less intelligent, and certainly more entertaining, than these were the dogs of our company, — brutes of diverse temperament, experience, and behavior. There were the captain's two, Trumpet and Jip, who, by virtue of their reflected rank and authority, held places of privilege and pickings under the table, and were jealous and overbearing as became a captain's favorites, snubbing and bullying their more accomplished and versatile guests, the circus dogs, with skipper-like growls and snarls and snaps. And there was our own true Bessy, — a Newfoundland, great and good, — discreet, reposeful, dignified, fastidious, not to be cajoled into confidences and familiarities with strange dogs, whether official or professional. Very human was her gentle countenance, and very loyal, I doubt not, her sense of responsibility, as she followed anxiously my boy and me, interpreting with her heart the thoughts she read in our faces, and responding with her sympathetic eyes.

In the afternoon, when we dined on deck, the land was plainly visible; and now, as with a favoring tide we glided toward the beautiful Meinam ("Mother of Waters"), the air grew brighter, and the picture lived and moved; trees *grew* on the banks, more and more verdure, monkeys swung from bough to bough, birds flashed and piped among the thickets.

Though the reddish-brown water over the "banks" is very shallow at low tide, craft of moderate burden, with the aid of a pilot, cast anchor commonly in the very heart of the capital, in from ten to twelve fathoms of water

The world has few rivers so deep, commodious, and safe as the Meinam; and when we arrived the authorities were contemplating the erection of beacons on the bar, as well as a lighthouse for the benefit of vessels entering the port of Bangkok. The stream is rich in fish of excellent quality and flavor, such as is found in most of the great rivers of Asia; and is especially noted for its *platoo*, a kind of sardine, so abundant and cheap that it forms a common seasoning to the laborer's bowl of rice. The Siamese are expert in modes of drying and salting fish of all kinds, and large quantities are exported annually to Java, Sumatra, Malacca, and China.

In half an hour from the time when the twin banks of the river, in their raiment of bright green, seemed to open their beautiful arms to receive us, we came to anchor opposite the mean, shabby, irregular town of Paknam, or Sumuttra P'hra-kan ("Ocean Affairs"). Here the captain went ashore to report himself to the Governor, and the officials of the custom-house, and the mail-boat came out to us. My boy became impatient for *couay* (cake); Moonshee, my Persian teacher, and Beebe, my gay Hindostanee nurse, expressed their disappointment and disgust, Moonshee being absurdly dramatic in his wrath, as, fairly shaking his fist at the town, he demanded, "What is this?"

Near this place are two islands. The one on the right is fortified, yet withal so green and pretty, and seemingly so innocent of bellicose designs, that one may fancy Nature has taken peculiar pains to heal and hide the disfigurements grim Art has made in her beauty. On the other, which at first I took for a floating shrine of white marble, is perhaps the most unique and graceful object of architecture in Siam; shining like a jewel on the broad bosom of the river, a temple all of purest white, its lofty spire, fantastic and gilded, flashing back the glory

of the sun, and duplicated in shifting, quivering shadows
in the limpid waters below. Add to these the fitful rip-
ple of the coquettish breeze, the burnished blazonry of
the surrounding vegetation, the budding charms of spring
joined to the sensuous opulence of autumn, and you
have a scene of lovely glamour it were but vain imper-
tinence to describe. Earth seemed to have gathered for
her adorning here elements more intellectual, poetic, and
inspiring than she commonly displays to pagan eyes.

These islands at the gateway of the river are, like the
bank in the gulf, but accumulations of the sand borne
down before the torrent, that, suddenly swollen by the
rains, rushes annually to the sea. The one on which the
temple stands is partly artificial, having been raised from
the bed of the Meinam by the king P'hra Chow Phra-sat-
thong, as a work of "merit." Visiting this island some
years later, I found that this temple, like all other py-
ramidal structures in this part of the world, consists of
solid masonry of brick and mortar. The bricks made
here are remarkable, being fully eight inches long and
nearly four broad, and of fine grain, — altogether not unlike the "tavellae" brick of the Egyptians and ancient
Romans. There are cornices on all sides, with steps to
ascend to the top, where a long inscription proclaims the
name, rank, and virtues of the founder, with dates of
the commencement of the island and the shrine. The
whole of the space, extending to the low stone breakwater
that surrounds the island, is paved with the same kind
of brick, and encloses, in addition to the P'hra-Cha-dei
("The Lord's Delight"), a smaller temple with a brass
image of the sitting Buddha. It also affords accommoda-
tion to the numerous retinue of princes, nobles, retainers,
and pages who attend the king in his annual visits to the
temple, to worship, and make votive offerings and dona-
tions to the priests.

A charming spot, yet not one to be contemplated with unalloyed pleasure; for here also are the wretched people, who pass up and down in boats, averting their eyes, pressing their hard, labor-grimed hands against their sweating foreheads, and lowly louting in blind awe to these whited bricks. Even the naked children hush and crouch, and lay their little foreheads against the bottom of the boat.

His Majesty Somdetch P'hra Paramendr Maha Mongkut, the late Supreme King, contributed interesting *souvenirs* to the enlargement and adornment of this temple.

The town, which the twin islands redeem from the ignominy it otherwise deserves, lies on the east bank of the river, and by its long lines of low ramparts that face the water seems to have been at one time substantially fortified; but the works are now dilapidated and neglected. They were constructed in the first instance, I am told, with fatal ingenuity; in the event of an attack the garrison would find them as dangerous to abandon as to defend. Paknam is indebted for its importance rather to its natural position, and its possibilities of improvement under the abler hands into which it is gradually falling, than to any advantage or promise in itself; for a more disgusting, repulsive place is scarcely to be found on Asian ground.

The houses are built partly of mud, partly of wood, and, as in those of Malacca, only the upper story is habitable, the ground floor being the abode of pigs, dogs, fowls, and noisome reptiles. The "Government House" was originally of stone, but all the more recent additions have been shabbily constructed of rough timber and mud. This is one of the few houses in Paknam which one may enter without mounting a ladder or a clumsy staircase, and which have rooms in the lower as well as in the upper story.

The Custom-House is an open *sala*, or shed, where

interpreters, inspectors, and tidewaiters lounge away the
day on cool mats, chewing areca, betel, and tobacco, and
extorting moneys, goods, or provisions from the unhappy
proprietors of native trading craft, large or small; but
Europeans are protected from their rascally and insolent
exactions by the intelligence and energy of their respective consuls.

The hotel is a whitewashed brick building, originally
designed to accommodate foreign ambassadors and other
official personages visiting the Court of Siam. The king's
summer-house, fronting the islands, is the largest edifice
to be seen, but it has neither dignity nor beauty. A
number of inferior temples and monasteries occupy the
background, and are crowded with a rabble of priests, in
yellow robes and with shaven pates; packs of mangy
pariah-dogs attend them. These monasteries consist of
many small rooms or cells, containing merely a mat and
wooden pillow for each occupant. The refuse of the food,
which the priests beg during the day, is cast to the dogs
at night; and what *they* refuse is left to putrefy. Unimaginable are the stenches the sun of Siam engenders
in such conditions.

A village so happily situated might, under better management, become a thriving and pleasing port; but neglect, cupidity, and misrule have shockingly deformed and
degraded it. Nevertheless, by its picturesque site and
surroundings of beauty, it retains its hold upon the regret-
ful admiration of many Europeans and Americans, who
in ill health have found strength and cheer in its sea-
breezes.

We heartily enjoyed the delightful freshness of the
evening air as we glided up the Meinam, though the river
view at this point is somewhat marred by the wooden piers
and quays that line it on either side, and the floating
houses, representing elongated A's. From the deck, at-a

convenient height above the level of the river and the narrow serpentine canals and creeks, we looked down upon conical roofs thatched with attaps, and diversified by the pyramids and spires and fantastic turrets of the more important buildings. The valley of the Meinam, not over six hundred miles in length, is as a long deep dent or fissure in the alluvial soil. At its southern extremity we have the climate and vegetation of the tropics, while its northern end, on the brow of the Yunan, is a region of perpetual snow. The surrounding country is remarkable for the bountiful productiveness of its unctuous loam. The scenery, though not wild nor grand, is very picturesque and charming in the peculiar golden haze of its atmosphere. I surveyed with more and more admiration each new scene of blended luxuriance and beauty, — plantations spreading on either hand as far as the eye could reach, and level fields of living green, billowy with crops of rice and maize, and sugar-cane and coffee, and cotton and tobacco; and the wide irregular river, a kaleidoscope of evanescent form and color, where land, water, and sky joined or parted in a thousand charming surprises of shapes and shadows.

The sun was already sinking in the west, when we caught sight of a tall roof of familiar European fashion; and presently a lowly white chapel with green windows, freshly painted, peeped out beside two pleasant dwellings. Chapel and homes belong to the American Presbyterian Mission. A forest of graceful boughs filled the background; the last faint rays of the departing sun fell on the Mission pathway, and the gentle swaying of the tall trees over the chapel imparted a promise of safety and peace, as the glamour of the approaching night and the gloom and mystery of the pagan land into which we were penetrating filled me with an indefinable dread. I almost trembled, as the unfriendly clouds drove out the lingering

tints of day. Here were the strange floating city, with
its stranger people on all the open porches, quays, and
jetties; the innumerable rafts and boats, canoes and gondolas, junks, and ships; the pall of black smoke from
the steamer, the burly roar of the engine, and the murmur
and the jar; the bewildering cries of men, women, and
children, the shouting of the Chinamen, and the barking
of the dogs, — yet no one seemed troubled but me. I
knew it was wisest to hide my fears. It was the old
story. How many of our sisters, how many of our daughters, how many of our hearts' darlings, are thus, without
friend or guide or guard or asylum, turning into untried
paths with untold stories of trouble and pain !

We dropped anchor in deep water near an island. In
a moment the river was alive with nondescript craft,
worked by amphibious creatures, half naked, swarthy, and
grim, who rent the air with shrill, wild jargon as they
scrambled toward us. In the distance were several hulks
of Siamese men-of-war, seemingly as old as the flood;
and on the right towered, tier over tier, the broad roofs of
the grand Royal Palace of Bangkok, — my future "home"
and the scene of my future labors.

The circus people are preparing to land; and the dogs,
running to and fro with anxious glances, have an air of
leave-taking also. Now the China coolies, with pigtails
braided and coiled round their low, receding brows, begin
their uncouth bustle, and into the small hours of the
morning enliven the time of waiting with frantic shouts
and gestures.

Before long a showy gondola, fashioned like a dragon,
with flashing torches and many paddles, approached;
and a Siamese official mounted the side, swaying himself
with an absolute air. The red *langoutee*, or skirt, loosely
folded about his person, did not reach his ankles; and
to cover his audacious chest and shoulders he had only

his own brown polished skin. He was followed by a dozen attendants, who, the moment they stepped from the gangway, sprawled on the deck like huge toads, doubling their arms and legs under them, and pressing their noses against the boards, as if intent on making themselves small by degrees and hideously less. Every Asiatic on deck, coolies and all, prostrates himself, except my two servants, who are bewildered. Moonshee covertly mumbles his five prayers, ejaculating between, *Mash-Allah! A Tala-yea kia hai?* * and Beebe shrinks, and draws her veil of spotted muslin jealously over her charms.

The captain stepped forward and introduced us. "His Excellency Chow Phya Sri Sury Wongse, Prime Minister of the Kingdom of Siam!"

Half naked as he was, and without an emblem to denote his rank, there was yet something remarkable about this native chief, by virtue of which he compelled our respect from the first glance, — a sensibly magnetic quality of tone or look. With an air of command oddly at variance with his almost indecent attire, of which he seemed superbly unconscious, he beckoned to a young attendant, who crawled to him as a dog crawls to an angry master. This was an interpreter, who at a word from his lord began to question me in English.

"Are you the lady who is to teach in the royal family?"

On my replying in the affirmative, he asked, "Have you friends in Bangkok?"

Finding I had none, he was silent for a minute or two; then demanded: "What will you do? Where will you sleep to-night?"

"Indeed I cannot tell," I said. "I am a stranger here. But I understood from his Majesty's letter that a resi-

* "Great God! what is this?"

1 *

dence would be provided for us on our arrival; and he has been duly informed that we were to arrive at this time."

"His Majesty cannot remember everything," said his Excellency; the interpreter added, "You can go where you like." And away went master and slaves. I was dumfoundered, without even voice to inquire if there was a hotel in the city; and my servants were scornfully mute. My kind friend the captain was sorely puzzled. He would have sheltered us if he could; but a cloud of coal-dust and the stamping and screaming of a hundred and fifty Chinamen made hospitality impracticable; so I made a little bed for my child on deck, and prepared to pass the night with him under a canopy of stars.

The situation was as Oriental as the scene, — heartless arbitrary insolence on the part of my employers; homelessness, forlornness, helplessness, mortification, indignation, on mine. Fears and misgivings crowded and stunned me. My tears fell thick and fast, and, weary and despairing, I closed my eyes, and tried to shut out heaven and earth; but the reflection would return to mock and goad me, that by my own act, and against the advice of my friends, I had placed myself in this position.

The good captain of the Chow Phya, much troubled by the conduct of the minister, paced the deck (which usually, on these occasions, he left to the supercargo) for more than an hour. Presently a boat approached, and he hailed it. In a moment it was at the gangway, and with robust, hearty greetings on both sides, Captain B——, a cheery Englishman, with a round, ruddy, rousing face, sprang on board; in a few words our predicament was explained to him, and at once he invited us to share his house, for the night at least, assuring us of a cordial welcome from his wife. In the beautiful gondola of our "friend in need" we were pulled by four men, standing to their oars, through a dream-like scene, peculiar to this Venice of the East. Larger boats, in an endless variety of form and adornment, with prows high, tapering, and elaborately carved, and pretty little gondolas and canoes, passed us continually on the right and left; yet amid so many signs of life, motion, traffic, bustle, the sweet sound of the rippling waters alone fell on the ear. No rumbling of wheels, nor clatter of hoofs, nor clangor of bells, nor roar and scream of engines to shock the soothing fairy-like illusion. The double charm of stillness and starlight was perfect.

"By the by," broke in my cheery new friend, "you'll have to go with me to the play, ma'm; because my wife is there with the boys, and the house-key is in her pocket."

"To the play!"

"O, don't be alarmed, ma'm! It's not a regular theatre; only a catchpenny show, got up by a Frenchman, who came from Singapore a fortnight since. And having so little amusement here, we are grateful for anything that may help to break the monotony. The temporary playhouse is within the palace grounds of his Royal Highness Prince Krom Lhuang Wongse; and I hope to have an opportunity to introduce you to the Prince, who I believe is to be present with his family."

The intelligence was not gratifying, a Siamese prince had too lately disturbed my moral equilibrium; but I held my peace and awaited the result with resignation. A few strokes of the oars, seconded by the swift though silent current, brought us to a wooden pier surmounted by two glaring lanterns. Captain B—— handed us out. My child, startled from a deep sleep, was refractory, and would not trust himself out of my fond keeping. When finally I had struggled with him in my arms to the landing, I saw in the shadow a form coiled on a piece of striped matting. Was it a bear? No, a prince! For the clumsy mass of reddish-brown flesh unrolled and uplifted itself, and held out a human arm, with a fat hand at the end of it, when Captain B—— presented me to "his Royal Highness."   Near by was his Excellency the Prime Minister, in the identical costume that had disgraced our unpleasant interview on the Chow Phya ; he was smoking a European pipe, and plainly enjoying our terrors. My stalwart friend contrived to squeeze us, and even himself, first through a bamboo door, and then through a crowd of hot people, to seats fronting a sort of altar, consecrated to the arts of jugglery.   A number of Chinamen of respectable appearance occupied the more distant places, while those immediately behind us were filled by the ladies and gentlemen of the foreign community. On a raised dais hung with kincob * curtains, the ladies of the Prince's harem reclined ; while their children, shining in silk and ornaments of gold, laughed, prattled, and gesticulated, until the juggler appeared, when they were stunned with sudden wonder.   Under the eaves on all sides human heads were packed, on every head its cherished tuft of hair, like a stiff black brush inverted, in every mouth its delicious cud of areca-nut and betel, which the human cattle ruminated with industrious content.   The juggler, a keen little Frenchman, plied his arts nimbly, and what with his ventriloquial doll, his empty bag full of eggs, his stones that were candies, and his candies that were stones, and his stuffed birds that sang, astonished and delighted his unsophisticated patrons, whose applauding murmurs were diversified by familiarly silly shrieks — the true Siamese Did-you-ever ! — from behind the kincob curtains.

But I was weary and disheartened, and welcomed with a sigh of relief the closing of the show. As we passed out with our guide, the glare of many torches falling on the

* Silk, embroidered with gold flowers.

dark silent river made the swarthy forms of the boatmen weird and Charon-like. Mrs. B—— welcomed us with a pleasant smile to her little heaven of home across the river, and by the simplicity and gentleness of her manners dispelled in a measure my feeling of forlornness. When at last I found myself alone, I would have sought the sleep I so much needed, but the strange scenes of the day chased each other in agitating confusion through my brain. Then I quitted the side of my sleeping boy, triumphant in his dreamless innocence, and sat defeated by the window, to crave counsel and help from the ever-present Friend; and as I waited I sank into a tumultuous slumber, from which at last I started to find the long-tarrying dawn climbing over a low wall and creeping through a half-open shutter.

II.

A SIAMESE PREMIER AT HOME.

I STARTED up, arranged my dress, and smoothed my hair; though no water nor any after-touches could remove the shadow that night of gloom and loneliness had left upon my face. But my boy awoke with eager, questioning eyes, his smile bright and his hair lustrous. As we knelt together by the window at the feet of "Our Father," I could not but ask in the darkness of my trouble, did it need so bitter a baptism as ours to purify so young a soul?

In an outer room we met Mrs. B—— *en déshabillé*, and scarcely so pretty as at our first meeting, but for her smile, remarkable for its subtile, evanescent sweetness. At breakfast our host joined us, and, after laughing at our late predicament and fright, assured me of that which I have since experienced, — the genuine goodness of the Prince Krom Lhuang Wongse. Every foreign resident of Bangkok, who at any time has had friendly acquaintance or business with him, would, I doubt not, join me in expressions of admiration and regard for one who has maintained through circumstances so trying and under a system so oppressive an exemplary reputation for liberality, integrity, justice, and humanity.

Soon after breakfast the Prime Minister's boat, with the slave interpreter who had questioned me on the steamer, arrived to take us to his Excellency's palace.

In about a quarter of an hour we found ourselves in

THE PRIME MINISTER.

front of a low gateway, which opened on a wide court-
yard, or "compound," paved with rough-hewn slabs of
stone. A brace of Chinese mandarins of ferocious aspect,
cut in stone and mounted on stone horses, guarded the
entrance. Farther on, a pair of men-at-arms in bass-relief
challenged us; and near these were posted two living
sentries, in European costume, but without shoes.   On
the left was a pavilion for theatrical entertainments, one
entire wall being covered with scenic pictures. On the
right of this stood the palace of the Prime Minister,
displaying a semicircular *façade;* in the background a
range of buildings of considerable extent, comprising the
lodgings of his numerous wives.   Attached to the largest
of these houses was a charming garden of flowers, in the
midst of which a refreshing fountain played.   His Excellency's residence abounded within in carvings and gildings, elegant in design and color, that blended and har-
monized in pleasing effects with the luxurious draperies
that hung in rich folds from the windows.

We moved softly, as the interpreter led us through a
suite of spacious saloons, disposed in ascending tiers, and
all carpeted, candelabraed, and appointed in the most
costly European fashion. A superb vase of silver, em-
bossed and burnished, stood on a table inlaid with mother-
of-pearl and chased with silver. Flowers of great variety
and beauty filled the rooms with a delicious though
slightly oppressive fragrance. On every side my eyes
were delighted with rare vases, jewelled cups and boxes,
burnished chalices, dainty statuettes, — *objets de virtu,*
Oriental and European, antique and modern, blending the
old barbaric splendors with the graces of the younger
arts.

As we waited, fascinated and bewildered, the Prime
Minister suddenly stood before us, — the semi-nude barbarian of last night. I lost my presence of mind, and in

my embarrassment would have left the room. But he held out his hand, saying, "Good morning, *sir!* Take a seat, *sir!*" which I did somewhat shyly, but not without a smile for his comical "sir." I spied a number of young girls peeping at us from behind curtains, while the male attendants, among whom were his younger brothers, nephews, and cousins, crouched in the antechamber on all fours. His Excellency, with an expression of pleased curiosity, and that same grand unconsciousness of his alarming poverty of costume, approached us nearly, and, with a kindly smile patting Boy on the head, asked him his name. But the child cried aloud, "Mamma, come home! Please, mamma, come home!" and I found it not easy to quiet him.

Presently, mustering courage for myself also, I ventured to express my wish for a quiet house or apartments, where I might be free from intrusion, and at perfect liberty before and after school-hours.

When this reasonable request was interpreted to him — seemingly in a few monosyllables — he stood looking at me, smiling, as if surprised and amused that I should have notions on the subject of liberty. Quickly this look became inquisitive and significant, so that I began to fancy he had doubts as to the use I might make of my stipulated freedom, and was puzzled to conjecture why a woman should wish to be free at all. Some such thought must have passed through his mind, for he said abruptly, "You not married!"

I bowed.

"Then where will you go in the evening?"

"Not anywhere, your Excellency. I simply desire to secure for myself and my child some hours of privacy and rest, when my duties do not require my presence elsewhere."

"How many years your husband has been dead?" he asked.

I replied that his Excellency had no right to pry into my domestic concerns. His business was with me as a governess only ; on any other subject I declined conversing. I enjoyed the expression of blank amazement with which he regarded me on receiving this somewhat defiant reply. " *Tam chai !* " (" Please yourself ! ") he said, and proceeded to pace to and fro, but without turning his eyes from my face, or ceasing to smile. Then he said something to his attendants, five or six of whom, raising themselves on their knees, with their eyes fixed upon the carpet, crawled backward till they reached the steps, bobbed their heads and shoulders, started spasmodically to their feet, and fled from the apartment. My boy, who had been awed and terrified, began to cry, and I too was startled. Again he uttered the harsh gutturals, and instantly, as with an electric shock, another half-dozen of the prostrate slaves sprang up and ran. Then he resumed his mysterious promenade, still carefully keeping an eye upon us, and smiling by way of conversation. It was long before I could imagine what we were to do. Boy, fairly tortured, cried " Come home, mamma ! why don't you come home ? I don't like that man." His Excellency halted, and sinking his voice ominously, said, " You no can go ! " Boy clutched my dress, and hid his face and smothered his sobs in my lap ; and yet, attracted, fascinated, the poor little fellow from time to time looked up, only to shudder, tremble, and hide his face again. For his sake I was glad when the interpreter returned on all fours. Pushing one elbow straight out before the other, in the manner of these people, he approached his master with such a salutation as might be offered to deity ; and with a few more unintelligible utterances, his Excellency bowed to us, and disappeared behind a mirror. All the curious, peering eyes that had been directed upon us from every nook and corner where a curtain hung, instantly

B

vanished; and at the same time sweet, wild music, like the tinkling of silver bells in the distance, fell upon our ears.

To my astonishment the interpreter stood boldly upright, and began to contemplate his irresistible face and figure in a glass, and arrange with cool coxcombry his darling tuft of hair; which done, he approached us with a mild swagger, and proceeded to address me with a freedom which I found it expedient to snub. I told him that, although I did not require any human being to go down on his face and hands before me, I should nevertheless tolerate no familiarity or disrespect from any one. The fellow understood me well enough, but did not permit me to recover immediately from my surprise at the sudden change in his bearing and tone. As he led us to the two elegant rooms reserved for us in the west end of the palace, he informed us that he was the Premier's half-brother, and hinted that I would be wise to conciliate him if I wished to have my own way. In the act of entering one of the rooms, I turned upon him angrily, and bade him be off. The next moment this half-brother of a Siamese magnate was kneeling in abject supplication in the half-open doorway, imploring me not to report him to his Excellency, and promising never to offend again. Here was a miracle of repentance I had not looked for; but the miracle was sham. Rage, cunning, insolence, servility, and hypocrisy were vilely mixed in the minion.

Our chambers opened on a quiet piazza, shaded by fruit-trees in blossom, and overlooking a small artificial lake stocked with pretty, sportive fish.

To be free to make a stunning din is a Siamese woman's idea of perfect enjoyment. Hardly were we installed in our apartments when, with a pell-mell rush and screams of laughter, the ladies of his Excellency's private Utah reconnoitred us in force. Crowding in through the half-open door, they scrambled for me with eager curiosity, all trying at once to embrace me boisterously, and promiscuously chattering in shrill Siamese, — a bedlam of parrots; while I endeavored to make myself impartially agreeable in the language of signs and glances. Nearly all were young; and in symmetry of form, delicacy of feature, and fairness of complexion, decidedly superior to the Malay women I had been accustomed to. Most of them might have been positively attractive, but for their ingeniously ugly mode of clipping the hair and blackening the teeth.

The youngest were mere children, hardly more than fourteen years old. All were arrayed in rich materials, though the fashion did not differ from that of their slaves, numbers of whom were prostrate in the rooms and passages. My apartments were ablaze with their crimson, blue, orange, and purple, their ornaments of gold, their rings and brilliants, and their jewelled boxes. Two or three of the younger girls satisfied my Western ideas of beauty, with their clear, mellow, olive complexions, and their almond-shaped eyes, so dark yet glowing. Those among them who were really old were simply hideous and repulsive. One wretched crone shuffled through the noisy throng with an air of authority, and pointing to Boy lying in my lap, cried, " *Moolay, moolay !* " "Beautiful, beautiful!" The familiar Malay word fell pleasantly on my ear, and I was delighted to find some one through whom I might possibly control the disorderly bevy around me. I addressed her in Malay. Instantly my visitors were silent, and waiting in attitudes of eager attention.

She told me she was one of the many custodians of the harem. She was a native of Quedah; and "some sixty years ago," she and her sister, together with other young Malay girls, were captured while working in the fields by a party of Siamese adventurers. They were brought to Siam and sold as slaves. At first she mourned miserably for her home and parents. But while she was yet young and attractive she became a favorite of the late Somdetch Ong Yai, father of her present lord, and bore him two sons, just as "moolay, moolay" as my own darling. But they were dead. (Here, with the end of her soiled silk scarf she furtively wiped a tear from her face, no longer ugly.) And her gracious lord was dead also; it was he who gave her this beautiful gold betel-box.

"But how is it that you are still a slave?" I asked.

"I am old and ugly and childless: and therefore, to be trusted by my dead lord's son, the beneficent prince, upon whose head be blessings," — clasping her withered hands, and turning toward that part of the palace where, no doubt, he was enjoying a "beneficent" nap.

"And now it is my privilege to watch and guard these favored ones, that they see no man but their lord."

The repulsive uncomeliness of this woman had been wrought by oppression out of that which must have been beautiful once; for the spirit of beauty came back to her for a moment, with the passing memories that brought her long-lost treasures with them. In the brutal tragedy of a slave's experience, — a female slave in the harem of an Asian despot, — the native angel in her had been bruised, mutilated, defaced, deformed, but not quite obliterated.

Her story ended, the younger women, to whom her language had been strange, could no longer suppress their merriment, nor preserve the decorum due to her age and authority. Again they swarmed about me like bees, ply-ing me pertinaciously with questions, as to my age, hus-band, children, country, customs, possessions; and pres-ently crowned the inquisitorial performance by asking, in all seriousness, if I should not like to be the wife of the prince, their lord, rather than of the terrible Chow-che-witt.*

Here was a monstrous suggestion that struck me dumb. Without replying, I rose and shook them off, retiring with my boy into the inner chamber. But they pursued me without compunction, repeating the extraordinary "conundrum," and dragging the Malay duenna along with them to interpret my answer. The intrusion provoked me; but, considering their beggarly poverty of true life and liberty, of hopes and joys, and loves and memories, and holy fears and sorrows, with which a full and true response might have twitted them, I was ashamed to be vexed.

Seeing it impossible to rid myself of them, I promised to answer their question, on condition that they would leave me for that day. Immediately all eyes were fixed upon me.

"The prince, your lord, and the king, your Chow-che-witt, are pagans," I said. "An English, that is a Christian, woman would rather be put to the torture, chained and dungeoned for life, or suffer a death the slowest and most painful you Siamese know, than be the wife of either."

They remained silent in astonishment, seemingly with-held from speaking by an instinctive sentiment of respect; until one, more volatile than the rest, cried, "What! not if he gave you all these jewelled rings and boxes, and these golden things?"

When the old woman, fearing to offend, whispered this test question in Malay to me, I laughed at the earnest eyes around, and said : "No, not even then. I am only here to teach the royal family. I am not like you. You have nothing to do but to play and sing and dance for your master; but I have to work for my children; and

---

* *Chow-che-witt,* — " Prince of life," — the supreme king.

one little one is now on the great ocean, and I am very sad."

Shades of sympathy, more or less deep, flitted across the faces of my audience, and for a moment they regarded me as something they could neither convince nor comfort nor understand. Then softly repeating *Poot-thoo! Poot-thoo!* "Dear God! dear God!" they quietly left me. A minute more, and I heard them laughing and shouting in the halls.

Relieved of my curious and exacting visitors, I lay down and fell into a deep sleep, from which I was suddenly awakened, in the afternoon, by the cries of Beebe, who rushed into the chamber, her head bare, her fine muslin veil trampled under her feet, and her face dramatically expressive of terror and despair. Moonshee, her husband, ignorant alike of the topography, the language, and the rules of the place, had by mistake intruded in the sacred penetralia where lounged the favorite of the harem, to the lively horror of that shrinking Nourmahal, and the general wrath of the old women on guard, two of whom, the ugliest, fiercest, and most muscular, had dragged him, daft and trembling, to summary inquisition.

I followed Beebe headlong to an open sala, where we found that respectable servant of the Prophet, his hands tied, his turban off, woe-begone but resigned ; faithful and philosophic Moslem that he was, he only waited for his throat to be cut, since it was his *kismut*, his perverse destiny, that had brought him to such a region of *Kafirs*, (infidels). Assuring him that there was nothing to fear, I despatched a messenger in search of the interpreter, while Beebe wept and protested. Presently an imposing personage stalked upon the scene, whose appearance matched his temper and his conduct. This was the judge. In vain I strove to explain to him by signs and gestures that my servant had offended unwittingly ; he could not or would not understand me; but stormed away at our poor old man, who bore his abuse with the calm indifference of profound ignorance, having never before been cursed in a foreign language.

The loafers of the yards and porches shook off their lazy naps and gathered round us; and among them came the interpreter, insolent satisfaction beaming in his bad face. He coolly declined to interfere, protesting that it was not his business, and that the judge would be offended if he offered to take part in the proceedings. Moonshee was condemned to be stripped, and beaten with twenty strokes. Here was an end to my patience. Going straight up to the judge, I told him that if a single lash was laid upon the old man's back (which was bared as I spoke), he should suffer tenfold, for I would immediately lay the matter before the British Consul. Though I spoke in English, he caught the familiar words "British Consul," and turning to the interpreter, demanded the explanation he should have listened to before he pronounced sentence. But even as the interpreter was jabbering away to the unreasonable functionary, the assembly was agitated with what the French term a "sensation." Judge, interpreter, and all fell upon their faces, doubling themselves up; and there stood the Premier, who took in the situation at a glance, ordered Moonshee to be released, and permitted him at my request to retire to the room allotted to Beebe. While the slaves were alert in the execution of these benevolent commands, the interpreter slunk away on his face and elbows. But the old Moslem, as soon as his hands were free, picked up his turban, advanced, and laid it at the feet of his deliverer, with the graceful salutation of his people, "Peace be with thee, O Vizier of a wise king!" The mild and venerable aspect of the Moonshee, and his snow-white beard falling low upon his breast, must have inspired the Siamese statesman with abiding feelings of respect and consideration, for he was ever afterward indulgent to that Oriental Dominie Sampson of my little household.

Dinner at the Premier's was composed and served with the same incongruous blending of the barbaric and the refined, the Oriental and the European, that characterized the furniture and adornments of his palace. The saucy little pages who handled the dishes had cigarettes between their pouting lips, and from time to time hopped over the heads of Medusæ to expectorate. When I pointed reproachfully to the double peccadillo, they only laughed and scampered off. Another detachment of these lads brought in fruits, and, when they had set the baskets or dishes on the table, retired to sofas to lounge till we had dined. But finding I objected to such manners, they giggled gayly, performed several acrobatic feats on the carpet, and left us to wait on ourselves.

Twilight on my pretty piazza. The fiery sun is setting, and long pencils of color, from palettes of painted glass, touch with rose and gold the low brow and downcast eyes and dainty bosom of a bust of Clyte. Beebe and Moonshee are preparing below in the open air their evening meal; and the smoke of their pottage is borne slowly, heavily on the hot still air, stirred only by the careless laughter of girls plunging and paddling in the dimpled lake. The blended gloom and brightness without enter, and interweave themselves with the blended gloom and brightness within, where lights and shadows lie half asleep and half awake, and life breathes itself sluggishly away, or drifts on a slumberous stream toward its ocean of death.

III

A SKETCH OF SIAMESE HISTORY.

BEFORE inducting the reader to more particular acquaintance with his Excellency Chow Phya Sri-Sury Wongse Samuha-P'hra Kralahome, I have thought that "an abstract and brief chronicle" of the times of the strange people over whom he is not less than second in dignity and power, would not be out of place.

In the opinion of Pickering, the Siamese are undoubtedly Malay; but a majority of the intelligent Europeans who have lived long among them regard the native population as mainly Mongolian. They are generally of medium stature, the face broad, the forehead low, the eyes black, the cheekbones prominent, the chin retreating, the mouth large, the lips thick, and the beard scanty. In common with most of the Asiatic races, they are apt to be indolent, improvident, greedy, intemperate, servile, cruel, vain, inquisitive, superstitious, and cowardly; but individual variations from the more repulsive types are happily not rare. In public they are scrupulously polite and decorous according to their own notions of good manners, respectful to the aged, affectionate to their kindred, and bountiful to their priests, of whom more than twenty thousand are supported by voluntary contributions in Bangkok alone. Marriage is contracted at sixteen for males, and fourteen for females, and polygamy is the common practice, without limit to the number of

2

wives except such as may be imposed by the humble estate or poverty of the husband; the women are generally treated with consideration.

The bodies of the dead are burned; and the badges of mourning are white robes for those of the family or kinfolk who are younger than the deceased, black for those who are older, and shaven heads for all who are in inferior degrees connected with the dead, either as descendants, dependents, servants, or slaves. When a king dies the entire population, with the exception of very young children, must display this tonsorial uniform.

Every ancient or famous city of Siam has a story of its founding, woven for it from tradition or fable; and each of these legends is distinguished from the others by peculiar features. The religion, customs, arts, and literature of a people naturally impart to their annals a spirit all their own. Especially is this the case in the Orient, where the most original and suggestive thought is half disguised in the garb of metaphor, and where, in spite of vivid fancies and fiery passions, the people affect taciturnity or reticence, and delight in the metaphysical and the mystic. Hence the early annals of the Siamese, or Sajamese, abound in fables of heroes, demigods, giants, and genii, and afford but few facts of practical value. Swayed by religious influences, they joined, in the spirit of the Hebrews, the name of God to the titles of their rulers and princes, whom they almost deified after death. But the skeleton sketch of the history of Siam that follows is of comparatively modern date, and may be accepted as in the main authentic.

In the year 712 of the Siamese, and 1350 of the Christian era, Phya-Othong founded, near the river Meinam, about sixty miles from the Gulf of Siam, the city of Ayudia or Ayuthia ("the Abode of the Gods"); at the same time he assumed the title of P'hra Rama Thibodi.

This capital and stronghold was continually exposed to storms of civil war and foreign invasion; and its turreted battlements and ponderous gates, with the wide deep moat spanned by drawbridges, where now is a forest of great trees, were but the necessary fences behind which court and garrison took shelter from the tempestuous barbarism in the midst of which they lived. But before any portion of the city, except that facing the river, could boast of a fortified enclosure, hostile enterprises were directed against it. Birman pirates, ascending the Meinam in formidable flotillas, harassed it. Thrice they ravaged the country around; but on the last of these occasions great numbers of them were captured and put to cruel death by P'hra Rama Suen, successor to Thibodi, who pursued the routed remnant to the very citadel of Chiengmai, then a tributary of the Birman Empire. Having made successful war upon this province, and impressed thousands of Laotian captives, he next turned his arms against Cambodia, took the capital by storm, slew every male capable of bearing arms, and carried off enormous treasures in plate gold, with which, on his return to his kingdom, he erected a remarkable pagoda, called to this day "The Mountain of Gold."

P'hra Rama Suen was succeeded by his son Phya Ram, who reigned fourteen years, and was assassinated by his uncle, Inthra Racha, the governor or feudal lord of the city, who had snatched the reins of government and sent three of his sons to rule over the northern provinces. At the death of Inthra Racha, in 780, two of these princes set out simultaneously, with the design of seizing and occupying the vacant throne. Mounted on elephants, they met in the dusk of evening on a bridge leading to the Royal Palace; and each instantly divining his brother's purpose, they dismounted, and with their naked swords fell upon each other with such fury that both were slain on the spot.

The political and social disorganization that prevailed
at this period was aggravated by the vulnerable condition
of the monarchy, then recently transferred to a new line.
Princes of the blood royal were for a long time engaged,
brother against brother, in fierce family feuds. Ayuthia
suffered gravely from these unnatural contentions, but
even more from the universal license and riot that reigned
among the nobility and the proud proprietors of the soil.
In the distracted and enfeebled state of all authority,
royal and magisterial, the fields around remained for many
years untilled; and the only evidence the land presented
of the abode of man was here and there the bristling den
of some feudal chief, a mere outlaw and dacoit, who rarely
sallied from it but to carry torch and pillage wherever
there was aught to sack or burn.

In 834 the undisputed sovereignty of the kingdom fell
to another P'hra Rama Thibodi, who reigned thirty years,
and is famous in Siamese annals for the casting of a great
image of Buddha, fifty cubits high, of gold very moderately alloyed with copper. On an isolated hill, in a sacred
enclosure, he erected for this image a stately temple of
the purest white marble, approached by a graceful flight
of steps.   From the ruins of its eastern front, which are
still visible, it appears to have had six columns at either
end and thirteen on each side; the eastern pediment is
adorned with sculptures, as are also the ten metopes.

P'hra Rama Thibodi was succeeded by his son, P'hra
Racha Kuman, whose reign was short, and chiefly memorable for a tremendous conflagration that devastated
Ayuthia.   It raged three days, and destroyed more than a
hundred thousand houses.

This monarch left at his death but one son, P'hra Yot-
Fa, a lad of twelve, whose mother, the Queen Sisudah-
Chand, was appointed regent during his minority.

The devil of ambition has rarely possessed the heart

of an Eastern queen more absolutely than it did that of
this infamous woman, — infamous even in heathen annals.
She is said to have graced her exalted station alike by
the beauty of her person and the charm of her manner ;
but in pursuit of the most arbitrary and audacious purposes she moved with the recklessness their nature demanded, and with equal impatience trampled on friend
and rival.   Blind superstition was the only weak point in
her character ; but though her deference to the imaginary
instructions or warnings of the stars was slavish, it does
not seem to have deterred her from any false or cruel
course ; indeed, a cunning astrologer of her court, by
scaring her with visionary perils, contrived to obtain a
monstrous ascendency over her mind, only to plunge her
into crime more deeply than by her own weight of wick-
edness she might have sunk.   She ordered the secret
assassination of every member of the royal household
(not excepting her mother and sisters), who, however
mildly, opposed her will.   Besotted with fear, that fruitful
mother of crime, she ended by putting to death the young
king, her son, and publicly calling her paramour (the court
astrologer, in whose thoughts, she believed, were hidden
all the secrets of divination) to the throne of the P'hra-
batts.

This double crime filled the measure of her impunity.
The nobility revolted.   The strength of their faction lay,
not within the palace, which was filled with the queen's
parasites, but with the feudal proprietors of the soil, who,
exasperated by the abominations of the court, only
waited for a chance to crush it.   One day, as the queen
and her paramour were proceeding in a barge on their
customary visit to her private pagoda and garden, — a
paradise of all the floral wonders of the tropics, — a nobleman, who had followed them, hailed the royal gondola,
as if for instructions, and, being permitted to approach,

suddenly sprang upon the guilty pair, drew his sword, and dispatched them both, careless of their loud cries for help. Almost simultaneously with the performance of this tragic exploit, the nobles offered the crown to an uncle of the murdered heir, who had fled from the court and taken refuge in a monastery. Having accepted it and assumed the title of Maha-Chakrapât Racha-therat, he invaded Pegu with a hundred thousand men-at-arms, five thousand war elephants, and seven thousand horse. With this mighty host he marched against Hongzawadi, the capital of Pegu, laying waste the country as he went with fire and sword. The king of Pegu came out to meet him, accompanied by his romantic and intrepid queen, Maha Chandra, and supported by the few devoted followers that on so short a notice he could bring together. In consideration of this great disparity of forces, the two kings agreed, in the chivalric spirit of the time, to decide the fortune of the day by single combat. Hardly had they encountered, when the elephant on which the king of Pegu was mounted took fright and fled the field; but his queen promptly took his place, and fighting rashly, fell, speared through the right breast. She was borne off amid the clash of cymbals and flourish of trumpets that hailed the victor.

Maha-Chakrapât Racha-therat was a great prince. His wisdom, valor, and heroic exploits supplied the native bards with inspiring themes. By his magnanimity he extinguished the envy of the neighboring princes and transformed rivals into friends. Jealous rulers became his willing vassals, not from fear of his power, but in admiration for his virtues. Malacca, Tenasserim, Ligor, Thavai, Martaban, Maulmain, Songkhla, Chantaboon, Phitsanulok, Look-Kho-Thai, Phi-chi, Savan Khalok, Phechit, Cambodia, and Nakhon Savan were all dependencies of Siam under his reign.

In the year 1568 of the Christian era the Siamese territory was invaded and laid under tribute by a Birman
king named Mandanahgri, who must have been a warrior
of Napoleonic genius, for he extended his dominion as
far as the confines of China. It is remarkable that the
flower of his army was composed of several thousand Portuguese, tried troops in good discipline, commanded by
the noted Don Diego Suanes. These, like the famous
Scotch Legion of Gustavus Adolphus in the Thirty Years'
War, were mercenaries, and doubtless contributed import-
antly to the success of the Birman arms. Theirs is by
no means the only case of Portuguese soldiers serving for
hire in the armies of the East. Their commander, Suanes, seems to have been a brave and accomplished officer,
and to have been intrusted with undivided control of the
Birmese forces.

Mandanahgri held the queen of Siam and her two sons
as hostages for the payment of the tribute he had levied;
but the princes were permitted to return to Siam after a
few years of captivity in Birmah, and in 1583 their cap-
tor died. His successor struggled with an uncle for possession of the throne, and the king of Siam, seizing the
opportunity, declared himself independent; wherefore a
more formidable army was shortly sent against him, under
command of the eldest son of the king of Birmah. But
one of the young princes who had been led into captivity by Mandanahgri now sat on the throne of Siam.
In his youth he had been styled "the Black Prince," a
title of distinction which seems to have fitted his characteristics not less appropriately than it did those of the
English Edward. Undismayed by the strength and fury
of the enemy, he attacked and routed them in a pitched
battle, killing their leader with his own hands, invaded
Pegu, and besieged its capital; but was finally compelled
to retire with considerable loss. The Black Prince was

succeeded by "the White King," who reigned peacefully
for many years.

The next monarch especially worthy of notice is P'hra
Narai, who sent ambassadors to Goa, the most important
of the Portuguese trading-stations in the East Indies,
chiefly to invite the Portuguese of Malacca to establish
themselves in Siam for mutual advantages of trade.   The
welcome emissaries were sumptuously entertained, and a
Dominican friar accompanied them on their return, with
costly presents for the king.   This friar found P'hra Narai
much more liberal in his ideas than later ambassadors,
even to this day, have found any other ruler of Siam.
He agreed not only to permit all Portuguese merchants
to establish themselves anywhere in his dominions, but to
exempt their goods and wares from duty.   The Dominican monks were likewise invited to build churches and
preach Christianity in Siam.

Soon after this extraordinary display of liberal states-
manship P'hra Narai narrowly escaped death by a strange
conspiracy.   Four or five .hundred Japanese adventurers
were secretly introduced into the country by an ambitious
feudal proprietor, who had conceived the mad design of
dethroning the monarch and reigning in his stead; but
the king, warned of the planned attack upon the palace,
seized the native conspirator and put him to death.   The
Japanese, on the contrary, were enrolled as a kind of
prætorian guard, or janissaries ; in this character, however, their pride and power became so formidable that the
king grew uneasy and disbanded them.

P'hra Narai, from all accounts, was a man to be re-
spected and esteemed.   The events and the *dramatis
personæ* of his reign form a story so romantic, so excep-
tional even in Eastern annals, that, but for the undoubted
authenticity of this chapter of Siamese history, it would
be incredible.   It was during his reign that the whimsical

attempt was made by Louis XIV. to conquer Siam and proselyte her king.   An extraordinary spectacle !   One of the most licentious monarchs of France, who to the last breathed an atmosphere poisoned with scepticism, and more than Buddhism itself subversive of the true principles of Christianity, is suddenly inspired with an apparently devout longing to be the instrument of converting to the true faith the princes of the East.   To this end he employs that wily, powerful, and indefatigable body of daring priests, the Jesuits, who were then in the very ardor of their missionary schemes.

Ostensibly for the purpose of propagating the Gospel, but with more reality aspiring to extend their subtile influence over all mankind, this society, with means the most slender and in the face of obstacles the most disheartening, have, with indomitable courage and supernatural patience, accomplished labors unparalleled in the achievements of mind.   Now, in the wilds of Western America, taming and teaching races of whose existence the world of refinement had never heard ; now climbing the icy steeps and tracking the wastes and wildernesses of Siberia, or with the evangel of John in one hand and the art of Luke in the other, bringing life to the bodies and souls of perishing multitudes under a scorching equatorial sun, — there is not a spot of earth in which European civilization has taken root where traces of Jesuit forethought and careful, patient husbandry may not be found.   So in Siam, we discover a monarch of consummate acumen, more European than Asiatic in his ideas, sedulously cultivating the friendship of these foreign workers of wonders ; and finally we find a Greek adventurer officiating as prime minister to this same king, and conducting his affairs with that ability and success which must have commanded intellectual admiration, even if they had not been inspired and promoted by motives of

2*   c

integrity toward the monarch who had so implicitly con-
fided in his wisdom and fidelity.

Constantine Phaulkon was the son of respectable parents, natives of the island of Cephalonia, where he was
born in 1630. The geography, if not the very name, of
the kingdom whose affairs he was destined to direct was
quite unknown to his compatriots of the Ionian Isles, —
even when as a mariner, wrecked on the coast of Malabar,
he became a fellow-passenger with a party of Siamese
officials, his companions in disaster, who were returning
to their country from an embassy. The facile Greek
quickly learned to talk with his new-found friends in
their own tongue, and by his accomplishments and adroitness made a place for himself in their admiration and
influence, so that he was received with flattering consideration at the Court of P'hra Narai, and very soon invited to take service under government. By his sagacity,
tact, and diligence in the management of all affairs intrusted to him, he rapidly rose in favor with his patron,
who finally elevated him to the highest post of honor in
the state : he was made premier.

The star of the Cephalonian waif and adventurer had
now mounted to the zenith, and was safe to shine for
many years with unabated brilliancy ; to this day he is
remembered by the expressive term *Vicha-yen*, "the cool
wisdom." The French priests, elated at his success,
spared no promises or arts to retain him secretly in their
interest. Under circumstances so extraordinary and auspicious, the plans of the Jesuits for the conversion of
all Eastern Asia were put in execution. From the Vat-
ican bishops were appointed, and sent out to Cochin
China, Cambodia, Siam, and Pegu, while the people of
those several kingdoms were yet profoundly ignorant of
the amiable intentions of the Pope. Francis Pallu, M.
De la Motte Lambert, and Ignatius Cotolendy were the

respective exponents of this pious idea, under the imposing titles of Bishops of Heliopolis, Borytus, Byzantium, and Metellopolis, — all Frenchmen, for Louis XIV. insisted that the glory of the enterprise should be ascribed exclusively to France and to himself.

But all their efforts to convert the king were of no avail. The Jesuits, however, opened schools, and have ever since labored assiduously and with success to introduce the ideas and the arts of Europe into those countries.

After some years P'hra Narai sent an embassy to the Court of Louis, who was so sensible of the flattery that he immediately reciprocated with an embassy of his own, with more priests, headed by the Chevalier De Chaumont and the Père Tachard. The French fleet of five ships cast anchor in the Meinam on the 27th of September, 1687, and the Chevalier and his reverend colleague, attended by Jesuits, were promptly and graciously received by the king, who, however, expressed his "fears" that the chief object of their mission might not prove so easy of attainment as they had been led to believe. As for Phaulkon, he had adroitly deceived the Jesuits from the first, and made all parties instruments to promote his own shrewd and secret plans.

De Chaumont, disheartened by his failure, sailed back to France, where he arrived in 1688, in the height of the agitation attending the English Revolution of that year.

Phaulkon, finding that he could no longer conceal from the Jesuits the king's repugnance to their plans for his conversion, placed himself under their direction and control; for though he had not as yet conceived the idea of seizing upon the crown, it was plain that he aspired to honors higher than the premiership. Then rumors of disaffection among the nobles were diligently propagated by the French priests, who, although not sufficiently powerful to dethrone the king, were nevertheless dangerous inciters of rebellion among the common people.

Meanwhile the king of Johore, then a tributary of Siam, instigated by the Dutch, who, from the first, had watched with jealousy the machinations of the French, sent envoys to P'hra Narai, to advise the extermination or expulsion of the French, and to proffer the aid of his troops; but the proposition was rejected with indignation.

These events were immediately followed by another, known in Siamese history as the Revolt of the Macassars, which materially promoted the ripening of the revolution of which the French had sown the seeds. Celebes, a large, irregular island east of Borneo, includes a district known as Macassar, the ruler of which had been arbitrarily dethroned by the Dutch; and the sons of the injured monarch, taking refuge in Siam, secretly encouraged the growing enmity of the nobles against the French.

Meanwhile Phaulkon, by his address, and skilful management of public affairs, continued to exercise paramount influence over the mind of the king. He persuaded P'hra Narai to send another embassy to France, which arrived happily (the former having been shipwrecked off the Cape of Good Hope) at the Court of Louis XIV. in 1689. He also diligently and ably advanced the commercial strength of the country; merchants from all parts of the world were invited to settle in Siam, and factories of every nation were established along the banks of the Meinam. Both Ayudia and Lophaburee became busy and flourishing. He was careful to keep the people employed, and applied himself with vigor to improving the agriculture of the country. Rice, sugar, corn, and palm-oil constituting the most fruitful and regular source of revenue, he wisely regulated the traffic in those staples, and was studious to promote the security and happiness of the great body of the population engaged or concerned in their production. The laws he framed were so sound and stable, and at the same time so wisely conformable to the interests alike of king and subject, that to this day they constitute the fundamental law of the land.

Phaulkon designed and built the palaces at Lopha-buree, consisting of two lofty edifices, square, with pillars on all sides; each pillar was made to represent a succession of shafts by the intervention of salient blocks, forming capitals to what they surmounted and pedestals to what they supported. The apartments within were gorgeously gilt and sumptuously furnished. There yet remains, in remarkable preservation, a vermilion chamber looking toward the east; though, otherwise, a forest of stately trees and several broken arches alone mark the spot where dwelt in regal splendor this foreign favorite of P'hra Narai.

He also erected the famous castle on the west of the town, on a piece of ground, near the north bank of the river, which formerly belonged to a Buddhist monastery.

Finally, to keep off the Birman invaders, he built a wall, surmounted along its whole extent by a parapet, and fortified with towers at regular intervals of forty fathoms, as well as by four larger ones at its extremities on the banks of the river, below the two bridges. Its gates appear to have been twelve or thirteen in number, and the extent of the southern portion is fixed at two thousand fathoms. Suburban villages still exist on both sides of the river, and, beyond these, the religious buildings, which have been restored, but which now display the fantastic rather than the grand style which distinguished the architecture of this consummate Grecian, whom the people name with wonder, — all marvellous works being by them attributed to gods, genii, devils, or the " Vicha-yen."

But the luxury in which the haughty statesman revelled, his towering ambition, and the wealth he lavished on his private abodes, joined to the lofty, condescending air he assumed toward the nobles, soon provoked their jealous murmurings against him and his too partial master; and when, at last, the king, falling ill, repaired to the premier's palace at Lophaburee, some of the more disaffected nobles, headed by a natural son of P'hra Narai and the two princes of Macassar, forced their way into the palace to slay the monarch. But the brave old man, at a glance divining their purpose, leaped from his couch and, seizing his sword, threw himself upon it, and died as his assassins entered.

In the picturesque drama of Siamese history no figure appears so truly noble and brilliant as this king, not merely renowned by the glory of his military exploits and the happy success of his more peaceful undertakings, but beloved for his affectionate concern for the welfare of his subjects, his liberality, his moderation, his modesty, his indifference to the formal honors due to his royal state, and (what is most rare in Asiatic character) his sincere aversion to flattery, his shyness even toward deserved and genuine praise.

Turning from the corpse of the king, the baffled regicides dashed at the luxurious apartment where Phaulkon slumbered, as was his custom of an afternoon, unattended save by his fair young daughter Constantia. Breaking in, they tore the sleeping father from the arms of his agonized child, who with piteous implorings offered her life for his, bound him with cords, dragged him to the woods beyond his garden, and there, within sight of the lovely little Greek chapel he had erected for his private devotions, first tortured him like fiends, and then, dispatching him, flung his body into a pit. His daughter, following them, clung fast to her father, and, though her heart bled and her brain grew numb between the gashes and the groans, she still cheered him with her passionate endearments; and, holding before his eyes a cross of gold that always hung on her bosom, inspired him to die like a brave man and a Christian. After that the lovely heroine was dragged into slavery and concubinage by the infamous Chow Dua, one of the bloodiest of the gang.

Even pagan chroniclers do not fail to render homage to so brave a man, of whom they tell that " he bore all with a fortitude and defiance that astounded the monsters who slew him, and convinced them that he derived his supernatural courage and contempt of pain from the miraculous virtues of his daughter's golden cross."

After the death of the able premier, the Birmese again overran the land, laying waste the fields, and besieging the city of Ayuthia for two years. Finding they could not reduce it by famine, they tried flames, and the burning is said to have lasted two whole months. One of the feudal lords of Siam, Phya Tâk, a Chinese adventurer, who had amassed wealth, and held the office of governor of the northern provinces under the late king, seeing the impending ruin of the country, assembled his personal followers and dependants, and with about a thousand hardy and resolute warriors retired to the mountain fastness of Naghon Najok, whence from time to time he swooped down to harass the encampments of the Birmese, who were almost invariably worsted in the skirmishes he provoked. He then moved upon Bangplasoi, and the people of that place came out with gifts of treasure and hailed him as their sovereign. Thence he sailed to Rajong, strengthened his small force with volunteers in great numbers, marched against Chantaboon, whose governor had disputed his authority, and executed that indiscreet official; levied another large army; built and equipped a hundred vessels of war;

and set sail — a part of his army preceding him overland — for Kankhoa, on the confines of Cochin China,
which place he brought to terms in less than three hours.
Thence he pushed on to Cambodia, and arriving there on
the Siamese Sabâto, or Sabbath, he issued a solemn proclamation to his army, assuring them that he would that
evening worship in the temple of the famous emerald
idol, P'hra Këau.   Every man was ordered to arm as if
for battle, but to wear the sacred robe, — white for the
laity, yellow for the clergy; and all the priests who followed his fortunes were required to lead the way into
the grand temple through the southern portico, over
which stood a triple-headed tower.   Then the conqueror,
having prepared himself by fasting and purification, clad
in his sacred robes and armed to the teeth, followed and
made his words good.

Almost his first act was to send his ships to the adjacent provinces for supplies of rice and grain, which he
dispensed so bountifully to the famishing people that
they gratefully accepted his rule.

This king is described as an enthusiastic and indefatigable warrior, scorning palaces, and only happy in camp
or at the head of his army.   His people found in him a
true friend, he was ever kind and generous to the poor,
and to his soldiers he paid fivefold the rates of former
reigns.   But toward the nobles he was haughty, rude,
exacting.   It is supposed that his prime minister, fearing
to oppose him openly, corrupted his chief concubine, and
with her assistance drugged his food; so that he was rendered insane, and, imagining himself a god, insisted that
sacrifices and offerings should be made to him, and began
to levy upon the nobility for enormous sums, often putting them to the torture to extort treasure.   Instigated
by their infuriated lords, the people now rebelled against
their lately idolized master, and attacked him in his pal-

ace, from which he fled by a secret passage to an adjoining monastery, in the disguise of a priest. But the premier, to whom he was presently betrayed, had him put to death, on the pretext that he might cause still greater scandal and disaster, but in reality to establish himself in undisputed possession of the throne, which he now usurped under the title of P'hra-Phuthi-Chow-Lhuang, and removed the palace from the west to the east bank of the Meinam. During his reign the Birmese made several attempts to invade the country, but were invariably repulsed with loss.

This brings us to the uneventful reign of P'hēn-din-Klang; and by his death, in 1825, to the beginning of the story of his Majesty, Maha Mongkut, the late supreme king, and my employer, with whom, in these pages, we shall have much to do.

IV.

HIS EXCELLENCY'S HAREM AND HELPMEET.

WHEN the Senabawdee, or Royal Council, by elevating to the throne the priest-prince Chowfa Mongkut, frustrated the machinations of the son of his predecessor, they by the same stroke crushed the secret hopes of Chow Phya Sri Sury Wongse, the present premier. It is whispered to this day — for no native, prince or peasant, may venture to approach the subject openly — that, on the day of coronation, his Excellency retired to his private chambers, and there remained, shut up with his chagrin and grief, for three days. On the fourth, arrayed in his court robes and attended by a numerous retinue, he presented himself at the palace to take part in the ceremonies with which the coronation was celebrated. The astute young king, who in his priestly character had penetrated many state secrets, advanced to greet him, and with the double purpose of procuring the adherence and testing the fidelity of this discontented and wavering son of his stanch old champion, the Duke Somdetch Ong Yai, appointed him on the spot to the command of the army, under the title of Phya P'hra Kralahome.

This flattering distinction, though it did not immediately beguile him from his moodiness, for a time diverted his dangerous fancies into channels of activity, and he found a safe expression for his annoyance in a useful restlessness. But after he had done more than any of his predecessors to remodel and perfect the army, he relapsed into morbid melancholy, from which he was once more aroused by the call of his royal master, who invited him to share the labors and the honors of government in the highest civil office, that of prime minister. He accepted, and has ever since shown himself prolific in devices to augment the revenue, secure the co-operation of the nobility, and confirm his own power. His remarkable executive faculty, seconding the enlightened policy of the king, would doubtless have inaugurated a golden age for his country, but for the aggressive meddling of French diplomacy in the quarrels between the princes of Cochin China and Cambodia ; by which exasperating measure Siam is in the way to lose one of her richest possessions,* and may in time become, herself, the brightest and most costly jewel in the crown of France.

Such was Chow Phya Sri Sury Wongse when I was first presented to him : a natural king among the dusky forms that surrounded him, the actual ruler of that semi-barbarous realm, and the prime contriver of its arbitrary policy. Black, but comely, robust, and vigorous, neck short and thick, nose large and nostrils wide, eyes inquisitive and penetrating, his was the massive brain proper to an intellect deliberate and systematic. Well found in the best idioms of his native tongue, he expressed strong, discriminative thoughts in words at once accurate and abundant. His only vanity was his English, with which he so interlarded his native speech, as often to impart the effect of levity to ideas that, in themselves, were grave, judicious, and impressive.

Let me conduct the reader into one of the saloons of the palace, where we shall find this intellectual sensualist in the moral relaxation of his harem, with his latest pets and playthings about him.

Peering into a twilight, studiously contrived, of dimly-

* Cambodia.

lighted and suggestive shadows, we discover in the centre of the hall a long line of girls with skins of olive, — creatures who in years and physical proportions are yet but children, but by training developed into women and accomplished actresses.   There are some twenty of them, in transparent draperies with golden girdles, their arms and bosoms, wholly nude, flashing, as they wave and heave, with barbaric ornaments of gold.   The heads are modestly inclined, the hands are humbly folded, and the eyes droop timidly beneath long lashes.   Their only garment, the lower skirt, floating in light folds about their limbs, is of very costly material bordered heavily with gold.   On the ends of their fingers they wear long "nails" of gold, tapering sharply like the claws of a bird.   The apartment is illuminated by means of candelabras, hung so high that the light falls in a soft hazy mist on the tender faces and pliant forms below.

Another group of maidens, comely and merry, sit behind musical instruments, of so great variety as to recall the "cornet, flute, sackbut, harp, psaltery, and dulcimer" of Scripture.   The "head wife" of the premier, earnestly engaged in creaming her lips, reclines apart on a dais, attended by many waiting-women.

From the folds of a great curtain a single flute opens the entertainment with low tender strains, and from the recesses twelve damsels appear, bearing gold and silver fans, with which, seated in order, they fan the central group.

Now the dancers, a burst of joyous music being the signal, form in two lines, and simultaneously, with military precision, kneel, fold and raise their hands, and bow till their foreheads touch the carpet before their lord. Then suddenly springing to their feet, they describe a succession of rapid and intricate circles, tapping the carpet with their toes in time to the music.   Next follows a miracle of art, such as may be found only among pupils of the highest physical training; a dance in which every motion is poetry, every attitude an expression of love, even rest but the eloquence of passion overcome by its own fervor. The music swelling into a rapturous tumult preludes the choral climax, wherein the dancers, raising their delicate feet, and curving their arms and fingers in seemingly impossible flexures, sway like withes of willow, and agitate all the muscles of the body like the fluttering of leaves in a soft breeze. Their eyes glow as with an inner light; the soft brown complexion, the rosy lips half parted, the heaving bosom, and the waving arms, as they float round and round in wild eddies of dance, impart to them the aspect of fair young fiends.

And there sits the Kralahome, like the idol of ebony before the demon had entered it! while around him these elfin worshippers, with flushed cheeks and flashing eyes, tossing arms and panting bosoms, whirl in their witching waltz. He is a man to be wondered at, — stony and grim, his huge hands resting on his knees in statuesque repose, as though he supported on his well-poised head the whole weight of the Maha Mongkut * itself, while at his feet these brown leaves of humanity lie quivering.

Is it all *maya*, — delusion? I open wide my eyes, then close them, then open them again. There still lie the living puppets, not daring to look up to the face of their silent god, where scorn and passion contend for place. The dim lights, the shadows blending with them, the fine harmony of colors, the wild harmony of sounds, the fantastic phantoms, the overcoming sentiment, all the poetry and the pity of the scene, — the formless longing, the undefined sense of wrong! Poor things, poor things!

The prime minister of Siam enjoys no exemption from that mocking law which condemns the hero strutting on

* "The Mighty Crown."

the stage of the world to cut but a sorry figure at home. Toward these helpless slaves of his nod his deportment was studiously ungracious and mean. No smile of pleased surprise or approbation ever brightened his gloomy countenance. True, the fire of his native ardor burns there still, but through no crevice of the outward man may one catch a glimpse of its light. Though he rage as a fiery furnace within, externally he is calm as a lake, too deep to be troubled by the skipping, singing brooks that flow into it. Rising automatically, he abruptly retired, bored. And those youthful, tender forms, glowing and panting there, — in what glorious robes might not their proper loveliness have arrayed them, if only their hearts had looked upward in freedom, and not, like their trained eyes, downward in blind homage.

Koon Ying Phan (literally, "The Lady in One Thousand") was the head wife of the Premier. He married her, after repudiating the companion of his more grateful years, the mother of his only child, a son — the legitimacy of whose birth he doubted, and so, for a grim jest, named the lad *My Chi*, "Not So." He would have put the mother to death, but finding no real grounds for his suspicion, let her off with a public "putting away." The divorced woman, having nothing left but her disowned baby, carefully changed the *My Chi* to *Ny Chi* ("Not So" to "Master So"), — a cunning trick of pride, but a doubtful improvement.

Koon Ying Phan had neither beauty nor grace; but her habits were domestic, and her temper extremely mild. When I first knew her she was perhaps forty years old, — stout, heavy, dark, — her only attraction the gentle expression of her eyes and mouth. Around her pretty residence, adjoining the Premier's palace, bloomed the most charming garden I saw in Siam, with shrubberies, fountains, and nooks, designed by a true artist; though the work of the native florists is usually fantastic and grotesque, with an excess of dwarfed trees in Chinese vases. There was, besides, a cool, shaded walk, leading to a more extensive garden, adorned with curious lattice-work, and abounding in shrubs of great variety and beauty. Koon Ying Phan had a lively love for flowers, which she styled the children of her heart; "for my lord is childless," she whispered.

In her apartments the same subdued lights and mellow half-tints prevailed that in her husband's saloons imparted a pensive sentiment to the place. There were neither carpets nor mirrors; and the only articles of furniture were some sofa-beds, low marble couches, tables, and a few arm-chairs, but all of forms antique and delicate. The combined effect was one of delicious coolness, retirement, and repose, even despite the glaring rays that strove to invade the sweet refuge through the silken window-nets.

This lady, to whom belonged the undivided supervision of the premier's household, was kind to the younger women of her husband's harem, in whose welfare she manifested a most amiable interest, — living among them happily, as a mother among her daughters, sharing their confidences, and often pleading their cause with her lord and theirs, over whom she exercised a very cautious but positive influence.

I learned gladly and with pride to admire and love this lady, to accept her as the type of a most precious truth. For to behold, even afar off, "silent upon a peak" of sympathy, the ocean of love and pathos, of passion and patience, on which the lives of these our pagan sisters drift, is to be gratefully sensible of a loving, pitying, and sufficing Presence, even in the darkness of error, superstition, slavery, and death.

Shortly after her marriage, Koon Ying Phan, moved partly by compassion for the wrongs of her predecessor, partly by the "aching void" of her own life, adopted the disowned son of the premier, and called him, with reproachful significance, P'hra Nah Why, "the Lord endures." And her strong friend, Nature, who had already knit together, by nerve and vein and bone and sinew, the father and the child, now came to her aid, and united them by the finer but scarcely weaker ties of habit and companionship and home affections.

The Temple of the Sleeping Idol.

V

THE TEMPLES OF THE SLEEPING AND THE EMERALD IDOLS.

THE day had come for my presentation to the supreme king. After much preliminary talk between the Kralahome and myself, through the medium of the interpreter, it had been arranged that my straightforward friend, Captain B——, should conduct us to the royal palace, and procure the interview. Our cheerful escort arrived duly, and we proceeded up the river, — my boy maintaining an ominous silence all the while, except once, when he shyly confessed he was afraid to go.

At the landing we found a large party of priests, some bathing, some wringing their yellow garments; graceful girls balancing on their heads vessels of water; others, less pleasing, carrying bundles of grass, or baskets of fruit and nuts; noblemen in gilded sedans, borne on men's shoulders, hurrying toward the palace; in the distance a troop of horsemen, with long glittering spears.

Passing the covered gangway at the landing, we came upon a clean brick road, bounded by two high walls, the one on the left enclosing the abode of royalty, the other the temple Watt Poh, where reposes in gigantic state the wondrous Sleeping Idol. Imagine a reclining figure one hundred and fifty feet long and forty feet high, entirely overlaid with plate gold; the soles of its monstrous feet covered with bass-reliefs inlaid with mother-of-pearl and chased with gold; each separate design distinctly

3   D

representing one of the many transmigrations of Buddha whereby he obtained Niphan. On the nails are graven his divine attributes, ten in number:

1. Arahang, — Immaculate, Pure, Chaste.

2. Samma Sam-Putho, — Cognizant of the laws of Nature, Infallible, Unchangeable, True.

3. Vicharanah Sampanoh, — Endowed with all Knowledge, all Science.

4. Lukha-tho, — Excellence, Perfection.

5. Lôk-havi-tho, — Cognizant of the mystery of Creation.

6. Annutharo, — Inconceivably Pure, without Sin.

7. Purisah tham-mah Sarathi, — Unconquerable, Invincible, before whom the angels bow.

8. Sassahdah, — Father of Beatitude, Teacher of the ways to bliss.

9. Poodh-tho, — Endowed with boundless Compassion, Pitiful, Tender, Loving, Merciful, Benevolent.

10. Pâk-havah, — Glorious, endowed with inconceivable Merit, Adorable.

Leaving this temple, we approached a low circular fort near the palace, — a miniature model of a great citadel, with bastions, battlements, and towers, showing confusedly over a crenellated wall. Entering by a curious wooden gate, bossed with great flat-headed nails, we reached by a stony pathway the stables (or, more correctly, the palace) of the White Elephant, where the huge creature — indebted for its " whiteness " to tradition rather than to nature — is housed royally. Passing these, we next came to the famous Watt P'hra Këau, or temple of the Emerald Idol.

An inner wall separates this temple from the military depot attached to the palace; but it is connected by a secret passage with the most private apartments of his Majesty's harem, which, enclosed on all sides, is accessible only to women. The temple itself is unquestionably one of the most remarkable and beautiful structures of its class in the Orient; the lofty octagonal pillars, the quaint Gothic doors and windows, the tapering and gilded roofs, are carved in an infinite variety of emblems, the lotos and the palm predominating. The adornment of the exterior is only equalled in its profusion by the pictorial and hieroglyphic embellishment within. The ceiling is covered with mythological figures and symbols. Most conspicuous among the latter are the luminous circles, resembling the mystic orb of the Hindoos, and representing the seven constellations known to the ancients; these revolve round a central sun in the form of a lotos, called by the Siamese *Dok Âthit* (sun-flower), because it expands its leaves to the rising sun and contracts them as he sets. On the cornices are displayed the twelve signs of the zodiac.

The altar is a wonder of dimensions and splendor, — a pyramid one hundred feet high, terminating in a fine spire of gold, and surrounded on every side by idols, all curious and precious, from the bijou image in sapphire to the colossal statue in plate gold. A series of trophies these, gathered from the triumphs of Buddhism over the proudest forms of worship in the old pagan world. In the pillars that surround the temple, and the spires that taper far aloft, may be traced types and emblems borrowed from the Temple of the Sun at Baalbec, the proud fane of Diana at Ephesus, the shrines of the Delian Apollo; but the Brahminical symbols and interpretations prevail. Strange that it should be so, with a sect that suffered by the slayings and the outcastings of a ruthless persecution, at the hands of their Brahmin fathers, for the cause of restoring the culture of that simple and pure philosophy which flourished before pantheism! The floor is paved with diamonds of polished brass,

which reflect the light of tall tapers that have burned on
for more than a hundred years, so closely is the sacred
fire watched. The floods of light and depths of shadow
about the altar are extreme, and the effect overwhelming.

The Emerald Idol is about twelve inches high and
eight in width. Into the virgin gold of which its hair
and collar are composed must have been stirred, while the
metal was yet molten, crystals, topazes, sapphires, rubies,
onyxes, amethysts, and diamonds, — the stones crude, or
rudely cut, and blended in such proportions as might
enhance to the utmost imaginable limit the beauty and
the cost of the adored effigy. The combination is as harmonious as it is splendid. No wonder it is commonly
believed that Buddha himself alighted on the spot in the
form of a great emerald, and by a flash of lightning
conjured the glittering edifice and altar in an instant
from the earth, to house and throne him there !

On either side of the eastern entrance — called *Patoo
Ngam,* " The Beautiful Gate " — stands a modern statue ;
one of Saint Peter, with flowing mantle and sandalled
feet, in an attitude of sorrow, as when " he turned away
his face and wept " ; the other of Ceres, scattering flowers.
The western entrance, which admits only ladies, is styled
Patoo Thavâdah, " The Angels' Gate," and is guarded by
genii of ferocious aspect.

At a later period, visiting this temple in company with
the king and his family, I called his Majesty's attention
to the statue at the Beautiful Gate, as that of a Christian
saint with whose story he was not unfamiliar. Turning
quickly to his children, and addressing them gently, he
bade them salute it reverently. " It is Mam's P'hra,"*
he said ; whereupon the tribe of little ones folded their
hands devoutly, and made obeisance before the effigy of
Saint Peter.

* Saint, or Lord.

THE BEAUTIFUL GATE OF THE TEMPLE.

As often as my thought reverts to this inspiring shrine, reposing in its lonely loveliness amid the shadows and the silence of its consecrated groves, I cannot find it in my heart to condemn, however illusive the object, but rather I rejoice to admire and applaud, the bent of that devotion which could erect so proud and beautiful a fane in the midst of moral surroundings so ignoble and un-lovely, — a spiritual remembrance perhaps older and truer than paganism, ennobling the pagan mind with the idea of an architectural Sabbath, so to speak, such as a heathen may purely enjoy and a Christian may not wisely despise.

VI.

THE KING AND THE GOVERNESS.

IN 1825 a royal prince of Siam (his birthright wrested from him, and his life imperilled) took refuge in a Buddhist monastery and assumed the yellow garb of a priest. His father, commonly known as P'hēn-din-Klang, first or supreme king of Siam, had just died, leaving this prince, Chowfa Mongkut, at the age of twenty, lawful heir to the crown; for he was the eldest son of the acknowledged queen, and therefore by courtesy and honored custom, if not by absolute right, the legitimate successor to the throne of the P'hra-batts.* But he had an elder half-brother, who, through the intrigues of his mother, had already obtained control of the royal treasury, and now, with the connivance, if not by the authority, of the Senabawdee, the Grand Council of the kingdom, proclaimed himself king. He had the grace, however, to promise his plundered brother — such royal promises being a cheap form of propitiation in Siam — to hold the reins of government only until Chowfa Mongkut should be of years and strength and skill to manage them. But, once firmly seated on the throne, the usurper saw in his patient but proud and astute kinsman only a hindrance and a peril in the path of his own cruder and fiercer aspirations. Hence the forewarning and the flight, the cloister and the yellow robes. And so the usurper continued to reign, unchallenged by any claim from the king that should be, until

* The Golden-footed.

March, 1851, when, a mortal illness having overtaken him, he convoked the Grand Council of princes and nobles around his couch, and proposed his favorite son as his successor. Then the safe asses of the court kicked the dying lion with seven words of sententious scorn, — "The crown has already its rightful owner"; whereupon the king literally cursed himself to death, for it was almost in the convulsion of his chagrin and rage that he came to his end, on the 3d of April.

In Siam there is no such personage as an heir-apparent to the throne, in the definite meaning and positive value which attaches to that phrase in Europe, — no prince with an absolute and exclusive title, by birth, adoption, or nomination, to succeed to the crown. And while it is true that the eldest living son of a Siamese sovereign by his queen or queen consort is recognized by all custom, ancient and modern, as the *probable* successor to the high seat of his royal sire, he cannot be said to have a clear and indefeasible right to it, because the question of his accession has yet to be decided by the electing voice of the Senabawdee, in whose judgment he may be ineligible, by reason of certain physical, mental, or moral disabilities, — as extreme youth, effeminacy, imbecility, intemperance, profligacy. Nevertheless, the election is popularly expected to result in the choice of the eldest son of the queen, though an interregnum or a regency is a contingency by no means unusual.

It was in view of this jurisdiction of the Senabawdee, exercised in deference to a just and honored usage, that the voice of the oracle fell upon the ear of the dying monarch with a disappointing and offensive significance; for he well knew who was meant by the "rightful owner" of the crown. Hardly had he breathed his last when, in spite of the busy intrigues of his eldest son (whom we find described in the *Bangkok Recorder* of July 26, 1866, as "most honorable and promising"), in spite of the bitter vexation of his lordship Chow Phya Sri Sury Wongse, so soon to be premier, the prince Chowfa Mongkut doffed his sacerdotal robes, emerged from his cloister, and was crowned, with the title of Somdetch Phra Paramendr Maha Mongkut.*

For twenty-five years had the true heir to the throne of the P'hra-batts, patiently biding his time, lain *perdu* in his monastery, diligently devoting himself to the study of Sanskrit, Pali, theology, history, geology, chemistry, and especially astronomy. He had been a familiar visitor at the houses of the American missionaries, two of whom (Dr. House and Mr. Mattoon) were, throughout his reign and life, gratefully revered by him for that pleasant and profitable converse which helped to unlock to him the secrets of European vigor and advancement, and to make straight and easy the paths of knowledge he had started upon. Not even the essential arrogance of his Siamese nature could prevent him from accepting cordially the happy influences these good and true men inspired ; and doubtless he would have gone more than half-way to meet them, but for the dazzle of the golden throne in the distance which arrested him midway between Christianity and Buddhism, between truth and delusion, between light and darkness, between life and death.

In the Oriental tongues this progressive king was eminently proficient; and toward priests, preachers, and teachers, of all creeds, sects, and sciences, an enlightened exemplar of tolerance. It was likewise his peculiar vanity to pass for an accomplished English scholar, and to this end he maintained in his palace at Bangkok a private printing establishment, with fonts of English type, which, as may be perceived presently, he was at no loss to keep in "copy." Perhaps it was the printing-office

---

* Duke, and royal bearer of the great crown.

which suggested, quite naturally, an English governess for the *élite* of his wives and concubines, and their offspring, — in number amply adequate to the constitution of a royal school, and in material most attractively fresh and romantic. Happy thought! Wherefore, behold me, just after sunset on a pleasant day in April, 1862, on the threshold of the outer court of the Grand Palace, accompanied by my own brave little boy, and escorted by a compatriot.

A flood of light sweeping through the spacious Hall of Audience displayed a throng of noblemen in waiting. None turned a glance, or seemingly a thought, on us, and, my child being tired and hungry, I urged Captain B—— to present us without delay. At once we mounted the marble steps, and entered the brilliant hall unannounced. Ranged on the carpet were many prostrate, mute, and motionless forms, over whose heads to step was a temptation as drolly natural as it was dangerous. His Majesty spied us quickly, and advanced abruptly, petulantly screaming, " Who? who? who ? "

Captain B—— (who, by the by, is a titled nobleman of Siam) introduced me as the English governess, engaged for the royal family. The king shook hands with us, and immediately proceeded to march up and down in quick step, putting one foot before the other with mathematical precision, as if under drill. " Forewarned, forearmed !" my friend whispered that I should prepare myself for a sharp cross-questioning as to my age, my husband, children, and other strictly personal concerns. Suddenly his Majesty, having cogitated sufficiently in his peculiar manner, with one long final stride halted in front of us, and, pointing straight at me with his forefinger, asked, " How old shall you be ? "

Scarcely able to repress a smile at a proceeding so absurd, and with my sex's distaste for so serious a question, I demurely replied, " One hundred and fifty years old."

3*

Had I made myself much younger, he might have ridiculed or assailed me; but now he stood surprised and embarrassed for a few moments, then resumed his queer march; and at last, beginning to perceive the jest, coughed, laughed, coughed again, and in a high, sharp key asked, "In what year were you borned?"

Instantly I struck a mental balance, and answered, as gravely as I could, "In 1788."

At this point the expression of his Majesty's face was indescribably comical. Captain B—— slipped behind a pillar to laugh; but the king only coughed, with a significant emphasis that startled me, and addressed a few words to his prostrate courtiers, who smiled at the carpet, —all except the prime minister, who turned to look at me. But his Majesty was not to be baffled so: again he marched with vigor, and then returned to the attack with *élan*.

"How many years shall you be married?"

"For several years, your Majesty."

He fell into a brown study; then, laughing, rushed at me, and demanded triumphantly:—

"Ha! How many grandchildren shall you now have? Ha, ha! How many? How many? Ha, ha, ha!"

Of course we all laughed with him; but the general hilarity admitted of a variety of constructions.

Then suddenly he seized my hand, and dragged me, *nolens volens*, my little Louis holding fast by my skirt, through several sombre passages, along which crouched duennas, shrivelled and grotesque, and many youthful women, covering their faces, as if blinded by the splendor of the passing Majesty. At length he stopped before one of the many-curtained recesses, and, drawing aside the hangings, disclosed a lovely, childlike form. He stooped and took her hand, (she naïvely hiding her face), and placing it in mine, said, "This is my wife, the Lady Tâlâp.

She desires to be educated in English. She is as pleasing for her talents as for her beauty, and it is our pleasure to make her a good English scholar. You shall educate her for me."

I replied that the office would give me much pleasure; for nothing could be more eloquently winning than the modest, timid bearing of that tender young creature in the presence of her lord. She laughed low and pleasantly as he translated my sympathetic words to her, and seemed so enraptured with the graciousness of his act that I took my leave of her with a sentiment of profound pity.

He led me back by the way we had come; and now we met many children, who put my patient boy to much childish torture for the gratification of their startled curiosity.

"I have sixty-seven children," said his Majesty, when we had returned to the Audience Hall. "You shall educate them, and as many of my wives, likewise, as may wish to learn English. And I have much correspondence in which you must assist me. And, moreover, I have much difficulty for reading and translating French letters; for French are fond of using gloomily deceiving terms. You must undertake; and you shall make all their murky sentences and gloomily deceiving propositions clear to me. And, furthermore, I have by every mail foreign letters whose writing is not easily read by me. You shall copy on round hand, for my readily perusal thereof."

Nil desperandum; but I began by despairing of my ability to accomplish tasks so multifarious. I simply bowed, however, and so dismissed myself for that evening.

One tempting morning, when the air was cool, my boy and I ventured some distance beyond the bounds of our usual cautious promenade, close to the palace of the premier. Some forty or fifty carpenters, building boats

under a long low shed, attracted the child's attention.
We tarried awhile, watching their work, and then strolled
to a stone bridge hard by, where we found a gang of repulsive wretches, all men, coupled by means of iron
collars and short but heavy fetters, in which they moved
with difficulty, if not with positive pain.   They were
carrying stone from the canal to the bridge, and as they
stopped to deposit their burdens, I observed that most of
them had hard, defiant faces, though here and there were
sad and gentle eyes that bespoke sympathy.   One of
them approached us, holding out his hand, into which
Boy dropped the few coins he had.   Instantly, with a
greedy shout, the whole gang were upon us, crowding us
on all sides, wrangling, yelling.   I was exceedingly
alarmed, and having no more money there, knew not
what to do, except to take my child in my arms, and
strive again and again to break through the press; but
still I fell back baffled, and sickened by the insufferable
odors that emanated from their disgusting persons; and
still they pressed and scrambled and screamed, and clanked
their horrid chains.   But behold! suddenly, as if struck
by lightning, every man of them fell on his face, and
officers flew among them pell-mell, swingeing with hard,
heavy thongs the naked wincing backs.

It was with a sense of infinite relief that we found
ourselves safe in our rooms at last; but the breakfast
tasted earthy and the atmosphere was choking, and our
very hearts were parched.   At night Boy lay burning on
his little bed, moaning for *aiyer sujok* (cold water), while
I fainted for a breath of fresh, sweet air.   But God
blesses these Eastern prison-houses not at all; the air
that visits them is no better than the life within,—
heavy, stifling, stupefying.   For relief I betook me to the
study of the Siamese language, an occupation I had found
very pleasant and inspiring.   As for Boy, who spoke

Malay fluently, it was wonderful with what aptness he acquired it.

When next I waited on the king, I was accompanied by the premier's sister, a fair and friendly woman, whose whole stock of English was, " Good morning, sir"; and with this somewhat irrelevant greeting, a dozen times in an hour, though the hour were night, she relieved her pent-up feelings, and gave expression to her sympathy and regard for me.

Mr. Hunter, private secretary to the premier, had informed me, speaking for his Excellency, that I should prepare to enter upon my duties at the royal palace without delay. Accordingly, next morning, the elder sister of the Kralahome came for us. She led the way to the river, followed by slave-girls bearing a gold teapot, a pretty gold tray containing two tiny porcelain cups with covers, her betel-box, also of gold, and two large fans. When we were seated in the closely covered basket-boat, she took up one of the books I had brought with me, and, turning over the leaves, came upon the alphabet; whereat, with a look of pleased surprise, she began repeating the letters. I helped her, and for a while she seemed amused and gratified; but presently, growing weary of it, she abruptly closed the book, and, offering me her hand, said, " Good morning, sir!" I replied with equal cordiality, and I think we bade each other good morning at least a dozen times before we reached the palace.

We landed at a showy pavilion, and after traversing several covered passages came to a barrier guarded by Amazons, to whom the old lady was evidently well known, for they threw open the gate for us, and " squatted" till we passed. A hot walk of twenty minutes brought us to a curious oval door of polished brass, which opened and shut noiselessly in a highly ornate frame.

This admitted us to a cool retreat, on one side of which were several temples or chapels in antique styles, and on the other a long dim gallery. On the marble floor of this pavilion a number of interesting children sat or sprawled, and quaint babies slept or frolicked in their nurses' arms. It was, indeed, a grateful change from the oppressive, irritating heat and glare through which we had just passed.

The loungers started up to greet our motherly guide, who humbly prostrated herself before them; and then refreshments were brought in on large silver trays, with covers of scarlet silk in the form of a bee-hive. As no knife or fork or spoon was visible, Boy and I were fain to content ourselves with oranges, wherewith we made ourselves an unexpected but cheerful show for the entertainment and edification of those juvenile spectators of the royal family of Siam. I smiled and held out my hand to them, for they were, almost without exception, attractive children; but they shyly shrank from me.

Meanwhile the "child-wife," to whom his Majesty had presented me at my first audience, appeared, and after saluting profoundly the sister of the Kralahome, and conversing with her for some minutes, lay down on the cool floor, and, using her betel-box for a pillow, beckoned to me. As I approached, and seated myself beside her, she said: "I am very glad to see you. It is long time I not see. Why you come so late?" to all of which she evidently expected no reply. I tried baby-talk, in the hope of making my amiable sentiments intelligible to so infantile a creature, but in vain. Seeing me disappointed and embarrassed, she oddly sang a scrap of the Sunday-school hymn, "There is a Happy Land, far, far away"; and then said, "I think of you very often. In the beginning, God created the heavens and the earth."

This meritorious but disjointed performance was followed by a protracted and trying silence, I sitting patient, and Boy wondering in my lap. At last she half rose, and, looking around, cautiously whispered, " Dear Mam Mattoon ! I love you. I think of you. Your boy dead, you come-to palace ; you cry — I love you" ; and laying her finger on her lips, and her head on the betel-box again, again she sang, " There is a Happy Land, far, far away ! "

Mrs. Mattoon is the wife of that good and true American apostle who has nobly served the cause of missions in Siam as a co-laborer with the excellent Dr. Samuel House. While the wife of the latter devoted herself indefatigably to the improvement of schools for the native children whom the mission had gathered round it, Mrs. Mattoon shared her labors by occasionally teaching in the palace, which was for some time thrown open to the ladies of her faithful sisterhood. Here, as elsewhere, the blended force and gentleness of her character wrought marvels in the impressible and grateful minds to which she had access.

So spontaneous and ingenuous a tribute of reverence and affection from a pagan to a Christian lady was inexpressibly charming to me.

Thus the better part of the day passed. The longer I rested dreaming there, the more enchanted seemed the world within those walls. I was aroused by a slight noise proceeding from the covered gallery, whence an old lady appeared bearing a candlestick of gold, with branches supporting four lighted candles. I afterward learned that these were daily offerings, which the king, on awakening from his forenoon slumber, sent to the Watt P'hra Këau. This apparition was the signal for much stir. The Lady Tâlâp started to her feet and fled, and we were left alone with the premier's sister and the slaves in waiting. The entire household seemed to awake on the in-

stant, as in the "Sleeping Palace" of Tennyson, at the
kiss of the Fairy Prince, —

> "The maid and page renewed their strife ;
> The palace banged, and buzzed, and clackt ;
> And all the long-pent stream of life
> Dashed downward in a cataract."

A various procession of women and children — some
pale and downcast, others bright and blooming, more
moody and hardened — moved in the one direction ; none
tarried to chat, none loitered or looked back ; the lord
was awake.

> "And last with these the king awoke,
> And in his chair himself upreared,
> And yawned, and rubbed his face, and spoke."

Presently the child-wife reappeared, — arrayed now in
dark blue silk, which contrasted well with the soft olive
of her complexion, — and quickly followed the others,
with a certain anxious alacrity expressed in her baby
face. I readily guessed that his Majesty was the awful
cause of all this careful bustle, and began to feel uneasy
myself, as my ordeal approached. For an hour I stood
on thorns. Then there was a general frantic rush. Attendants, nurses, slaves, vanished through doors, around
corners, behind pillars, under stairways ; and at last, preceded by a sharp, "cross" cough, behold the king !

We found his Majesty in a less genial mood than at my
first reception. He approached us coughing loudly and
repeatedly, a sufficiently ominous fashion of announcing
himself, which greatly discouraged my darling boy, who
clung to me anxiously. He was followed by a numerous
"tail" of women and children, who formally prostrated
themselves around him. Shaking hands with me coldly,
but remarking upon the beauty of the child's hair, half
buried in the folds of my dress, he turned to the premier's sister, and conversed at some length with her, she

apparently acquiescing in all that he had to say. He
then approached me, and said, in a loud and domineer-
ing tone : —

" It is our pleasure that you shall reside within this
palace with our family."

I replied that it would be quite impossible for me to
do so; that, being as yet unable to speak the language,
and the gates being shut every evening, I should feel like
an unhappy prisoner in the palace.

" Where do you go every evening ? " he demanded.

" Not anywhere, your Majesty. I am a stranger here."

" Then why you shall object to the gates being shut ? "

" I do not clearly know," I replied, with a secret shudder at the idea of sleeping within those walls ; " but I
am afraid I could not do it. I beg your Majesty will remember that in your gracious letter you promised me ' a
residence adjoining the royal palace,' not within it."

He turned and looked at me, his face growing almost
purple with rage. " I do not know I have promised. I
do not know former condition. I do not know anything
but you are our servant; and it is our pleasure that you
must live in this palace, and — *you shall obey*." Those
last three words he fairly screamed.

I trembled in every limb, and for some time knew not
how to reply. At length I ventured to say, " I am prepared to obey all your Majesty's commands within the
obligation of my duty to your family, but beyond that I
can promise no obedience."

" You *shall* live in palace," he roared, — " you *shall* live
in palace ! I will give woman slaves to wait on you.
You shall commence royal school in this pavilion on
Thursday next. That is the best day for such undertaking, in the estimation of our astrologers."

With that, he addressed, in a frantic manner, commands, unintelligible to me, to some of the old women

B

about the pavilion. My boy began to cry; tears filled my own eyes; and the premier's sister, so kind but an hour before, cast fierce glances at us both. I turned and led my child toward the oval brass door. We heard voices behind us crying, "Mam! Mam!" I turned again, and saw the king beckoning and calling to me. I bowed to him profoundly, but passed on through the brass door. The prime minister's sister bounced after us in a distraction of excitement, tugging at my cloak, shaking her finger in my face, and crying, "*My dee! my dee!*" * All the way back, in the boat, and on the street, to the very door of my apartments, instead of her jocund "Good morning, sir," I had nothing but *my dee.*

But kings, who are not mad, have their sober second-thoughts like other rational people. His Golden-footed Majesty presently repented him of his arbitrary "cantankerousness," and in due time my ultimatum was accepted.

* "Bad, bad!"

VII.

MARBLE HALLS AND FISH-STALLS.

WELL! by this time I was awake to the realities of time, place, and circumstance. The palace and its spells, the impracticable despot, the impassible premier, were not the phantasms of a witching night, but the hard facts of noonday. Here were the very Apollyons of paganry in the way, and only the Great Hearts of a lonely woman and a loving child to challenge them.

With a heart heavy with regret for the comparatively happy home I had left in Malacca, I sought an interview with the Kralahome, and told him (through his secretary, Mr. Hunter) how impossible it would be for me and my child to lodge within the walls of the Grand Palace; and that he was bound in honor to make good the conditions on which I had been induced to leave Singapore. At last I succeeded in interesting him, and he accorded me a gracious hearing. My objection to the palace, as a place of residence as well as of business, seemed to strike him as reasonable enough; and he promised to plead my cause with his Majesty, bidding me kindly "give myself no further trouble about the matter, for he would make it right."

Thus passed a few days more, while I waited monotonously under the roof of the premier, teaching Boy, studying Siamese, paying stated visits to the good Koon Ying Phan, and suffering tumultuous invasions from my "intimate enemies" of the harem, who came upon us like a flight of locusts, and rarely left without booty, in the shape of trifles they had begged of me. But things get themselves done, after a fashion, even in Siam; and so, one morning, came the slow but welcome news that the king was reconciled to the idea of my living outside the palace, that a house had been selected for me, and a messenger waited to conduct me to it.

Hastily donning our walking-gear, we found an elderly man, of somewhat sinister aspect, in a dingy red coat with faded facings of yellow, impatient to guide us to our unimaginable quarters. As we passed out, we met the premier, whose countenance wore a quizzing expression, which I afterward understood; but at the moment I saw in it only the characteristic conundrum that I had neither the time nor the talent to guess. It was with a lively sense of relief that I followed our conductor, in whom, by a desperate exploit of imagination, I discovered a promise of privacy and "home."

In a long, slender boat, with a high, uneven covering of wood, we stowed ourselves in the Oriental manner, my dress and appearance affording infinite amusement to the ten rowers as they plied their paddles, while our escort stood in the entrance chewing betel, and looking more ill-omened than ever. We alighted at the king's pavilion facing the river, and were led, by a long, circuitous, and unpleasant road, through two tall gates, into a street which, from the offensive odors that assailed us, I took to be a fish-market. The sun burned, the air stifled, the dust choked us, the ground blistered our feet; we were parching and suffocating, when our guide stopped at the end of this most execrable lane, and signed to us to follow him up three broken steps of brick. From a pouch in his dingy coat he produced a key, applied it to a door, and opened to us two small rooms, without a window in either, without a leaf to shade, without bath-closet or kitchen.   And this was the residence sumptuously appointed for the English governess to the royal family of Siam!

And furnished! and garnished! In one room, on a remnant of filthy matting, stood the wreck of a table, superannuated, and maimed of a leg, but propped by two chairs that with broken arms sympathized with each other.   In the other, a cheap excess of Chinese bedstead, that took the whole room to itself; and a mattress!—a mutilated epitome of a Lazarine hospital.

My stock of Siamese words was small, but strong.   I gratefully recalled the emphatic monosyllables wherewith the premier's sister had so berated me; and turning upon the king's messenger with her tremendous *my dee ! my dee!* dashed the key from his hand, as, inanely grinning, he held it out to me, caught my boy up in my arms, cleared the steps in a bound, and fled anywhere, anywhere, until I was stopped by the crowd of men, women, and children, half naked, who gathered around me, wondering. Then, remembering my adventure with the chain-gang, I was glad to accept the protection of my insulted escort, and escape from that suburb of disgust.   All the way back to the premier's our guide grinned at us fiendishly, whether in token of apology or ridicule I knew not; and landing us safely, he departed to our great relief, still grinning.

Straight went I to the Kralahome, whose shy, inquisitive smile was more and more provoking.   In a few sharp words I told him, through the interpreter, what I thought of the lodging provided for me, and that nothing should induce me to live in such a slum.   To which, with cool, deliberate audacity, he replied that nothing prevented me from living where I was.   I started from the low seat I had taken (in order to converse with him at my ease, he sitting on the floor), and not without difficulty found voice to say that neither his palace nor the den in the fish-market would suit me, and that I demanded suitable and independent accommodations, in a respectable neighborhood, for myself and my child. My rage only amused him. Smiling insolently, he rose, bade me, "'Never mind: it will be all right by and by," and retired to an inner chamber.

My head throbbed with pain, my pulse bounded, my throat burned. I staggered to my rooms, exhausted and despairing, there to lie, for almost a week, prostrated with fever, and tortured day and night with frightful fancies and dreams. Beebe and the gentle Koon Ying Phan nursed me tenderly, bringing me water, deliciously cool, in which the fragrant flower of the jessamine had been steeped, both to drink and to bathe my temples. As soon as I began to recover, I caressed the soft hand of the dear pagan lady, and implored her, partly in Siamese, partly in English, to intercede for me with her husband, that a decent home might be provided for us. She assured me, while she smoothed my hair and patted my cheek as though I were a helpless child, that she would do her best with him, begging me meanwhile to be patient. But that I could not be ; and I spared no opportunity to expostulate with the premier on the subject of my future abode and duties, telling him that the life I was leading under his roof was insupportable to me ; though, indeed, I was not ungrateful for the many offices of affection I received from the ladies of his harem, who in my trouble were sympathetic and tender. From that time forth the imperturbable Kralahome was ever courteous to me. Nevertheless, when from time to time I grew warm again on the irrepressible topic, he would smile slyly, tap the ashes from his pipe, and say, "Yes, sir ! Never mind, sir ! You not like, you can live in fish-market, sir ! " ·

The apathy and supineness of these people oppressed me intolerably. Never well practised in patience, I chafed at the *sang-froid* of the deliberate premier. Without compromising my dignity, I did much to enrage him; but he bore all with a *nonchalance* that was the more irritating because it was not put on.

Thus more than two months passed, and I had desperately settled down to my Oriental studies, content to snub the Kralahome with his own indifference, whilst he, on the other hand, blandly ignored our existence, when, to my surprise, he paid me a visit one afternoon, complimented me on my progress in the language, and on my "great heart,"— or *chi yai,* as he called it,— and told me his Majesty was highly incensed at my conduct in the affair of the fish-market, and that he had found me something to do. I thanked him so cordially that he expressed his surprise, saying, " Siamese lady no like work; love play, love sleep. Why you no love play ? "

I assured him that I liked play well enough when I was in the humor for play; but that at present I was not disposed to disport myself, being weary of my life in his palace, and sick of Siam altogether. He received my candor with his characteristic smile and a good-humored " Good by, sir ! "

Next morning ten Siamese lads and a little girl came to my room. The former were the half-brothers, nephews, and other " encumbrances " of the Kralahome ; the latter their sister, a simple child of nine or ten. Surely it was with no snobbery of condescension that I received these poor children, but rather gratefully, as a comfort and a wholesome discipline.

And so another month went by, and still I heard nothing from his Majesty. But the premier began to interest me. The more I saw of him the more he puzzled me. It was plain that all who came in contact with him both feared and loved him.   He displayed a kind of passive amiability of which he seemed always conscious, which he made his *forte*.   By what means he exacted such prompt obedience, and so completely controlled a people whom he seemed to drive with reins so loose and careless, was a mystery to me.   But that his influence and the prestige of his name penetrated to every nook of that vast yet undeveloped kingdom was the phenomenon which slowly but surely impressed me.   I was but a passing traveller, surveying from a distance and at large that vast plain of humanity; but I could see that it was systematically tilled by one master mind.

VIII.

OUR HOME IN BANGKOK.

REBUKED and saddened, I abandoned my long-cher-
ished hope of a home, and resigned myself with
no good grace to my routine of study and instruction.
Where were all the romantic fancies and proud anticipa-
tions with which I had accepted the position of governess to the royal family of Siam? Alas! in two squalid
rooms at the end of a Bangkok fish-market. I failed to
find the fresh strength and courage that lay in the hope
of improving the interesting children whose education
had been intrusted to me, and day by day grew more
and more desponding, less and less equal to the simple
task my "mission" had set me. I was fairly sick at
heart and ready to surrender that morning when the good
Koon Ying Phan came unannounced into our rooms to
tell us that a tolerable house was found for us at last. I
cannot describe with what an access of joy I heard the
glad tidings, nor how I thanked the messenger, nor how in
a moment I forgot all my chagrin and repining, and hugged
my boy and covered him with kisses. It was not until
that "order for release" arrived, that I truly felt how
offensive and galling had been the life I had led in the
premier's palace. It was with unutterable gladness that
I followed a half-brother of the Kralahome, Moonshee
leading Boy by the hand, to our new house. Passing
several streets, we entered a walled enclosure, abounding
in broken bricks, stone, lime, mortar, and various rubbish.

4

A tall, dingy storehouse occupied one side of the wall; in the other, a low door opened toward the river; and at the farther end stood the house, sheltered by a few fine trees, that, drooping over the piazza, made the place almost picturesque. On entering, however, we found ourselves face to face with overpowering filth. Poor Moonshee stood aghast. " It must be a paradise," he had said when we set out, " since the great Vizier bestows it upon the Mem Sahib, whom he delights to honor." Now he cursed his fate, and reviled all viziers. I turned to see to whom his lamentations were addressed, and beheld another Mohammedan seated on the floor, and attending with an attitude and air of devout respect. The scene reminded Boy and me of our old home, and we laughed heartily. On making a tour of inspection, we found nine rooms, some of them pleasant and airy, and with every " modern convenience " (though somewhat Oriental as to style) of bath, kitchen, etc. It was clear that soap and water without stint would do much here toward the making of a home for us. Beebe and Boy were hopeful, and promptly put a full stop to the rhetorical outcry of Moonshee by requesting him to enlist the services of his admiring friend and two China coolies to fetch water. But there were no buckets. With a few dollars that I gave him, Moonshee, with all a Moslem's resignation to any new turn in his fate, departed to explore for the required utensils, while the brother of the awful Kralahome, perched on the piazza railing, adjusted his anatomy for a comfortable oversight of the proceedings. Boy, with his " pinny " on, ran off in glee to make himself promiscuously useful, and I sat down to plan an attack.

Where to begin? — that was the question. It was such filthy filth, so monstrous in quantity and kind, — dirt to be stared at, defied, savagely assaulted with rage and havoc. Suddenly I arose, shook my head dangerously at the prime minister's brother,—who, fascinated, had advanced into the room,—marched through a broken door, hung my hat and mantle on a rusty nail, doffed my neat half-mourning, slipped on an old wrapper, dashed at the vile matting that in ulcerous patches afflicted the floor, and began fiercely tearing it up.

In good time Moonshee and his new friend returned with half a dozen buckets, but no coolies; in place of the latter came a neat and pleasant Siamese lady, Mrs. Hunter, wife of the premier's secretary, bringing her slaves to help, and some rolls of fresh, sweet China matting for the floor. How quickly the general foulness was purified, the general raggedness repaired, the general shabbiness made "good as new"! The floors, that had been buried under immemorial dust, arose again under the excavating labors of the sweepers; and the walls, that had been gory with expectorations of betel, hid their "damnéd spots" under innocent veils of whitewash.

Moonshee, who had evidently been beguiled by a cheap and spurious variety of the wine of Shiraz, and now sat maudlin on the steps, weeping for his home in Singapore, I despatched peremptorily in search of Beebe, bedsteads, and boxes. But the Kralahome's brother had vanished, doubtless routed by the brooms.

Bright, fresh, fragrant matting; a table neither too low to be pretty nor too high to be useful; a couple of arm-chairs, hospitably embracing; a pair of silver candle-sticks, quaint and homely; a goodly company of pleasant books; a piano, just escaping from its travelling-cage, with all its pent-up music in its bosom; a cosey little cot clinging to its ampler mother; a stream of generous sunlight from the window gilding and gladdening all,—behold our home in Siam!

I worked exultingly till the setting sun slanted his long shadows across the piazza. Then came comfortable

Beebe with the soup and dainties she had prepared with
the help of a "Bombay man." Boy slept soundly in an
empty room, overcome by the spell of its sudden sweetness, his hands and face as dirty as a healthy, well-regu-
lated boy could desire. Triumphantly I bore him to his
own pretty couch, adjusted my hair, resumed my royal
robes of mauve muslin, and prepared to queen it in my
own palace.

And even as I stood, smiling at my own small grandeur,
came tender memories crowding thick upon me, — of a
soft, warm lap, in which I had once loved to lay my
head; of a face, fair, pensive, loving, lovely; of eyes
whose deep and quiet light a shadow of unkindness never
crossed; of lips that sweetly crooned the songs of a far-
off, happy land; of a presence full of comfort, hope,
strength, courage, victory, peace, that perfect harmony
that comes of perfect faith, — a child's trust in its mother.

Passionately I clasped my child in my arms, and awoke
him with pious promises that took the form of kisses.
Beebe, soup, teapot, candlesticks, teacups, and dear faithful Bessy, looked on and smiled.

Hardly had we finished this, our first and finest feast,
in celebration of our glorious independence, when our late
guide of fish-market fame, he of the seedy red coat and
faded yellow facings, appeared on the piazza, saluted us
with that vacant chuckle and grin wherefrom no inference could be drawn, and delivered his Majesty's order
that I should now come to the school.

Unterrified and deliberate, we lingered yet a little over
that famous breakfast, then rose, and prepared to follow
the mechanical old ape. Boy hugged Bessy fondly by
way of good-by, and, leaving Beebe on guard, we went
forth. The same long, narrow, tall, and very crank boat
received us. The sun was hot enough to daunt a sepoy;

down the bare backs of the oarsmen flowed miniature
Meinams of sweat, as they tugged, grunting, against the
strong current.   We landed at the familiar (king's) pavilion, the front of which projects into the river by a low
portico.   The roof, rising in several tiers, half shelters, half
bridges the detached and dilapidated parts of the structure, which presents throughout a very ancient aspect,
parts of the roof having evidently been renewed, and the
gables showing traces of recent repairs, while the rickety
pillars seem to protest with groans against the architectural anachronism that has piled so many young heads
upon their time-worn shoulders.

IX.

OUR SCHOOL IN THE PALACE.

THE fact is remarkable, that though education in its higher degrees is popularly neglected in Siam, there is scarcely a man or woman in the empire who cannot read and write. Though a vain people, they are neither bigoted nor shallow; and I think the day is not far off when the enlightening influences applied to them, and accepted through their willingness, not only to receive instruction from Europeans, but even to adopt in a measure their customs and their habits of thought, will raise them to the rank of a superior nation.

The language of this people advances but slowly in the direction of grammatical perfection. Like many other Oriental tongues, it was at first purely monosyllabic; but as the Pali or Sanskrit has been liberally engrafted on it, polysyllabic words have been formed. Its pronouns and particles are peculiar, its idioms few and simple, its metaphors very obvious. It is copious to redundancy in terms expressive of royalty, rank, dignity — in fact, a distinct phraseology is required in addressing personages of exalted station; repetitions of word and phrase are affected, rather than shunned. Sententious brevity and simplicity of expression belong to the pure spirit of the language, and when employed impart to it much dignity and beauty; but there is no standard of orthography, nor any grammar, and but few rules of universal application. Every Siamese writer spells to please

A PUPIL OF THE ROYAL SCHOOL.

himself, and the purism of one is the slang or gibberish of another.

The Siamese write from left to right, the words running together in a line unbroken by spaces, points, or capitals ; so that, as in ancient Sanskrit, an entire paragraph appears as one protracted word,

"That, like a wounded snake, drags its slow length along."

When not written with a reed on dark native paper, the characters are engraved with a style (of brass or iron, one end sharp for writing, the other flat for erasing) on palm-leaves prepared for the purpose.

In all parts of the empire the boys are taught by priests to read, write, and cipher. Every monastery is provided with a library, more or less standard. The more elegant books are composed of tablets of ivory, or of palmyra leaves delicately prepared ; the characters engraved on these are gilt, the margins and edges adorned with heavy gilding or with flowers in bright colors.

The literature of the Siamese deals principally with religious topics. The " Kammarakya," or Buddhist Ritual, — a work for the priesthood only, and therefore, like others of the Vinnâyâ, little known, — contains the vital elements of the Buddhist Moral Code, and, *per se*, is perfect ; on this point all writers, whether partial or captious, are of one mind. Spence Hardy, a Wesleyan missionary, speaking of that part of the work entitled " Dhammâ-Padam," * which is freely taught in the schools attached to the monasteries, admits that a compilation might be made from its precepts, " which in the purity of its ethics could hardly be equalled from any other heathen author."

M. Laboulaye, one of the most distinguished members of the French Academy, remarks, in the *Débats* of April 4,

* Properly *Dharmna,* — " Footsteps of the Law."

1853, on a work known by the title of "Dharmna Maitrî," or "Law of Charity".: —

"It is difficult to comprehend how men, not aided by revelation, could have soared so high and approached so near the truth. Beside the five great commandments, — not to kill, not to steal, not to commit adultery, not to lie, not to get drunk, — every shade of vice, hypocrisy, anger, pride, suspicion, greed, gossip, cruelty to animals, is guarded against by special precepts. Among the virtues commended we find, not only reverence for parents, care for children, submission to authority, gratitude, moderation in time of prosperity, resignation and fortitude in time of trial, equanimity at all times, but virtues unknown to any heathen system of morality, such as the duty of forgiving insults, and of rewarding evil with good."

All virtues, we are told, spring from *maitrî*, and this *maitrî* can only be rendered by charity and love.

"I do not hesitate," says Burnouf, in his *Lotus de la Bonne Loi,* "to translate by 'charity' the word *maitrî*, which expresses, not merely friendship, or the feeling of particular affection which a man has for one or more of his fellow-creatures, but that universal feeling which inspires us with good-will toward all men and a constant willingness to help them."

I may here add the testimony of Barthélemy Saint-Hilaire : "I do not hesitate to add," he writes, "that, save the Christ alone, there is not among the founders of religion a figure more pure, more touching, than that of Buddha. His life is without blemish ; his constant heroism equals his conviction ; and if the theory he extols is false, the personal examples he affords are irreproachable. He is the accomplished model of all the virtues he preaches ; his abnegation, his charity, his unalterable sweetness, never belie themselves. At the age of twenty-nine he retires from the court of the king, his father, to become a devotee and a beggar. He silently prepares his doctrine by six years of seclusion and meditation. He propagates it, by the unaided power of speech and persuasion, for more than half a century ; and when he dies in the arms of his disciples, it is with the serenity of a sage who has practised goodness all his life, and knows that he has found Truth."

Another work, as sacred and more mystic, is the " Parajikâ," read in the temples with closed doors by the chief priests exclusively, and only to such devotees as have entered the monastic schools for life.

Then there are the " P'ra-jana Para-mita," (the " Accomplishment of Reason," or " Transcendental Wisdom,)" and other works in abstruse philosophy. The " Lalita Vistara " contains the life of Buddha, and is esteemed the highest authority as to the more remarkable events in the career of the great reformer. The " Saddharma-pundikara " (or *pundariki* in Ceylon), " The White Lotos of the True Religion," presents the incidents of Buddha's life in the form of legend and fable.

The " Ganda-Veyuha," but little known, consists of remarkable and very beautiful forms of prayer and thanksgiving, with psalms of praise addressed to the Perfection of the Infinite and to the Invisible, by Sakya Muni, the Buddha. The " Nirwana " treats of the end of material existence, and is universally read, and highly esteemed by Buddhists as a treatise of rare merit.

But the most important parts of the theological study of the Siamese priesthood are found in a work revered under the titles of "Tautras " and " Kala-Chakara," — that is, " Circles of Time, Matter, Space " ; probably a translation of the Sanskrit symbolic word, *Om*, " Circle." There are twenty-two volumes, treating exclusively of mystics and mystical worship.

4 *

The libraries of the monasteries are rich in works on the theory and practice of medicine; but very poor in historical books, the few preserved dealing mainly with the lives and actions of Siamese rulers, oddly associated with the genii and heroes of the Hindoo mythology. Like the early historians of Greece and Rome, the writers are careful to furnish a particular account of all signs, omens, and predictions relating to the several events recorded. They possess also a few translated works in Chinese history.

The late king was an authority on all questions of religion, law, and custom, and was familiar with the writings of Pythagoras and Aristotle.

The Siamese have an extravagant fondness for the drama, and for poetry of every kind. In all the lyric form predominates, and their compositions are commonly adapted for instrumental accompaniment. Their dramatic entertainments are mainly musical, combining rudely the opera with the ballet, — monotonous singing, and listless, mechanical dancing. Dialogue is occasionally introduced, the favorite subjects being passages from the Hindoo Avatars, the epic "Ramayana," and the "Mahabharata"; or from legends, peculiar to Siam, of gods, heroes, and demons. Throughout their literature, mythology is the all-pervading element; history, science, arts, customs, conversation, opinion, doctrine, are alike colored and flavored with it.

With so brief and meagre a sketch of the literature of Siam, I would fain prepare the reader to appreciate the peculiarities of an English classical school in the Royal Palace at Bangkok. In Siam, all schools, literary societies, monasteries, even factories, all intellectual and progressive enterprises of whatever nature and intention, are opened and begun on Thursday, "One P'ra Hatt"; because that day is sacred to the goddess of Mind or Wisdom, probably the Hindoo Saraswati. On the Thursday appointed for the opening of my classes in the palace, one of the king's barges conveyed us across the Meinam. At the landing I was met by slave-girls, who conducted me to the palace through the gate called Patoo Sap, " Gate of Knowledge." Here I was received by some Amazons, who in turn gave notice to other slave-girls waiting to escort us to a pavilion — or, more correctly, temple — dedicated to the wives and daughters of Siam.* The profound solitude of this refuge, embowered in its twilight grove of orange and palm trees, was strangely tranquillizing. The religion of the place seemed to overcome us, as we waited among the tall, gilded pillars of the temple. On one side was an altar, enriched with some of the most curious and precious offerings of art to be found in the East. There was a gilded rostrum also, from which the priests daily officiated; and near by, on the summit of a curiously carved trunk of an old Bho tree,† the goddess of Mind presided.

The floor of this beautiful temple was a somewhat gaudy mosaic of variegated marble and precious stones; but the gilded pillars, the friezes that surmounted them, and the vaulted roof of gilded arabesques, seemed to tone down the whole to their own chaste harmony of design.

In the centre of the temple stood a long table, finely carved, and some gilt chairs. The king and most of the nobler ladies of the court were present, with a few of the chief priests, among whom I recognized, for the first time, his Lordship Chow Khoon Sâh.

His Majesty received me and my little boy most kindly. After an interval of silence he clapped his hands lightly, and instantly the lower hall was filled with female slaves.

* *Watt Khoon Choom Manda Thai*, — "Temple of the Mothers of the Free."

† The sacred tree under which Guadama discoursed with his disciples.

A word or two, dropped from his lips, bowed every head and dispersed the attendants. But they presently returned laden, some with boxes containing books, slates, pens, pencils, and ink; others with lighted tapers and vases filled with the white lotos, which they set down before the gilded chairs.

At a signal from the king, the priests chanted a hymn from the "P'ra-jana Para-mita";* and then a burst of music announced the entrance of the princes and princesses, my future pupils. They advanced in the order of their ages. The Princess Ying You Wahlacks ("First-born among Women"), having precedence, approached and prostrated herself before her royal father, the others following her example. I admired the beauty of her skin, the delicacy of her form, and the subdued lustre of her dreamy eyes. The king took her gently by the hand, and presented me to her, saying simply, "The English teacher." Her greeting was quiet and self-possessed. Taking both my hands, she bowed, and touched them with her forehead; then, at a word from the king, retired to her place on the right. One by one, in like manner, all the royal children were presented and saluted me; and the music ceased.

His Majesty then spoke briefly, to this effect: "Dear children, as this is to be an English school, you will have to learn and observe the English modes of salutation, address, conversation, and etiquette; and each and every one of you shall be at liberty to sit in my presence, unless it be your own pleasure not to do so." The children all bowed, and touched their foreheads with their folded palms, in acquiescence.

Then his Majesty departed with the priests; and the moment he was fairly out of sight, the ladies of the court began, with much noise and confusion, to ask questions,

---

* "Accomplishment of Reason," or "Transcendental Wisdom."

turn over the leaves of books, and chatter and giggle together. Of course, no teaching was possible in such a din ; my young princes and princesses disappeared in the arms of their nurses and slaves, and I retired to my apartments in the prime minister's palace. But the serious business of my school began on the following Thursday.

On that day a crowd of half-naked children followed me and my Louis to the palace gates, where our guide gave us in charge to a consequential female slave, at whose request the ponderous portal was opened barely wide enough to admit one person at a time. On entering we were jealously scrutinized by the Amazonian guard, and a "high private" questioned the propriety of admitting my boy ; whereat a general tittering, and we passed on. We advanced through the noiseless oval door, and entered the dim, cool pavilion, in the centre of which the tables were arranged for school. Away flew several venerable dames who had awaited our arrival, and in about an hour returned, bringing with them twenty-one scions of Siamese royalty, to be initiated into the mysteries of reading, writing, and arithmetic, after the European, and especially the English manner.

It was not long before my scholars were ranged in chairs around the long table, with Webster's far-famed spelling-books before them, repeating audibly after me the letters of the alphabet. While I stood at one end of the table, my little Louis at the other, mounted on a chair, the better to command his division, mimicked me with a fidelity of tone and manner very quaint and charming. Patiently his small finger pointed out to his class the characters so strange to them, and not yet perfectly familiar to himself.

About noon, a number of young women were brought to me, to be taught like the rest. I received them sym-

pathetically, at the same time making a memorandum of
their names in a book of my own. This created a general
and lively alarm, which it was not in my power immediately to allay, my knowledge of their language being confined to a few simple sentences; but when at last their
courage and confidence were restored, they began to take
observations and an inventory of me that were by no
means agreeable. They fingered my hair and dress, my
collar, belt, and rings. One donned my hat and cloak,
and made a promenade of the pavilion; another pounced
upon my gloves and veil, and disguised herself in them,
to the great delight of the little ones, who laughed boisterously. A grim duenna, who had heard the noise, bus-
tled wrathfully into the pavilion. Instantly hat, cloak,
veil, gloves, were flung right and left, and the young women dropped on the floor, repeating shrilly, like truant
urchins caught in the act, their " ba, be, bi, bo."

One who seemed the infant phenomenon of the royal
harem, so juvenile and artless were her looks and ways,
despising a performance so rudimentary as the a, b, c, demanded to be steered at once into the mid-ocean of the
book; but when I left her without pilot in an archipelago
of hard words, she soon showed signals of distress.

At the far end of the table, bending over a little prince,
her eyes riveted on the letters my boy was naming to her,
stood a pale young woman, whose aspect was dejected and
forlorn. She had entered unannounced and unnoticed, as
one who had no interest in common with the others; and
now she stood apart and alone, intent only on mastering
the alphabet with the help of her small teacher. When
we were about to dismiss the school, she repeated her lesson to my wise lad, who listened with imposing gravity,
pronounced her a " very good child," and said she might
go now. But when she perceived that I observed her
curiously, she crouched almost under the table, as though

owning she had no right to be there, and was worthy to pick only the crumbs of knowledge that might fall from it. She was neither very young nor pretty, save that her dark eyes were profound and expressive, and now the more interesting by their touching sadness. Esteeming it the part of prudence as well as of kindness to appear unconscious of her presence, and so encourage her to come again, I left the palace without accosting her, before his Majesty had awakened from his forenoon nap. This crushed creature had fallen under the displeasure of the king, and the after chapters of her story, which shall be related in their proper connection, were romantic and mournful.

X.

MOONSHEE AND THE ANGEL GABRIEL.

OUR blue chamber overlooked the attap roofs of a long row of houses, badly disfigured by the stains and wear of many a wet season, in which our next neighbor, a Mohammedan of patriarchal aspect and demeanor, stored bags of sugar, waiting for a rise in the market. This worthy paid us the honor of a visit every afternoon, and in the snug little eastern chamber consecrated to the studies and meditations of my Persian teacher propounded solemn problems from the Alkoran.

Under Moonshee's window the tops of houses huddled, presenting forms more or less fantastic according to the purse or caprice of the proprietors. The shrewd old man was not long in finding tenants for all these roofs, and could even tell the social status and the means of each. It tickled his vanity to find himself domiciled in so aristocratic a quarter. Our house — more Oriental than European in its architecture — was comparatively new, having been erected upon the site of the old palace, the *débris* of which had furnished the materials of which it was constructed. Among the loose slabs of marble and fragments of pottery that turned up with the promiscuous rubbish every day, we sometimes found surfaces of stone bearing Siamese or Cambodian inscriptions ; others with grotesque figures in bass-relief, taken from the mythology of the Hindoos. Had these relics a charm for Moonshee, and was he animated by the antiquarian's en-

thusiasm, that he delved away hour after hour, unearth-
ing, with his spade, bricks and stones and tiles and slabs?
I was at a loss to account for this new freak in the old
man ; but seeing him infatuated with his eccentric pursuit, and Boy enraptured over grubs and snails and bits
of broken figures, the resurrections of the nimble spade,
I left them to their cheap and harmless bliss.

One evening, as I sat musing in the piazza, with my
book unopened on my lap, I heard Boy's clear voice ring-
ing in happy, musical peals of laughter that drew me to
him. On the edge of a deep hole, in a corner of the
compound, sat Moonshee, an effigy of doleful disappointment, and beside him stood the lad, clapping his little
hands and laughing merrily. The old child had taken
the young one into his confidence, and by their joint exertions they had dug this hole in search of treasure ; and
lo ! at the bottom lay something that looked like a rusty
purse. With a long look and a throbbing heart Moonshee, after several empty hauls, had fished it up ; and it
was — a toad ! a huge, unsightly, yellow toad !

" May the foul fiend fly away with thee !" cried the en-
thusiast in his rage, as he flung the astonished reptile
back into the pit, and sat down to bewail his *kismut*,
while Boy made merry with his groans.

For some days the spade was neglected, though I
observed, from the cautious drift of his remarks at
the conclusion of our evening lesson, that Moonshee's
thoughts still harped on hidden treasure. The fervid
imagination of the child had uncovered to his mind's eye
mines of wealth, awaiting only the touch of the magic
spade to bare their golden veins to the needs of his Mem
Sahib and himself. There was no dispelling his golden
visions by any shock of hard sense ; the more he dreamed
the more he believed. But the spot ? the right spot ?
" Only wait."

Another week elapsed, and Boy and I worked harder than ever in our school in the cool pavilion. I had flung off the dead weight of my stubborn repinings, and my heart was light again. There were delightful discoveries of beauty in the artless, childish faces that greeted us every morning; and now the only wonder was that I had been so slow to penetrate the secret of their charm. That eager, radiant elf, the Princess Somdetch Chow Fâ-ying,* the king's darling (of whom, by and by, I shall have a sadder tale to tell), had become a sprite of sunshine and gladness amid the sombre shadows of those walls. In her deep, dark, lustrous eyes, her simple, trusting ways, there was a springtide of refreshment, a pure, pervading radiance, that brightened the darkest thing it touched. Even the grim hags of the harem felt its influence, and softened in her presence.

As Boy was reciting his tasks one morning before breakfast, Moonshee entered the room with one of his profoundest salaams, and an expression at once so earnest and so comical that I anxiously asked him what was the matter. Panting alike with the eagerness of childhood and the feebleness of age, he stammered, " I have something of the greatest importance to confide to you, Mem Sahib! Now is the time! Now you shall prove the devotion of your faithful Moonshee, who swears by Allah not to touch a grain of gold without your leave, in all those bursting sacks, if Mem Sahib will but lend him ten ticals, only ten ticals, to buy a screw-driver !"

" What in the world can you want with a screw-driver, Moonshee ? "

" O Mem, listen to me !" he cried, his face glowing with the very rapture of possession ; " I have discovered the exact spot on which the old duke, Somdetch Ong

---

* " First-Born of the Skies."

Yai, expired. It is a secret, a wonderful secret, Mem Sahib; not a creature in all Siam knows it."

"Then how came you by it," I inquired, "seeing that you know not one word of the language, which you have bravely scorned as unworthy to be uttered by the Faithful, and of no use on earth but to confound philosophers and Moonshees?"

"*Sunnoh, sunnoh!** Mem Sahib! No human tongue revealed it to me. It was the Angè Gibhrayeel.† He came to me last night as I slept, and said, 'O son of Jaffur Khan! to your prayers is granted the knowledge that, for all these years, has been denied to Kafirs. Arise! obey! and with humility receive the treasures reserved for thee, thou faithful follower of the Prophet!' And so saying he struck the golden palms he bore in his hand; and though I was now awake, Mem Sahib, I was so overpowered by the beauty and effulgence of his person, that I was as one about to die. The radiant glory of his wings, which were of the hue of sapphires, blinded my vision; I could neither speak nor see. But I felt the glow of his presence and heard the rustle of his pinions, as once more he beat the golden palms and cried, 'Behold, O son of Jaffur Khan! behold the spot where lie the treasures of that haughty Kafir chief!' I arose, and immediately the angel flashed from my sight; and as I gazed there appeared a luminous golden hen with six golden chickens, which pecked at bits of blazing coal that, as they cooled, became nuggets of pure gold. When suddenly I beheld a great light as of *rooshnees,*‡ and it burst upon the spot where the hen had been; and then all was darkness again. Mem Sahib, your servant ran down and placed a stone upon that spot, and kneeling on that stone, with his face to the south, repeated his five Kalemahs."§

* "Listen, listen!"   ‡ Fire-balls.
† The Angel Gabriel.   § Thanksgivings.

I am ashamed to say I laughed; whereat the old man was so mortified that he vowed the next time the angel appeared to him, he would call us all to see. I accepted the condition; and even promised that if I saw the nuggets of pure gold that Gabriel's chickens pecked, I would immediately accommodate him with the ten ticals to invest in a screw-driver. So perfect was his faith in the vision, that he accepted the promise with complete satisfaction.

Not many nights after this extraordinary apparition, we were aroused by Beebe and her husband calling, "Awake, awake!" Thinking the house was on fire, I threw on my dressing-gown and ran into the next room with Boy in my arms. There was indeed a fire, but it was in a distant corner of the yard. The night was dark, a thick mist rose from the river, and the gusty puffs of wind that now and then swept through the compound caused the wood fire to flare up and flicker, casting fitful and fantastic shadows around. Moonshee stared, with fixed eyes, expecting every moment the reappearance of the supernatural poultry; but I, being as yet sceptical, descended the stairs, followed by my trembling household, and approached the spot.

On a remnant of matting, with a stone for a pillow, lay an old Siamese woman asleep. Driven by the heat to the relief of the open air, she had kindled a fire to keep off the mosquitoes.

"Now, Moonshee," said I, "here is your Angel Gabriel. Don't you ever again trouble me for ticals to invest in screw-drivers."

XI.

THE WAYS OF THE PALACE.

THE city of Bangkok is commonly supposed to have inherited the name of the ancient capital, Ayudia; but in the royal archives, to which I have had free access, it is given as Krung Thèp'ha Maha-Nakhon Si-ayut-thia Maha-dilok Racha-thani, — "The City of the Royal, Invincible, and Beautiful Archangel." It is ramparted with walls within and without, which divide it into an inner and an outer city, the inner wall being thirty feet high, and flanked with circular forts mounted with cannon, making a respectable show of defence. Centre of all, the heart of the citadel, is the grand palace, encompassed by a third wall, which encloses only the royal edifice, the harems, the temple of Watt P'hra Këau, and the Maha P'hrasat.

The Maha Phrasat is an immense structure of quadrangular façades, surmounted by a tall spire of very chaste and harmonious design. It is consecrated; and here dead sovereigns of Siam lie in state, waiting twelve months for their cremation; here also their ashes are deposited, in urns of gold, after that fiery consummation. In the Maha Phrasat the supreme king is crowned and all court ceremonies performed. On certain high holidays and occasions of state, the high-priest administers here a sort of mass, at which the whole court attend, even the chief ladies of the harem, who, behind heavy curtains of silk and gold that hang from the ceiling to the floor, whisper and giggle and peep and chew betel, and have the wonted little raptures of their sex over furtive, piquant glimpses of the world; for, despite the strict confinement and jealous surveillance to which they are subject, the outer life, with all its bustle, passion, and romance, will now and then steal, like a vagrant, curious ray of light, into the heart's darkness of these tabooed women, thrilling their childish minds with eager wonderment and formless longings.

Within these walls lurked lately fugitives of every class, profligates from all quarters of the city, to whom discovery was death; but here their "sanctuary" was impenetrable. Here were women disguised as men, and men in the attire of women, hiding vice of every vileness and crime of every enormity, — at once the most disgusting, the most appalling, and the most unnatural that the heart of man has conceived. It was death in life, a charnel-house of quick corruption; a place of gloom and solitude indeed, wherefrom happiness, hope, courage, liberty, truth, were forever excluded, and only mother's love was left.

The king * was the disk of light and life round which these strange flies swarmed. Most of the women who composed his harem were of gentle blood, — the fairest of the daughters of Siamese nobles and of princes of the adjacent tributary states; the late queen consort was his own half-sister. Beside many choice Chinese and Indian girls, purchased annually for the royal harem by agents stationed at Peking, Foo-chou, and different points in Bengal, enormous sums were offered, year after year, through "solicitors" at Bangkok and Singapore, for an English woman of beauty and good parentage to crown the sensational collection; but when I took my leave of Bangkok, in 1868, the coveted specimen had not yet appeared in the

---

* All that is here written applies to Maha Mongkut, the supreme king, who died October, 1868; not to his successor (and my pupil), the present king.

market. The cunning *commissionnaires* contrived to keep their places and make a living by sending his Majesty, now and then, a piquant photograph of some British Nourmahal of the period, freshly caught, and duly shipped, in good order for the harem ; but the goods never arrived.

Had the king's tastes been Gallic, his requisition might have been filled. I remember a score of genuine offers from French demoiselles, who enclosed their *cartes* in billets more surprising and enterprising than any other "proposals" it was my office to translate. But his whimsical Majesty entertained a lively horror of French intrigue, whether of priests, consuls, or *lionnes*, and stood in vigilant fear of being beguiled, through one of these adventurous sirens, into fathering the innovation of a Franco-Siamese heir to the throne of the celestial P'hrabatts.

The king, as well as most of the principal members of his household, rose at five in the morning, and immediately partook of a slight repast, served by the ladies who had been in waiting through the night ; after which, attended by them and his sisters and elder children, he descended and took his station on a long strip of matting, laid from one of the gates through all the avenues to another. On his Majesty's left were ranged, first, his children in the order of rank ; then the princesses, his sisters ; and, lastly, his concubines, his maids of honor, and their slaves. Before each was placed a large silver tray containing offerings of boiled rice, fruit, cakes, and the seri leaf ; some even had cigars.

A little after five, the Patoo Dharmina (" Gate of Merit," called by the populace "Patoo Boon") was thrown open and the Amazons of the guard drawn up on either side. Then the priests entered, always by that gate, — one hundred and ninety-nine of them, escorted on the right and left by men armed with swords and clubs, — and as they entered they chanted: "Take thy meat, but think it dust! Eat but to live, and but to know thyself, and what thou art below! And say withal unto thy heart, It is earth I eat, that to the earth I may new life impart."

Then the chief priest, who led the procession, advanced with downcast eyes and lowly mien, and very simply presented his bowl (slung from his neck by a cord, and until that moment quite hidden under the folds of his yellow robe) to the members of the royal household, who *offered* their fruit or cakes, or their spoonfuls of rice or sweetmeats. In like manner did all his brethren. If, by any chance, one before whom a tray was placed was not ready and waiting with an offering, no priest stopped, but all continued to advance slowly, taking only what was freely offered, without thanks or even a look of acknowledgment, until the end of the royal train was reached, when the procession retired, chanting as before, by the gate called Dinn, or, in the Court language, *Prithvi*, "Gate of Earth."

After this, the king and all his company repaired to his private temple, Watt Sasmiras Manda-thung,* so called because it was dedicated by his Majesty to the memory of his mother. This is an edifice of unique and charming beauty, decorated throughout by artists from Japan, who have represented on the walls, in designs as diverse and ingenious as they are costly, the numerous metempsychoses of Buddha.

Here his Majesty ascended alone the steps of the altar, rang a bell to announce the hour of devotion, lighted the consecrated tapers, and offered the white lotos and the roses. Then he spent an hour in prayer, and in reading texts from the P'ra-jana Para-mita and the P'hra-ti-Moksha.

This service over, he retired for another nap, attended

* "Temple in Memory of Mother."

by a fresh detail of women, — those who had waited the night before being dismissed, not to be recalled for a month, or at least a fortnight, save as a peculiar mark of preference or favor to some one who had had the good fortune to please or amuse him; but most of that party voluntarily waited upon him every day.

His Majesty usually passed his mornings in study, or in dictating or writing English letters and despatches. His breakfast, though a repast sufficiently frugal for Oriental royalty, was served with awesome forms. In an ante-chamber adjoining a noble hall, rich in grotesque carvings and gildings, a throng of females waited, while his Majesty sat at a long table, near which knelt twelve women before great silver trays laden with twelve varieties of viands, — soups, meats, game, poultry, fish, vegetables, cakes, jellies, preserves, sauces, fruits, and teas. Each tray, in its order, was passed by three ladies to the head wife or concubine, who removed the silver covers, and at least seemed to taste the contents of each dish; and then, advancing on her knees, she set them on the long table before the king.

But his Majesty was notably temperate in his diet, and by no means a gastronome. In his long seclusion in a Buddhist cloister he had acquired habits of severe simplicity and frugality, as a preparation for the exercise of those powers of mental concentration for which he was remarkable. At these morning repasts it was his custom to detain me in conversation relating to some topic of interest derived from his studies, or in reading or translating. He was more systematically educated, and a more capacious devourer of books and news, than perhaps any man of equal rank in our day. But much learning had made him morally mad; his extensive reading had engendered in his mind an extreme scepticism concerning all existing religious systems. In inborn integrity and stead-

5

fast principle he had no faith whatever. He sincerely
believed that every man strove to compass his own ends,
per fas et nefas. The *mens sibi conscia recti* was to him
an hallucination, for which he entertained profound contempt; and he honestly pitied the delusion that pinned
its faith on human truth and virtue. He was a provoking *mélange* of antiquarian attainments and modern scepticism. When, sometimes, I ventured to disabuse his
mind of his darling scorn for motive and responsibility, I
had the mortification to discover that I had but helped
him to an argument against myself: it was simply "my
peculiar interest to do so." Money, money, money! that
could procure anything.

But aside from the too manifest bias of his early education and experience, it is due to his memory to say that
his practice was less faithless than his profession, toward
those persons and principles to which he was attracted by
a just regard. In many grave considerations he displayed
soundness of understanding and clearness of judgment, —
a genuine nobility of mind, established upon universal
ethics and philosophic reason, — where his passions were
not dominant; but when these broke in between the man
and the majesty, they effectually barred his advance in
the direction of true greatness; beyond them he could not,
or would not, make way.

Ah, if this man could but have cast off the cramping
yoke of his intellectual egotism, and been loyal to the free
government of his own true heart, what a demi-god might
he not have been among the lower animals of Asiatic
royalty!

At two o'clock he bestirred himself, and with the aid
of his women bathed and anointed his person. Then he
descended to a breakfast-chamber, where he was served
with the most substantial meal of the day. Here he
chatted with his favorites among the wives and concu-

bines, and caressed his children, taking them in his arms, embracing them, plying them with puzzling or funny questions, and making droll faces at the babies : the more agreeable the mother, the dearer the child. The love of children was the constant and hearty virtue of this forlorn despot. They appealed to him by their beauty and their trustfulness, they refreshed him with the bold innocence of their ways, so frolicsome, graceful, and quaint.

From this delusive scene of domestic condescension and kindliness he passed to his Hall of Audience to consider official matters. Twice a week at sunset he appeared at one of the gates of the palace to hear the complaints and petitions of the poorest of his subjects, who at no other time or place could reach his ear. It was most pitiful to see the helpless, awe-stricken wretches, prostrate and abject as toads, many too terrified to present the precious petition after all.

At nine he retired to his private apartments, whence issued immediately peculiar domestic bulletins, in which were named the women whose presence he particularly desired, in addition to those whose turn it was to " wait " that night.

And twice a week he held a secret council, or court, at midnight. Of the proceedings of those dark and terrifying sittings I can, of course, give no exact account. I permit myself to speak only of those things which were but too plain to one who lived for six years in or near the palace.

In Siam, the king — Maha Mongkut especially — is not merely enthroned, he is enshrined. To the nobility he is omnipotence, and to the rabble mystery. Since the occupation of the country by the Jesuits, many foreigners have fancied that the government is becoming more and more silent, insidious, secretive ; and that this midnight council is but the expression of a " policy of stifling." It is an inquisition, — not overt, audacious, like that of Rome, but nocturnal, invisible, subtle, ubiquitous, like that of Spain ; proceeding without witnesses or warning; kidnapping a subject, not arresting him, and then incarcerating, chaining, torturing him, to extort confession or denunciation.   If any Siamese citizen utter one word against the " San Luang," (the royal judges), and escape, forthwith his house is sacked and his wife and children kidnapped.   Should he be captured, he is brought to secret trial, to which no one is admitted who is not in the patronage and confidence of the royal judges.   In themselves the laws are tolerable ; but in their operation they are frustrated or circumvented by arbitrary and capricious power in the king, or craft or cruelty in the Council.   No one not initiated in the mystic *séances* of the San Luang can depend upon Siamese law for justice.   No man will consent to appear there, even as a true witness, save for large reward.   The citizen who would enjoy, safe from legal plunder, his private income, must be careful to find a patron and protector in the king, the prime minister, or some other formidable friend at court.   Spies in the employ of the San Luang penetrate into every family of wealth and influence.   Every citizen suspects and fears always his neighbor, sometimes his wife.   On more than one occasion when, vexed by some act of the king's, more than usually wanton and unjust, I instinctively gave expression to my feelings by word or look in the presence of certain officers and courtiers, I observed that they rapped, or tapped, in a peculiar and stealthy manner.   This I afterward discovered was one of the secret signs of the San Luang; and the warning signal was addressed to me, because they imagined that I also was a member of the Council.

En passant, a word as to the ordinary and familiar costumes of the palace.   Men and women alike wear a sort of kilt, like the *pu'sho* of the Birmans, with a short upper tunic, over which the women draw a broad silk scarf, which is closely bound round the chest and descends in long, waving folds almost to the feet. Neither sex wears any covering on the head. The uniform of the Amazons of the harem is green and gold, and for the soldiers scarlet and purple.

There are usually four meals : breakfast about sunrise ; a sort of tiffin at noon ; a more substantial repast in the afternoon ; and supper after the business of the day is over. Wine and tea are drunk freely, and perfumed liquors are used by the wealthy. An indispensable preparation for polite repast is by bathing and anointing the body. When guests are invited, the sexes are never brought together ; for Siamese women of rank very rarely appear in strange company ; they are confined to remote and unapproachable halls and chambers, where nothing human, being male, may ever enter. The convivial entertainments of the Court are usually given on occasions of public devotion, and form a part of these.

XII.

SHADOWS AND WHISPERS OF THE HAREM.

AS, month after month, I continued to teach in the palace, — especially as the language of my pupils, its idioms and characteristic forms of expression, began to be familiar to me, — all the dim life of the place "came out" to my ken, like a faint picture, which at first displays to the eye only a formless confusion, a chaos of colors, but by force of much looking and tracing and joining and separating, first objects and then groups are discovered in their proper identity and relation, until the whole stands out, clear, true, and informing in its coherent significance of light and shade. Thus, by slow processes, as one whose sight has been imperceptibly restored, I awoke to a clearer and truer sense of the life within "the city of the beautiful and invincible angel."

Sitting at one end of the table in my school-room, with Boy at the other, and all those far-off faces between, I felt as though we were twenty thousand miles away from the world that lay but a twenty minutes' walk from the door; the distance was but a speck in space, but the separation was tremendous. It always seemed to me that here was a sudden, harsh suspension of nature's fundamental law, — the human heart arrested in its functions, ceasing to throb, and yet alive.

The fields beyond are fresh and green, and bright with flowers. The sun of summer, rising exultant, greets them with rejoicing; and evening shadows, falling soft among

PRESENTATION OF A PRINCESS.

the dewy petals, linger to kiss them good-night.   There
the children of the poor — naked, rude, neglected though
they be — are rich in the freedom of the bounteous earth,
rich in the freedom of the fair blue sky, rich in the freedom of the limpid ocean of air above and around them.
But within the close and gloomy lanes of this city within
a city, through which many lovely women are wont to
come and go, many little feet to patter, and many baby
citizens to be borne in the arms of their dodging slaves,
there is but cloud and chill, and famishing and stinting,
and beating of wings against golden bars.   In the order
of nature, evening melts softly into night, and darkness
retreats with dignity and grace before the advancing triumphs of the morning; but here light and darkness are
monstrously mixed, and the result is a glaring gloom that
is neither of the day nor of the night, nor of life nor of
death, nor of earth nor of — yes, hell !

In the long galleries and corridors, bewildering with
their everlasting twilight of the eye and of the mind,
one is forever coming upon shocks of sudden sunshine or
shocks of sudden shadow, — the smile yet dimpling in a
baby's face, a sister bearing a brother's scourging ; a
mother singing to her "sacred infant,"* a slave sobbing
before a deaf idol.   And O, the forlornness of it all !
You who have never beheld these things know not the
utterness of loneliness.   Compared with the predicament
of some who were my daily companions, the sea were a
home and an iceberg a hearth.

How I have pitied those ill-fated sisters of mine, imprisoned without a crime ! If they could but have rejoiced once more in the freedom of the fields and woods,
what new births of gladness might have been theirs, —
they who with a gasp of despair and moral death first entered those royal dungeons, never again to come forth

* *Phra-ong.*

alive! And yet have I known more than one among them who accepted her fate with a repose of manner and a sweetness of smile that told how dead must be the heart under that still exterior. And I wondered at the sight. Only twenty minutes between bondage and freedom, — such freedom as may be found in Siam! only twenty minutes between those gloomy, hateful cells and the fair fields and the radiant skies! only twenty minutes between the cramping and the suffocation and the fear, and the full, deep, glorious inspirations of freedom and safety!

I had never beheld misery till I found it here; I had never looked upon the sickening hideousness of slavery till I encountered its features here; nor, above all, had I comprehended the perfection of the life, light, blessedness and beauty, the all-sufficing fulness of the love of God as it is in Jesus, until I felt the contrast here, — pain, deformity, darkness, death, and eternal emptiness, a darkness to which there is neither beginning nor end, a living which is neither of this world nor of the next. The misery which checks the pulse and thrills the heart with pity in one's common walks about the great cities of Europe is hardly so saddening as the nameless, mocking wretchedness of these women, to whom poverty were a luxury, and houselessness as a draught of pure, free air.

And yet their lot is light indeed compared with that of their children. The single aim of such a hapless mother, howsoever tender and devoted she may by nature be, is to form her child after the one strict pattern her fate has set her, — her master's will; since, otherwise, she dare not contemplate the perils which might overtake her treasure. Pitiful indeed, therefore, is the pitiless inflexibility of purpose with which she wrings from her child's heart all the dangerous endearments of childhood, — its merry laughter, its sparkling tears, its trustfulness, its artlessness, its engaging waywardness; and in their place instils silence, submission, self-constraint, suspicion, cunning, carefulness, and an ever-vigilant fear. And the result is a spectacle of unnatural discipline simply appalling. The life of such a child is an egg-shell on an ocean; to its helpless speck of experience all horrors are possible. Its passing moment is its eternity; and that overwhelmed with terrors, real or imaginary, what is left but that poor little floating wreck, a child's despair?

I was often alone in the school-room, long after my other charges had departed, with a pale, dejected woman, whose name translated was " Hidden-Perfume." As a pupil she was remarkably diligent and attentive, and in reading and translating English her progress was extraordinary. Only in her eager, inquisitive glances was she child-like; otherwise, her expression and demeanor were anxious and aged. She had long been out of favor with her "lord"; and now, without hope from him, surrendered herself wholly to her fondness for a son she had borne him in her more youthful and attractive days. In this young prince, who was about ten years old, the same air of timidity and restraint was apparent as in his mother, whom he strikingly resembled, only lacking that cast of pensive sadness which rendered her so attractive, and her pride, which closed her lips upon the past, though the story of her wrongs was a moving one.

It was my habit to visit her twice a week at her residence,* for I was indebted to her for much intelligent assistance in my study of the Siamese language. On going to her abode one afternoon, I found her absent; only the young prince was there, sitting sadly by the window.

" Where is your mother, dear ? " I inquired.

" With his Majesty up stairs, I think," he replied, still

* Each of the ladies of the harem has her own exclusive domicile, within the inner walls of the palace.

looking anxiously in one direction, as though watching for her.

This was an unusual circumstance for my sad, lonely friend, and I returned home without my lesson for that day.

Next morning, passing the house again, I saw the lad sitting in the same attitude at the window, his eyes bent in the same direction, only more wistful and weary than before. On questioning him, I found his mother had not yet returned. At the pavilion I was met by the Lady Tâlâp, who, seizing my hand, said, "Hidden-Perfume is in trouble."

"What is the matter?" I inquired.

"She is in prison," she whispered, drawing me closely to her. "She is not prudent, you know, — like you and me," in a tone which expressed both triumph and fear.

"Can I see her?" I asked.

"Yes, yes! if you bribe the jailers. But don't give them more than a tical each. They'll demand two; give them only one."

In the pavilion, which served as a private chapel for the ladies of the harem, priests were reading prayers and reciting homilies from that sacred book of Buddha called *Sâsânâh Thai*, "The Religion of the Free"; while the ladies sat on velvet cushions with their hands folded, a vase of flowers in front of each, and a pair of odoriferous candles, lighted. Prayers are held daily in this place, and three times a day during the Buddhist Lent. The priests are escorted to the pavilion by Amazons, and two warriors, armed with swords and clubs, remain on guard till the service is ended. The latter, who are eunuchs, also attend the priests when they enter the palace, in the afternoon, to sprinkle the inmates with consecrated water.

Leaving the priests reciting and chanting, and the rapt

worshippers bowing, I passed a young mother with a sleeping babe, some slave-girls playing at *sabâh* * on the stone pavement, and two princesses borne in the arms of their slaves, though almost women grown, on my way to the palace prison.

If it ever should be the reader's fortune, good or ill, to visit a Siamese dungeon, whether allotted to prince or peasant, his attention will be first attracted to the rude designs on the rough stone walls (otherwise decorated only with moss and fungi and loathsome reptiles) of some night-mared painter, who has exhausted his dyspeptic fancy in portraying hideous personifications of Hunger, Terror, Old Age, Despair, Disease, and Death, tormented by furies and avengers, with hair of snakes and whips of scorpions, — all beyond expression devilish.   Floor it has none, nor ceiling, for, with the Meinam so near, neither boards nor plaster can keep out the ooze.   Underfoot, a few planks, loosely laid, are already as soft as the mud they are meant to cover; the damp has rotted them through and through.   Overhead, the roof is black, but not with smoke; for here, where the close steam of the soggy earth and the reeking walls is almost intolerable, no fire is needed in the coldest season.   The cell is lighted by one small window, so heavily grated on the outer side as effectually to bar the ingress of fresh air.   A pair of wooden trestles, supporting rough boards, form a makeshift for a bedstead, and a mat (which may be clean or dirty, the ticals of the prisoner must settle that) is all the bed.

In such a cell, on such a couch, lay the concubine of a supreme king and the mother of a royal prince of Siam, her feet covered with a silk mantle, her head supported by a pillow of glazed leather, her face turned to the clammy wall.

There was no door to grate upon her quivering nerves;

---

* Marbles, played with the knee instead of the fingers.

a trap-door in the street overhead had opened to the magic of silver, and I had descended a flight of broken steps of stone.   At her head, a little higher than the pillow, were a vase of flowers, half faded, a pair of candles burning in gold candlesticks, and a small image of the Buddha.   She had brought her god with her.   Well, she needed his presence.

I could hardly keep my feet, for the footing was slippery and my brain swam.   Touching the silent, motionless form, in a voice scarcely audible I pronounced her name.   She turned with difficulty, and a slight sound of clanking explained the covering on the feet.   She was chained to one of the trestles.

Sitting up, she made room for me beside her.   No tears were in her eyes; only the habitual sadness of her face was deepened.   Here, truly, was a perfect work of misery, meekness, and patience.

Astonished at seeing me, she imagined me capable of yet greater things, and folding her hands in an attitude of supplication, implored me to help her.   The offence for which she was imprisoned was briefly this: —

She had been led to petition, through her son,* that an appointment held by her late uncle, Phya Khien, might be bestowed on her elder brother, not knowing that another noble had already been preferred to the post by his Majesty.

Had she been guilty of the gravest crime, her punishment could not have been more severe.   It was plain that a stupid grudge was at the bottom of this cruel business. The king, on reading the petition, presented by the trembling lad on his knees, became furious, and, dashing it back into the child's face, accused the mother of plotting to undermine his power, saying he knew her to be at heart a rebel, who hated him and his dynasty with all the

* A privilege granted to all the concubines.

rancor of her Peguan ancestors, the natural enemies of
Siam. Thus lashing himself into a rage of hypocritical
patriotism, and seeking to justify himself by condemning
her, he sent one of his judges to bring her to him. But
before the myrmidon could go and come, concluding to
dispense with forms, he anticipated the result of that
mandate with another, — to chain and imprison her. No
sooner was she dragged to this deadly cell, than a third
order was issued to flog her till she confessed her treacherous plot; but the stripes were administered so tenderly,*
that the only confession they extorted was a meek protes-
tation that she was "his meanest slave, and ready to give
her life for his pleasure."

"Beat her on the mouth with a slipper for lying!"
roared the royal tiger; and they did, in the letter, if not
in the spirit, of the brutal sentence. She bore it meekly,
hanging down her head. "I am degraded forever!"
she said to me.

When once the king was enraged, there was nothing to
be done but to wait in patience until the storm should
exhaust itself by its own fury. But it was horrible to
witness such an abuse of power at the hands of one who
was the only source of justice in the land. It was a
crime against all humanity, the outrage of the strong
upon the helpless. His madness sometimes lasted a
week; but weeks have their endings. Besides, he really
had a conscience, tough and shrunken as it was; and
she had, what was more to the purpose, a whole tribe of
powerful connections.

As for myself, there was but one thing I could do;
and that was to intercede privately with the Kralahome.
The same evening, immediately on returning from my
visit to the dungeon, I called on him; but when I ex-

---

* In these cases the executioners are women, who generally spare each
other if they dare.

plained the object of my visit he rebuked me sharply
for interfering between his Majesty and his wives.

"She is my pupil," I replied.   "But I have not inter-
fered; I have only come to you for justice.   She did not
know of the appointment until she had sent in her petition; and to punish one woman for that which is permitted and encouraged in another is gross injustice."   Thereupon he sent for his secretary, and having satisfied himself that the appointment had not been published, was
good enough to promise that he would explain to his Majesty that "there had been delay in making known to the
Court the royal pleasure in this matter"; but he spoke
with indifference, as if thinking of something else.

I felt chilled and hurt as I left the premier's palace,
and more anxious than ever when I thought of the weary
eyes of the lonely lad watching for his mother's return;
for no one dared tell him the truth.   But, to do the premier justice, he was more troubled than he would permit
me to discover at the mistake the poor woman had made;
for there was good stuff in the moral fabric of the man,
— stern rectitude, and a judgment, unlike the king's, not
warped by passion.   That very night * he repaired to the
Grand Palace, and explained the delay to the king, without appearing to be aware of the concubine's punishment.

On Monday morning, when I came to school in the
pavilion, I found, to my great joy, that Hidden-Perfume
had been liberated, and was at home again with her child.
The poor creature embraced me ardently, glorifying me
with grateful epithets from the extravagant vocabulary of
her people; and, taking an emerald ring from her finger,
she put it upon mine, saying, "By this you will remember your thankful friend."

---

* All consultations on matters of state and of court discipline are
held in the royal palace at night.

On the following day she also sent me a small purse of gold thread netted, in which were a few Siamese coins, and a scrap of paper inscribed with cabalistic characters,— an infallible charm to preserve the wearer from poverty and distress.

Among my pupils was a little girl about eight or nine years old, of delicate frame, and with the low voice and subdued manner of one who had already had experience of sorrow. She was not among those presented to me at the opening of the school. Wanne Ratâna Kania was her name ("Sweet Promise of my Hopes"), and very engaging and persuasive was she in her patient, timid loveliness Her mother, the Lady Khoon Chom Kioa, who had once found favor with the king, had, at the time of my coming to the palace, fallen into disgrace by reason of her gambling, in which she had squandered all the patrimony of the little princess. This fact, instead of inspiring the royal father with pity for his child, seemed to attract to her all that was most cruel in his insane temper. The offence of the mother had made the daughter offensive in his sight; and it was not until long after the term of imprisonment of the degraded favorite had expired that Wanne ventured to appear at a royal *levée.* The moment the king caught sight of the little form, so piteously prostrated there, he drove her rudely from his presence, taunting her with the delinquencies of her mother with a coarseness that would have been cruel enough if she had been responsible for them and a gainer by them, but against one of her tender years, innocent toward both, and injured by both, it was inconceivably atrocious.

On her first appearance at school she was so timid and wistful that I felt constrained to notice and encourage her more than those whom I had already with me. But I found this no easy part to play; for very soon one of the court ladies in the confidence of the king took me quietly aside and warned me to be less demonstrative in favor of the little princess, saying, "Surely you would not bring trouble upon that wounded lamb."

It was a sore trial to me to witness the oppression of one so unoffending and so helpless. Yet our Wanne was neither thin nor pale. There was a freshness in her childish beauty, and a bloom in the transparent olive of her cheek, that were at times bewitching. She loved her father, and in her visions of baby faith beheld him almost as a god. It was true joy to her to fold her hands and bow before the chamber where he slept. With that steadfast hopefulness of childhood which can be deceived without being discouraged, she would say, "How glad he will be when I can read!" and yet she had known nothing but despair.

Her memory was extraordinary; she delighted in all that was remarkable, and with careful wisdom gathered up facts and precepts and saved them for future use. She seemed to have built around her an invisible temple of her own design, and to have illuminated it with the rushlight of her childish love. Among the books she read to me, rendering it from English into Siamese, was one called "Spring-time." On translating the line, "Whom He loveth he chasteneth," she looked up in my face, and asked anxiously: "Does thy God do that? Ah! lady, are *all* the gods angry and cruel? Has he no pity, even for those who love him? He must be like my father; *he* loves us, so he has to be *rye* (cruel), that we may fear evil and avoid it."

Meanwhile little Wanne learned to spell, read, and translate almost intuitively; for there were novelty and hope to help the Buddhist child, and love to help the English woman. The sad look left her face, her life had found an interest; and very often, on *fête* days, she was my only pupil; — when suddenly an ominous cloud obscured the sky of her transient gladness.

Wanne was poor; and her gifts to me were of the riches of poverty, — fruits and flowers.   But she owned some female slaves; and one among them, a woman of twenty-five perhaps (who had already made a place for herself in my regard), seemed devotedly attached to her youthful mistress, and not only attended her to the school day after day, but shared her scholarly enthusiasm, even studied with her, sitting at her feet by the table.   Steadily the slave kept pace with the princess.   All that Wanne learned at school in the day was lovingly taught to Mai Noie in the nursery at night; and it was not long before I found, to my astonishment, that the slave read and translated as correctly as her mistress.

Very delightful were the demonstrations of attachment interchanged between these two.   Mai Noie bore the child in her arms to and from the school, fed her, humored her every whim, fanned her naps, bathed and perfumed her every night, and then rocked her to sleep on her careful bosom, as tenderly as she would have done for her own baby.   And then it was charming to watch the child's face kindle with love and comfort as the sound of her friend's step approached.

Suddenly a change; the little princess came to school as usual, but a strange woman attended her, and I saw no more of Mai Noie there.   The child grew so listless and wretched that I was forced to ask the cause of her darling's absence; she burst into a passion of tears, but replied not a word.   Then I inquired of the stranger, and she answered in two syllables, — *My ru* (" I know not").

Shortly afterward, as I entered the school-room one day, I perceived that something unusual was happening. I turned toward the princes' door, and stood still, fairly holding my breath.   There was the king, furious, striding

H

up and down.   All the female judges of the palace were
present, and a crowd of mothers and royal children.   On
all the steps around, innumerable slave-women, old and
young, crouched and hid their faces.

But the object most conspicuous was little Wanne's
mother, manacled, and prostrate on the polished marble
pavement.   There, too, was my poor little princess, her
hands clasped helplessly, her eyes tearless but downcast,
palpitating, trembling, shivering.   Sorrow and horror had
transformed the child.

As well as I could understand, where no one dared explain, the wretched woman had been gambling again, and
had even staked and lost her daughter's slaves.   At last I
understood Wanne's silence when I asked her where Mai
Noie was.   By some means — spies probably — the whole
matter had come to the king's ears, and his rage was wild,
not because he loved the child, but that he hated the
mother.

Promptly the order was given to lash the woman; and
two Amazons advanced to execute it.   The first stripe
was delivered with savage skill; but before the thong
could descend again, the child sprang forward and flung
herself across the bare and quivering back of her mother.
Ti chan, Tha Moom! * *Poot-thoo ti chan, Tha Mom!*
("Strike *me*, my father!   Pray, strike me, O my father!")

The pause of fear that followed was only broken by
my boy, who, with a convulsive cry, buried his face desperately in the folds of my skirt.

There indeed was a case for prayer, *any* prayer! — the
prostrate woman, the hesitating lash, the tearless anguish
of the Siamese child, the heart-rending cry of the English
child, all those mothers with grovelling brows, but hearts
uplifted among the stars, on the wings of the Angel of
Prayer.   Who could behold so many women crouching,

---

* *Tha Mom* or *Moom,* used by children in addressing a royal father.

shuddering, stupefied, dismayed, in silence and darkness, animated, enlightened only by the deep whispering heart of maternity, and not be moved with mournful yearning?

The child's prayer was vain. As demons tremble in the presence of a god, so the king comprehended that he had now to deal with a power of weakness, pity, beauty, courage, and eloquence. "Strike *me*, O my father!" His quick, clear sagacity measured instantly all the danger in that challenge; and though his voice was thick and agitated (for, monster as he was at that moment, he could not but shrink from striking at every mother's heart at his feet), he nervously gave the word to remove the child, and bind her. The united strength of several women was not more than enough to loose the clasp of those loving arms from the neck of an unworthy mother. The tender hands and feet were bound, and the tender heart was broken. The lash descended then, unforbidden by any cry.

XIII.

FÂ-YING, THE KING'S DARLING.

"WILL you teach me to draw?" said an irresistible young voice to me, as I sat at the school-room table, one bright afternoon. "It is so much more pleasant to sit by you than to go to my Sanskrit class. My Sanskrit teacher is not like my English teacher; she bends my hands back when I make mistakes. I don't like Sanskrit, I like English. There are so many pretty pictures in your books. Will you take me to England with you, Mam cha?"* pleaded the engaging little prattler.

"I am afraid his Majesty will not let you go with me," I replied.

"O yes, he will!" said the child with smiling confidence. "He lets me do as I like. You know I am the Somdetch Chow Fâ-ying; he loves me best of all; he will let me go."

"I am glad to hear it," said I, "and very glad to hear that you love English and drawing. Let us go up and ask his Majesty if you may learn drawing instead of Sanskrit."

With sparkling eyes and a happy smile, she sprang from my lap, and, seizing my hand eagerly, said, "O yes! let us go now." We went, and our prayer was granted.

Never did work seem more like pleasure than it did to me as I sat with this sweet, bright little princess, day

* "Lady dear."

after day, at the hour when all her brothers and sisters were at their Sanskrit, drawing herself, as the humor seized her, or watching me draw; but oftener listening, her large questioning eyes fixed upon my face, as step by step I led her out of the shadow-land of myth into the realm of the truth as it is in Christ Jesus. "The wisdom of this world is foolishness with God"; and I felt that this child of smiles and tears, all unbaptized and unblessed as she was, was nearer and dearer to her Father in heaven than to her father on earth.

This was the Somdetch Chowfa Chandrmondol, best known in the palace by her pet name of Fâ-ying. Her mother, the late queen consort, in dying, left three sons and this one daughter, whom, with peculiar tenderness and anxiety, she commended to the loving-kindness of the king; and now the child was the fondled darling of the lonely, bitter man, having quickly won her way to his heart by the charm of her fearless innocence and trustfulness, her sprightly intelligence and changeful grace.

Morning dawned fair on the river, the sunshine flickering on the silver ripples, and gilding the boats of the market people as they softly glide up or down to the lazy swing of the oars. The floating shops were all awake, displaying their various and fantastic wares to attract the passing citizen or stranger. Priests in yellow robes moved noiselessly from door to door, receiving without asking and without thanks the alms wherewith their pious clients hoped to lay up treasures in heaven, or, in Buddhist parlance, to "make merit." Slaves hurried hither and thither in the various bustle of errands. Worshippers thronged the gates and vestibules of the many temples of this city of pagodas and *p'hra-cha-dees,* and myriads of fan-shaped bells scattered æolian melodies on the passing breeze.

As Boy and I gazed from our piazza on this strangely picturesque panorama, there swept across the river a royal barge filled with slaves, who, the moment they had landed, hurried up to me.

" My lady," they cried, " there is cholera in the palace ! Three slaves are lying dead in the princesses' court; and her Highness, the young Somdetch Chow Fâ-ying, was seized this morning. She sends for you. O, come to her, quickly !" and with that they put into my hand a scrap of paper ; it was from his Majesty.

" MY DEAR MAM, — Our well-beloved daughter, your favorite pupil, is attacked with cholera, and has earnest desire to see you, and is heard much to make frequent repetition of your name. I beg that you will favor her wish. I fear her illness is mortal, as there has been three deaths since morning. She is best beloved of my children.

"I am your afflicted friend,
                "S. S. P. P. MAHA MONGKUT."

In a moment I was in my boat. I entreated, I flattered, I scolded, the rowers. How slow they were !. how strong the opposing current ! And when we did reach those heavy gates, how slowly they moved, with what suspicious caution they admitted me ! I was fierce with impatience. And when at last I stood panting at the door of my Fâ-ying's chamber — too late ! even Dr. Campbell (the surgeon of the British consulate) had come too late.

There was no need to prolong that anxious wail in the ear of the deaf child, "P'hra-Arahang ! P'hra-Arahang !" *
She would not forget her way ; she would nevermore lose herself on the road to Heaven. Beyond, above the P'hra-

---

* One of the most sacred of the many titles of Buddha, repeated by the nearest relative in the ear of the dying till life is quite extinct.

Arahang, she had soared into the eternal, tender arms of the P'hra-Jesus, of whom she was wont to say in her infantine wonder and eagerness, *Mam cha, chân râk P'hra-Jesus mâk* ("Mam dear, I love your holy Jesus.")

As I stooped to imprint a parting kiss on the little face that had been so fair to me, her kindred and slaves exchanged their appealing "P'hra-Arahang" for a sudden burst of heart-rending cries.

An attendant hurried me to the king, who, reading the heavy tidings in my silence, covered his face with his hands and wept passionately. Strange and terrible were the tears of such a man, welling up from a heart from which all natural affections had seemed to be expelled, to make room for his own exacting, engrossing conceit of self.

Bitterly he bewailed his darling, calling her by such tender, touching epithets as the lips of loving Christian mothers use. What could I say? What could I do but weep with him, and then steal quietly away and leave the king to the Father?

"The moreover very sad & mournful Circular * from His Gracious Majesty Somdetch P'hra Paramendr Maha Mongkut, the reigning Supreme King of Siam, intimating the recent death of Her Celestial Royal Highness, Princess Somdetch Chowfa Chandrmondol Sobhon Baghiawati, who was His Majesty's most affectionate & well beloved 9th Royal daughter or 16th offspring, and the second Royal child by His Majesty's late Queen consort Rambery Bhamarabhiramy who deceased in the year 1861. Both mother and daughter have been known to many foreign friends of His Majesty.

"To all the foreign friends of His Majesty, residing or trading in Siam, or in Singapore, Malacca, Pinang, Ceylon, Batavia, Saigon, Macao, Hong-kong, & various regions in China, Europe, America, &c. &c. . . . .

* From the pen of the king.

" Her Celestial Royal Highness, having been born on the 24th April, 1855, grew up in happy condition of her royal valued life, under the care of her Royal parents, as well as her elder and younger three full brothers ; and on the demise of her royal mother on the forementioned date, she was almost always with her Royal father everywhere day & night. All things which belonged to her late mother suitable for female use were transferred to her as the most lawful inheritor of her late royal mother ; She grew up to the age of 8 years & 20 days.   On the ceremony of the funeral service of her elder late royal half brother forenamed, She accompanied her royal esteemed father & her royal brothers and sisters in customary service, cheerfully during three days of the ceremony, from the 11th to 13th May.   On the night of the latter day, when she was returning from the royal funeral place to the royal residence in the same sedan with her Royal father at 10 o'clock P. M. she yet appeared happy, but alas ! on her arrival at the royal residence, she was attacked by most violent & awful cholera, and sunk rapidly before the arrival of the physicians who were called on that night for treatment.   Her disease or illness of cholera increased so strong that it did not give way to the treatment of any one, or even to the Chlorodine administered to her by Doctor James Campbell the Surgeon of the British Consulate.   She expired at 4 o'clock P. M., on the 14th May, when her elder royal half brother's remains were burning at the funeral hall outside of the royal palace, according to the determined time for the assembling of the great congregation of the whole of the royalty & nobility, and native & foreign friends, before the occurrence of the unforeseen sudden misfortune or mournful event.

" The sudden death of the said most affectionate and lamented royal daughter has caused greater regret and

sorrow to her Royal father than several losses sustained
by him before, as this beloved Royal amiable daughter
was brought up almost by the hands of His Majesty
himself, since she was aged only 4 to 5 months, His Majesty has carried her to and fro by his hand and on the
lap and placed her by his side in every one of the Royal
seats, where ever he went; whatever could be done in the
way of nursing His Majesty has done himself, by feeding
her with milk obtained from her nurse, and sometimes
with the milk of the cow, goat &c. poured in a teacup
from which His Majesty fed her by means of a spoon, so
this Royal daughter was as familiar with her father in her
infancy, as with her nurses.

" On her being only aged six months, his Majesty took
this Princess with him and went to Ayudia on affairs
there; after that time when she became grown up His
Majesty had the princess seated on his lap when he was
in his chair at the breakfast, dinner & supper table, and
fed her at the same time of breakfast &c, almost every
day, except when she became sick of colds &c. until the
last days of her life she always eat at same table with her
father.   Where ever His Majesty went, this princess always accompanied her father upon the same, sedan, car-
riage, Royal boat, yacht &c. and on her being grown up
she became more prudent than other children of the same
age, she paid every affectionate attention to her affectionate and esteemed father in every thing where her ability
allowed; she was well educated in the vernacular Siamese literature which she commenced to study when she
was 3 years old, and in last year she commenced to study
in the English School where the schoolmistress, Lady
L—— has observed that she was more skillful than the
other royal Children, she pronounced & spoke English in
articulate & clever manner which pleased the schoolmistress exceedingly, so that the schoolmistress on the loss

6

of this her beloved pupil, was in great sorrow and wept much.

". . . . But alas! her life was very short. She was only aged 8 years & 20 days, reckoning from her birth day & hour, she lived in this world 2942 days & 18 hours. But it is known that the nature of human lives is like the flames of candles lighted in open air without any protection above & every side, so it is certain that this path ought to be followed by every one of human beings in a short or long while which cannot be ascertained by prediction, Alas!

"Dated Royal Grand Palace, Bangkok, 16th May, Anno Christi 1863."

Not long after our darling Fâ-ying was taken from us, the same royal barge, freighted with the same female slaves who had summoned us to her death-bed, came in haste to our house. His Majesty had sent them to find and bring us. We must hurry to the palace. On arriving there, we found the school pavilion strangely decorated with flowers. My chair of office had been freshly painted a glaring red, and on the back and round the arms and legs fresh flowers were twined. The books the Princess Fâ-ying had lately conned were carefully displayed in front of my accustomed seat, and upon them were laid fresh roses and fragrant lilies. Some of the ladies in waiting informed me that an extraordinary honor was about to be conferred on me. Not relishing the prospect of favors that might place me in a false position, and still all in the dark, I submitted quietly, but not without misgivings on my own part and positive opposition on Boy's, to be enthroned in the gorgeous chair, whereof the paint was hardly dry. Presently his Majesty sent to inquire if we had arrived, and being apprised of our presence, came down at once, followed by all my pupils and a formidable staff of noble dowagers, — his sisters, half-sisters, and aunts, paternal and maternal.

Having shaken hands with me and with my child, he proceeded to enlighten us. He was about to confer a distinction upon me, for my "courage and conduct," as he expressed it, at the death-bed of her Highness, his well-beloved royal child, the Somdetch Chow Fâ-ying. Then, bidding me "remain seated," much to the detriment of my white dress, in the sticky red chair, and carefully taking the ends of seven threads of unspun cotton (whereof the other ends were passed over my head, and over the dead child's books, into the hands of seven of his elder sisters), he proceeded to wind them round my brow and temples. Next he waved mysteriously a few gold coins, then dropped twenty-one drops of cold water out of a jewelled shell,* and finally, muttering something in Sanskrit, and placing in my hand a small silk bag containing a title of nobility and the number and description of the roods of lands pertaining to it, bade me rise, "Chow Khoon Crue Yai"!

My estate was in the district of Lophaburee and P'hra Batt, and I found afterward that to reach it I must perform a tedious journey overland, through a wild, dense jungle, on the back of an elephant. So, with wise munificence, I left it to my people, tigers, elephants, rhinoceroses, wild boars, armadillos, and monkeys to enjoy unmolested and untaxed, while I continued to pursue the even tenor of a "school-marm's" way, unagitated by my honorary title. In fact, the whole affair was ridiculous; and I was inclined to feel a little ashamed of the distinction, when I reflected on the absurd figure I must have cut, with my head in a string like a grocer's parcel, and Boy imploring me, with all his astonished eyes, not to submit to so silly an operation. So he and I tacitly agreed to hush the matter up between us.

Speaking of the "chank" shell, that is the name

* The conch or chank shell.

given in the East Indies to certain varieties of the *voluta
gravis*, fished up by divers in the Gulf of Manaar, on the
northwest coast of Ceylon.   There are two kinds, *payel*
and *patty*, — the one red, the other white ; the latter is of
small value.   These shells are exported to Calcutta and
Bombay, where they are sawed into rings of various sizes,
and worn on the arms, legs, fingers, and toes by the Hindoos, from whom the Buddhists have adopted the shell for
use in their religious or political ceremonies.   They employ, however, a third species, which opens to the right,
and is rare and costly.   The demand for these shells,
created by the innumerable poojahs and pageants of the
Hindoos and Buddhists, was formerly so great that a
bounty of sixty thousand rix dollars per annum was
paid to the British government for the privilege of fishing
for them ; but this demand finally ceased, and the revenue
became not worth collecting.   The fishing is now free to
all.

XIV.

AN OUTRAGE AND A WARNING.

ONE morning we were startled by a great outcry, from
which we presently began to pick out, here and
there, a coherent word, which, put together, signified that
Moonshee was once more in trouble. I ran down into the
compound, and found that the old man had been cruelly
beaten, by order of one of the premier's half-brothers, for
refusing to bow down before him. Exhausted as he was,
he found voice to express his sense of the outrage in in-
dignant iteration. "Am I a beast? Am I an unbeliev-
ing dog? O son of Jaffur Khan, how hast thou fallen!"

I felt so shocked and insulted that I went at once, and
without ceremony, to the Kralahome, and complained.
To my surprise and disgust, his Excellency made light of
the matter, saying that the old man was a fool; that he
had no time to waste upon such trifles; and that I must
not trouble him so often with my meddling in matters of
no moment, and which did not concern me.

When he was done with this explosion of petulance
and brow-beating, I endeavored to demonstrate to him the
unfairness of his remarks, and the disadvantage to himself
if he should appear to connive at the ruffianly behavior
of his people. But I assured him that in future I should
not trouble him with my complaints, but take them
directly to the British Consul. And so saying I left this
unreasonable prime minister, meeting the cause of all our
woes (the half-brother) coming in as I went out.

That same evening, as I sat in our little piazza, where it was cooler than in the house, embroidering a new coat for Boy to wear on his approaching birthday, I felt a violent blow on my head, and fell from my chair stunned, overturning the small table at which I was working, and the heavy Argand lamp that stood on it.

On recovering my senses I found myself in the dark, and Boy, with all his little strength, trying to lift me from the floor, while he screamed, " *Beebe maree ! Beebe maree !* " *　I endeavored to rise, but feeling dizzy and sick lay still for a while, taking Louis in my arms to reassure him.

When Beebe came from the river, where she had been bathing, she struck a light, and found that the mischief had been done with a large stone, about four inches long and two wide ; but by whom or why it had been thrown we could not for some time conjecture. Beebe raised the neighborhood with her cries : " First my husband, then my mistress ! It will be my turn next ; and then what will become of the *chota baba sahib ?* " †　But I begged her to have done with her din and help me to the couch, which she did with touching tenderness and quiet, bathing my head, which had bled so profusely that I sank, exhausted, into a deep sleep, though the sight of my boy's pale, anxious face, as he insisted on sharing Beebe's vigil, would have been more than enough to keep me awake at any other time. When I awoke in the morning, there sat the dear little fellow in a chair asleep, but dressed, his head resting on my pillow.

I now felt so much better, though my head was badly swollen, that I rose and paid a visit to Moonshee, who was really ill, though not dying, as his wife declared. The shame and outrage of his beating was the occasion of much sorrow and trouble to me, for my Persian teacher

---

* *Maree,* "Come here" (Malay).　　　† The little master.

now begged to be sent back to Singapore, and I thought that Beebe could not be persuaded to let him go alone, though my heart had been set on keeping them with me as long as I remained in Siam.   It was in vain that I tried to convince the terrified old man that such a catastrophe could hardly happen again; he would not be beguiled, but, shedding faithful tears at the sight of my bandaged head, declared we should all be murdered if we tarried another day in a land of such barbarous Kafirs.   I assured him that my wound was but skin-deep, and that I apprehended no further violence.   But all to no purpose; I was obliged to promise them that they should depart by the next trip of the Chow Phya steamer.

I deemed it prudent, however, to send for the premier's secretary, and warn him, in his official capacity, that if a repetition of the outrage already perpetrated upon members of my household should be attempted from any quarter, I would at once take refuge at the British consulate, and lodge a complaint against the government of Siam.

Mr. Hunter, who was always very serious when he was sober and very volatile when he was not, took the matter to heart, stared long and thoughtfully at my bandaged head and pallid countenance, and abruptly started for the premier's palace, whence he returned on the following day with several copies of a proclamation in the Siamese language, signed by his Excellency, to the effect that persons found injuring or in any way molesting any member of my household should be severely punished.   I desired him to leave one or two of them, in a friendly way, at the house of my neighbor on the left, the Kralahome's half-brother; for it was he, and no other, who had committed this most cowardly act of revenge.   The expression of Mr. Hunter's face, as the truth slowly dawned upon him, was rich in its blending of indignation, disgust, and contempt. "The pusillanimous rascal!" he exclaimed, as he hurried off in the direction indicated.

"The darkest hour is just before day." So the gloom now cast over our little circle by Moonshee's departure was quickly followed by the light of love in Beebe's tearful eyes as she bade her husband adieu. "How could she," she asked, "leave her Mem and the *chota baba sahib* alone in a strange land?"

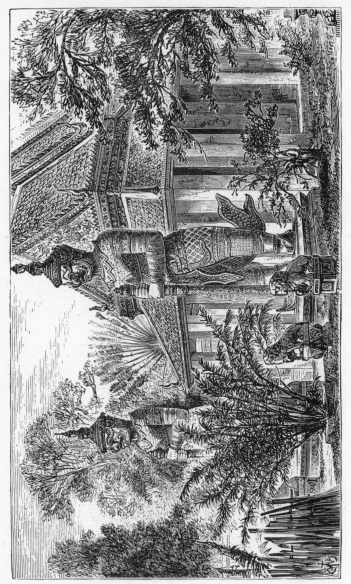

GATEWAY OF THE OLD PALACE.

XV.

THE CITY OF BANGKOK.

ASCENDING the Meinam (or Chow Phya) from the gulf, and passing Paknam, the paltry but picturesque seaport already described, we come next to Paklat Beeloo, or "Little Paklat," so styled to distinguish it from Paklat Boon, a considerable town higher up the river, which we shall presently inspect as we steam toward Bangkok. Though, strictly speaking, Paklat Beeloo is a mere cluster of huts, the humble dwellings of a colony of farmers and rice-planters, it is nevertheless a place of considerable importance as a depot for the products of the ample fields and gardens which surround it on every side. The rice and vegetables which these supply are shipped for the markets of Bangkok and Ayudia. At Paklat Beeloo that bustle of traffic begins which, more and more as we approach the capital, imparts to the river its characteristic aspect of activity and thrift, — an animated procession of boats of various form and size, deeply laden with grain, garden stuffs, and fruits, drifting with the friendly helping tide, and requiring little or no manual labor for their navigation, as they sweep along tranquilly, steadily, from bank to bank, from village to village.

Diverse as are the styles and uses of these boats, the most convenient, and therefore the most common, are the Rua-keng and the Rua-pêt. The former resembles in all respects the Venetian gondola, while the Rua-pêt has

6 *

either a square house with windows amidships, or (more commonly) a basket cover, long and round, like the tent-top of some Western wagons. The dimensions of many of these boats are sufficient to accommodate an entire family, with their household goods and merchandise, yet one seldom sees more than a single individual in charge of them. The tide, running strongly up or down, affords the motive-power; "the crew" has but to steer. Often unwieldy, and piled clumsily with cargo, one might reasonably suppose their safe piloting to be a nautical impossibility; yet so perfect is the skill — the instinct, rather — of these almost amphibious river-folk, that a little child, not uncommonly a girl, shall lead them. Accidents are marvellously rare, considering the thousands of large, heavy, handsome keng boats that ply continually between the gulf and the capital, now lost in a sudden bend of the stream, now emerging from behind a screen of man-groves, and in their swift descent threatening quick de-struction to the small and fragile market-boats, freighted with fish and poultry, fruit and vegetables.

Trom Paklat Beeloo a great canal penetrates to the heart of Bangkok, cutting off thirty Siamese miles, or *soks*, from the circuitous river route. But the traveller, faithful to the picturesque, will cling to the beautiful Meinam, which will entertain him with scenery more and more charming as he approaches the capital, — higher lands, a neater cultivation, hamlets and villages quaintly pretty, fantastic temples and pagodas dotting the plain, fine Oriental effects of form and color, scattered Edens of fruit-trees, — the mango, the mangostein, the bread-fruit, the durian, the orange, — their dark foliage contrasting boldly with the more lively and lovely green of the betel, the tama-rind, and the banana. Every curve of the river is beautiful with an unexpectedness of its own, — here the sugar-cane swaying gracefully, there the billow-like lights and shad-

ows of the supple, feathery bamboo, and everywhere ideal
paradises of refreshment and repose. As we drift on the
flowing thoroughfare toward the golden spires of Bangkok,
kaleidoscopic surprises of summer salute us on either hand.

Presently we come to Paklat Boon, a place of detached
cottages and orchards, fondly courting the river, the pretty
homesteads of husbandmen and gardeners. Here, too, is
a dock-yard for the construction of royal barges and war-
boats, some of them more than eighty feet long, with
less than twelve feet beam.

From Paklat Boon to Bangkok the scene is one of ever-
increasing splendor, the glorious river seeming to array
itself more and more grandly, as for the admiration of
kings, and proudly spreading its waters wide, as a courtier spreads his robes. Its lake-like expanses, without a
spiteful rock or shoal, are alive with ships, barks, brigs,
junks, proas, sampans, canoes; and the stranger is beset
by a flotilla of river pedlers, expertly sculling under the
stern of the steamer, and shrilly screaming the praises of
their wares; while here and there, in the thick of the
bustle and scramble and din, a cunning, quick-handed
Chinaman, in a crank canoe, ladles from a steaming cal-
dron his savory chow-chow soup, and serves it out in
small white bowls to hungry customers, who hold their
peace for a time and loll upon their oars, enraptured by
the penetrating brew.

Three miles below the capital are the royal dock-yards,
where most of the ships composing the Siamese navy and
merchant marine are built, under the supervision of English shipwrights. Here, also, craft from Hong-Kong,
Canton, Singapore, Rangoon, and other ports, that have
been disabled at sea, are repaired more thoroughly and
cheaply than in any other port in the East. There are,
likewise, several dry-docks, and, in fact, an establishment
completely equipped and intelligently managed.

A short distance below the dock-yards is the American Mission, comprising the dwellings of the missionaries and a modest school-house and chapel, the latter having a fair attendance of consuls and their children. Above the dock-yards is the Roman Catholic establishment, a quiet little settlement clustered about a small cross-crowned sanctuary.

Yet one more bend of the tortuous river, and the strange panorama of the floating city unrolls like a great painted canvas before us, — piers and rafts of open shops, with curious wares and fabrics exposed at the very water's edge; and beyond and above these the magnificent "watts" and pagodas with which the capital abounds.

These pagodas, and the *p'hra-cha-dees*, or minarets, that crown some of the temples, are in many cases true wonders of cunning workmanship and profuse adornment — displaying mosaics of fine porcelain, inlaid with ivory, gold, and silver, while the lofty doors and windows are overlaid with sculptures of grotesque figures from the Buddhist and Brahminical mythologies. Near the Grand Palace are three tall pillars of elegant design, everywhere inlaid with variegated stones, and so richly gilt that they are the wonder and the pride of all the country round. These monuments mark the places of deposit of a few charred bones that once were three demigods of Siam, — the kings P'hra Rama Thibodi, P'hra Narai, and P'hra Phya Tak, who did doughty deeds of valor and prowess in earlier periods of Siamese history.

The Grand Royal Palace, the semi-castellated residence of the Supreme King of Siam, with its roofs and spires pointed with what seem to be the horns of animals, towers pre-eminent over all the city. It is a great citadel, surrounded by a triplet of walls, fortified with many bastions. Each of the separate buildings it comprises is cruciform; and even the palace lately erected in the style of Windsor Castle forms with the old palace the arms of a cross, as the latter does with the Phrasat, — and so on down to an odd little conceit in architecture, in the Chinese style throughout.

In front of the old palace is an ample enclosure, paved, and surrounded with beautiful trees and rare plants. A gateway, guarded by a pair of colossal lions and two gigantic and frightful nondescripts, half demon, half human, leads to the old palace, now almost abandoned. Beyond this, and within the third or innermost wall, is the true heart of the citadel, the quarters of the women of, the harem. This is in itself a sort of miniature city, with streets, shops, bazaars, and gardens, all occupied and tended by women only. Outside are the observatory and watch-tower.

Some of the grandest and most beautiful temples and pagodas of Siam are in this part of the city. On one side of the palace are the temples and monasteries dedicated to the huge Sleeping Idol, and on the other the mass of buildings that constitute the palace and harem of the Second King. From these two palaces broad streets extend for several miles, occupied on either side by the principal shops and bazaars of Bangkok.

Leaving the Grand Palace, a short walk to the right brings us to the monuments, already mentioned, of the three warrior kings. From noble pedestals of fine black granite, adorned at top and bottom with cornices and rings of ivory, carved in mythological forms of animals, birds, and flowers, rise conical pillars about fifty feet high. The columns themselves are in mosaic, with diverse material inlaid upon the solid masonry so carefully that the cement can hardly be detected. No two patterns are the same, striking effects of form and color have been studied, and the result is beautiful beyond description. Close beside these a third pillar was lately in process of erection, to the memory of the good King P'hra-Phēn-den Klang, father of his late Majesty, Somdetch P'hra-Para-mendr Maha Mongkut.

On the outer skirt of the walled town stands the temple Watt Brahmanee Waid, dedicated to the divinity to whom the control of the universe has been ascribed from the most ancient times. His temple is the only shrine of a Brahminical deity that the followers of Buddha have not dared to abolish. Intelligent Buddhists hold that he exists in the latent forces of nature, that his only attribute is benevolence, though he is capable of a just indignation, and that within the scope of his mental vision are myriads of worlds yet to come. But he is said to have no form, no voice, no odor, no color, no active creative power, — a subtile, fundamental principle of nature, pervading all things, influencing all things. This belief in Brahma is so closely interwoven with all that is best in the morals and customs of the people, that it would seem as though Buddha himself had been careful to leave unchallenged this one idea in the mythology of the Hindoos. The temple includes a royal monastery, which only the sons of kings can enter.

Opposite the Brahmanee Watt, at the distance of about a mile, are the extensive grounds and buildings of Watt Sah Kâte, the great national burning-place of the dead. Within these mysterious precincts the Buddhist rite of cremation is performed, with circumstances more or less horrible, according to the condition or the superstition of the deceased. A broad canal surrounds the temple and yards, and here, night and day, priests watch and pray for the regeneration of mankind. Not alone the dead, but the living likewise, are given to be burned in secret here; and into this canal, at dead of night, are flung the rash wretches who have madly dared to oppose with speech or act the powers that rule in Siam. None but the initiated will approach these grounds after sunset, so universal and profound is the horror the place inspires, — a place the most frightful and offensive known to mortal eyes; for here the vows of dead men, howsoever ghoulish and monstrous, are consummated. The walls are hung with human skeletons and the ground is strewed with human skulls. Here also are scraped together the horrid fragments of those who have bequeathed their carcasses to the hungry dogs and vultures, that hover, and prowl, and swoop, and pounce, and snarl, and scream, and tear. The half-picked bones are gathered and burned by the outcast keepers of the temple (not priests), who receive from the nearest relative of the infatuated testator a small fee for that final service ; and so a Buddhist vow is fulfilled, and a Buddhist " deed of merit " accomplished.

Bangkok, the modern seat of government of Siam, has (according to the best authorities) two hundred thousand floating dwellings and shops, — to each house an average of five souls, — making the population of the city about one million ; of which number more than eighty thousand are Chinese, twenty thousand Birmese, fifteen thousand Arabs and Indians, and the remainder Siamese. These figures are from the latest census, which, however, must not be accepted as perfectly accurate.

The situation of the city is unique and picturesque. When Ayudia was "extinguished," and the capital established at Bangkok, the houses were at first built on the banks of the river. But so frequent were the invasions of cholera, that one of the kings happily commanded the people to build on the river itself, that they might have greater cleanliness and better ventilation. The result quickly proved the wisdom of the measure. The privilege of building on the banks is now confined to members of the royal family, the nobility, and residents of acknowledged influence, political or commercial.

At night the city is hung with thousands of covered lights, that illuminate the wide river from shore to shore. Lamps and lanterns of all imaginable shapes, colors, and sizes combine to form a fairy spectacle of enchanting brilliancy and beauty. The floating tenements and shops, the masts of vessels, the tall, fantastic pagodas and minarets, and, crowning all, the walls and towers of the Grand Palace, flash with countless charming tricks of light, and compose a scene of more than magic novelty and beauty. So oriental fancy and profusion deal with things of use, and make a wonder of a commonplace.

A double, and in some parts a triple, row of floating houses extends for miles along the banks of the river. These are wooden structures, tastefully designed and painted, raised on substantial rafts of bamboo linked together with chains, which, in turn, are made fast to great piles planted in the bed of the stream. The Meinam itself forms the main avenue, and the floating shops on either side constitute the great bazaar of the city, where all imaginable and unimaginable articles from India, China, Malacca, Birmah, Paris, Liverpool, and New York are displayed in stalls.

Naturally, boats and canoes are indispensable appendages to such houses; the nobility possess a fleet of them, and to every little water-cottage a canoe is tethered, for errands and visits. At all hours of the day and night processions of boats pass to and from the palace, and everywhere bustling traders and agents ply their dingy little craft, and proclaim their several callings in a Babel of cries.

Daily, at sunrise, a flotilla of canoes, filled with shaven men in yellow garments, visits every house along the banks. These are the priests gathering their various provender, the free gift of every inhabitant of the city. Twenty thousand of them are supported by the alms of the city of Bangkok alone.

At noon, all the clamor of the city is suddenly stilled, and perfect silence reigns. Men, women, and children are hushed in their afternoon nap. From the stifling heat of a tropical midday the still cattle seek shelter and repose under shady boughs, and even the crows cease their obstreperous clanging. The only sound that breaks the drowsy stillness of the hour is the rippling of the glaring river as it ebbs or flows under the steaming banks.

About three in the afternoon the sea-breeze sets in, bringing refreshment to the fevered, thirsty land, and reviving animal and vegetable life with its compassionate breath. Then once more the floating city awakes and stirs, and an animation rivalling that of the morning is prolonged far into the night, — the busy, gay, delightful night of Bangkok.

The streets are few compared with the number of canals that intersect the city in all directions. The most remarkable of the former is one that runs parallel with the Grand Palace, and terminates in what is now known as " Sanon Mai," or the New Road, which extends from Bangkok to Paknam, about forty miles, and crosses the canals on movable iron bridges. Almost every other house along this road is a shop, and at the close of the wet season Bangkok has no rival in the abundance of vegetables and fruits with which its markets are stocked.

I could wish for a special dispensation to pass without mention the public prisons of Bangkok, for their condition and the treatment of the unhappy wretches confined in them are the foulest blots on the character of the government. Some of these grated abominations are hung like bird-cages over the water ; and those on land, with their gangs of living corpses chained together like wild beasts, are too horrible to be pictured here. How European officials, representatives of Christian ideas of humanity and decency, can continue to countenance the apathy or wilful brutality of the prime minister, who, as the executive officer of the government in this department, is mainly responsible for the cruelties and outrages I may not even name, I cannot conceive.

The American Protestant missionaries have as yet made no remarkable impression on the religious mind of the Siamese. Devoted, persevering, and patient laborers, the field they have so faithfully tilled has rewarded them with but scanty fruits. Nor will the fact, thankless though it be, appear surprising to those whose privilege it has been to observe the Buddhist and the Roman Catholic side by side in the East, and to note how, even on the score of doctrine, they meet without a jar at many points. The average Siamese citizen, entering a Roman Catholic chapel in Bangkok, finds nothing there to shock his prejudices. He is introduced to certain forms and ceremonies, almost the counterpart of which he piously reveres in his own temple, — genuflections, prostrations, decorated shrines, lighted candles, smoking incense, holy water; while the prayers he hears are at least not less intelligible to him than those he hears mumbled in Pali by his own priests. He beholds familiar images too, and pictures of a Saviour in whom he charitably recognizes the stranger's Buddha. And if he happen to be a philosophic inquirer, how surprised and pleased is he to learn that the priests of this faith (like his own) are vowed to chastity, poverty, and obedience, and, like his own, devoted to the doing of good works, penance, and alms. There are many thousands of native converts to Catholicism in Siam; even the priests of Buddhism do not always turn a deaf ear to the persuasions of teachers bound with them in the bonds of celibacy, penance, and deeds of merit. And those teachers are quick to meet them half-way, happily recommending themselves by the alacrity with which they adopt, and make their own, usages which they may with propriety practise in common, whereby the Buddhist is flattered while the Christian is not offended. Such, for example, is the monastic custom of the uncovered head. As it is deemed sacrilege to touch the head of royalty, so the head of the priest may not without dishonor pass under anything less hallowed than the canopy of heaven; and in this Buddhist and Roman Catholic accord.

The residences of the British, French, American, and Portuguese Consuls are pleasantly situated in a bend of the river, where a flight of wooden steps in good repair leads directly to the houses of the officials and European merchants of that quarter. Most influential among the latter is the managing firm of the Borneo Company, whose factories and warehouses for rice, sugar, and cotton are extensive and prosperous.

The more opulent of the native merchants are grossly addicted to gambling and opium-smoking. Though the legal penalties prescribed for all who indulge in these destructive vices are severe, they do not avail to deter even respectable officers of the government from staking heavy sums on the turn of a card; and long before the game is ended the opium-pipe is introduced. One of the king's secretaries, who was a confirmed opium-smoker, assured me he would rather die at once than be excluded from the region of raptures his pipe opened to him.

XVI

THE WHITE ELEPHANT.

IT is commonly supposed that the Buddhists of Siam and Birmah regard the Chang Phoouk, or white elephant, as a deity, and worship it accordingly. The notion is erroneous, especially as it relates to Siam. The Buddhists do not recognize God in any material form whatever, and are shocked at the idea of adoring an elephant. Even Buddha, to whom they undoubtedly offer pious homage, they do not style "God," but on the contrary maintain that, though an emanation from a "sublimated ethereal being," he is by no means a deity. According to their philosophy of metempsychosis, however, each successive Buddha, in passing through a series of transmigrations, must necessarily have occupied in turn the forms of white animals of a certain class, — particularly the swan, the stork, the white sparrow, the dove, the monkey, and the elephant. But there is much obscurity and diversity in the views of their ancient writers on this subject. Only one thing is certain, that the forms of these nobler and purer creatures are reserved for the souls of the good and great, who find in them a kind of redemption from the baser animal life. Thus almost all white animals are held in reverence by the Siamese, because they were once superior human beings, and the white elephant, in particular, is supposed to be animated by the spirit of some king or hero. Having once been a great man, he is thought to be familiar with the dangers that

A War Elephant.

surround the great, and to know what is best and safest
for those whose condition in all respects was once his
own.   He is hence supposed to avert national calamity,
and bring prosperity and peace to a people.

From the earliest times the kings of Siam and Birmah
have anxiously sought for the white elephant, and having
had the rare fortune to procure one, have loaded it with
gifts and dignities, as though it were a conscious favorite
of the throne.   When the governor of a province of Siam
is notified of the appearance of a white elephant within
his bailiwick, he immediately commands that prayers and
offerings shall be made in all the temples, while he sends
out a formidable expedition of hunters and slaves to take
the precious beast, and bring it in in triumph.   As soon
as he is informed of its capture, a special messenger is
despatched to inform the king of its sex, probable age,
size, complexion, deportment, looks, and ways ; and in the
presence of his Majesty this bearer of glorious tidings un-
dergoes the painfully pleasant operation of having his
mouth, ears, and nostrils stuffed with gold.   Especially is
the lucky wight — perhaps some half-wild woodsman —
who was first to spy the illustrious monster munificently
rewarded.   Orders are promptly issued to the woons and
wongses of the several districts through which he must
pass to prepare to receive him royally, and a wide path is
cut for him through the forests he must traverse on his
way to the capital.   Wherever he rests he is sumptuously entertained, and everywhere he is escorted and
served by a host of attendants, who sing, dance, play
upon instruments, and perform feats of strength or skill
for his amusement, until he reaches the banks of the
Meinam, where a great floating palace of wood, surmounted by a gorgeous roof and hung with crimson curtains, awaits him.   The roof is literally thatched with
flowers ingeniously arranged so as to form symbols and

mottoes, which the superior beast is supposed to decipher with ease. The floor of this splendid float is laid with gilt matting curiously woven, in the centre of which his four-footed lordship is installed in state, surrounded by an obsequious and enraptured crowd of mere bipeds, who bathe him, perfume him, fan him, feed him, sing and play to him, flatter him. His food consists of the finest herbs, the tenderest grass, the sweetest sugar-cane, the mellowest plantains, the brownest cakes of wheat, served on huge trays of gold and silver; and his drink is perfumed with the fragrant flower of the *dok mallee*, the large native jessamine.

Thus, in more than princely state, he is floated down the river to a point within seventy miles of the capital, where the king and his court, all the chief personages of the kingdom, and a multitude of priests, both Buddhist and Brahmin, accompanied by troops of players and musicians, come out to meet him, and conduct him with all the honors to his stable-palace. A great number of cords and ropes of all qualities and lengths are attached to the raft, those in the centre being of fine silk (figuratively, "spun from a spider's web"). These are for the king and his noble retinue, who with their own hands make them fast to their gilded barges; the rest are secured to the great fleet of lesser boats. And so, with shouts of joy, beating of drums, blare of trumpets, boom of cannon, a hallelujah of music, and various splendid revelry, the great Chang Phoouk is conducted in triumph to the capital.

Here in a pavilion, temporary but very beautiful, he is welcomed with imposing ceremonies by the custodians of the palace and the principal personages of the royal household. The king, his courtiers, and the chief priests being gathered round him, thanksgiving is offered up; and then the lordly beast is knighted, after the an-

cient manner of the Buddhists, by pouring upon his forehead consecrated water from a chank-shell.

The titles reserved for the Chang Phoouk vary according to the purity of the complexion (for these favored creatures are rarely true albinos, — salmon or flesh-color being
the nearest approach to white in almost all the historic
"white elephants" of the courts of Birmah and Siam)
and the sex; for though one naturally has recourse to the
masculine pronoun in writing of a transmigrated prince
or warrior, it often happens that prince or warrior has, in
the medlied mask of metempsychosis, assumed a female
form. Such, in fact, was the case with the stately occupant
of the stable-palace at the court of Maha Mongkut; and
she was distinguished by the high-sounding appellation
of Mââ Phya Seri Wongsah Ditsarah Krasâat, — "August
and Glorious Mother, Descendant of Kings and Heroes."

For seven or nine days, according to certain conditions,
the Chang Phoouk is fêted at the temporary pavilion, and
entertained with a variety of dramatic performances; and
these days are observed as a general holiday throughout
the land. At the expiration of this period he is conducted with great pomp to his sumptuous quarters within
the precincts of the first king's palace, where he is received by his own court of officers, attendants, and slaves,
who install him in his fine lodgings, and at once proceed
to robe and decorate him. First, the court jeweller rings
his tremendous tusks with massive gold, crowns him with
a diadem of beaten gold of perfect purity, and adorns his
burly neck with heavy golden chains. Next his attendants robe him in a superb velvet cloak of purple, fringed
with scarlet and gold; and then his court prostrate themselves around him, and offer him royal homage.

When his lordship would refresh his portly person in
the bath, an officer of high rank shelters his noble head
with a great umbrella of crimson and gold, while others

wave golden fans before him. On these occasions he is invariably preceded by musicians, who announce his approach with cheerful minstrelsy and songs.

If he falls ill, the king's own leech prescribes for him, and the chief priests repair daily to his palace to pray for his safe deliverance, and sprinkle him with consecrated waters and anoint him with consecrated oils. Should he die, all Siam is bereaved, and the nation, as one man, goes into mourning for him. But his body is not burned; only his brains and heart are thought worthy of that last and highest honor. The carcass, shrouded in fine white linen, and laid on a bier, is carried down the river with much wailing and many mournful dirges, to be thrown into the Gulf of Siam.

In 1862 a magnificent white — or, rather, salmon-colored — elephant was " bagged," and preparations on a gorgeous scale were made to receive him. A temporary pavilion of extraordinary splendor sprang up, as if by magic, before the eastern gate of the palace; and the whole nation was wild with joy; when suddenly came awful tidings, — he had died !

No man dared tell the king. But the Kralahome — that man of prompt expedients and unfailing presence of mind — commanded that the preparations should cease instantly, and that the building should vanish with the builders. In the evening his Majesty came forth, as usual, to exult in the glorious work. What was his astonishment to find no vestige of the splendid structure that had been so nearly completed the night before. He turned, bewildered, to his courtiers, to demand an explanation, when suddenly the terrible truth flashed into his mind. With a cry of pain he sank down upon a stone, and gave vent to an hysterical passion of tears; but was presently consoled by one of his children, who, carefully prompted in his part, knelt before him and said : "Weep not, O my father ! The stranger lord may have left us but for a time." The stranger lord, fatally pampered, had succumbed to astonishment and indigestion.

A few days after this mournful event the king read to me a curious description of the defunct monster, and showed me parts of his skin preserved, and his tusks, which in size and whiteness surpassed the finest I had ever seen. " His (that is, the elephant's) eyes were light blue, surrounded by salmon-color ; his hair fine, soft, and white ; his complexion pinkish white ; his tusks like long pearls ; his ears like silver shields ; his trunk like a comet's tail ; his legs like the feet of the skies ; his tread like the sound of thunder ; his looks full of meditation ; his expression full of tenderness ; his voice the voice of a mighty warrior ; and his bearing that of an illustrious monarch."

That was a terrible affliction, to the people not less than to the king.

On all occasions of state, — court receptions, for example, — the white elephant, gorgeously arrayed, is stationed on the right of the inner gate of the palace, and forms an indispensable as well as a conspicuous figure in the picture.

When the Siamese ambassadors returned from England, the chief of the embassy — a man remarkable for his learning and the purity of his character, who was also first cousin to the Supreme King—published a quaint pamphlet, describing England and her people, their manners and customs and dwellings, with a very particular report of the presentation of the embassy at court. Speaking of the personal appearance of Queen Victoria, he says : " One cannot but be struck with the aspect of the august Queen of England, or fail to observe that she must be of pure descent from a race of goodly and warlike kings and rulers of the earth, in that her eyes, complexion, and above all her bearing, are those of a beautiful and majestic white elephant."

7

XVII.

THE CEREMONIES OF CORONATION.

ON the morning of the 3d of April, 1851, the Chowfa
Mongkut, after being formally apprised of his election by the Senabawdee to the supreme throne, was borne
in state to a residence adjoining the Phrasat, to await
the auspicious day of coronation, — the 15th of the following month, as fixed by the court astrologers; and when it
came it was hailed by all classes of the people with im-
moderate demonstrations of joy; for to their priest king,
more sacred than a conqueror, they were drawn by bonds
of superstition as well as of pride and affection.

The ceremony of coronation is very peculiar.

In the centre of the inner Hall of Audience of the
royal palace, on a high platform richly gilded and adorned,
is placed a circular golden basin, called, in the court language, *Mangala Baghavat-thong*, "the Golden Circlet of
Power." Within this basin is deposited the ancient *P'hra-
batt*, or golden stool, the whole being surmounted by a quadrangular canopy, under a tapering, nine-storied umbrella
in the form of a pagoda, from ten to twelve feet high and
profusely gilt. Directly over the centre of the canopy is
deposited a vase containing consecrated waters, which
have been prayed over nine times, and poured through
nine different circular vessels in their passage to the
sacred receptacle. These waters must be drawn from the
very sources of the chief rivers of Siam; and reservoirs
for their preservation are provided in the precincts of the
temples at Bangkok.

In the mouth of this vessel is a tube representing the pericarp of a lotos after its petals have fallen off; and this, called *Sukla Utapala Atmano*, "the White Lotos of Life," symbolizes the beauty of pure conduct.

The king elect, arrayed in a simple white robe, takes his seat on the golden stool. A Brahmin priest then presents to him some water in a small cup of gold, lotos-shaped. This water has previously been filtered through nine different forms of matter, commencing with earth, then ashes, wheaten flour, rice flour, powdered lotos and jessamine, dust of iron, gold, and charcoal, and finally flame ; each a symbol, not merely of the indestructibility of the element, but also of its presence in all animate or inanimate matter. Into this water the king elect dips his right hand, and passes it over his head. Immediately the choir join in an inspiring chant, the signal for the inverting, by means of a pulley, of the vessel over the canopy ; and the consecrated waters descend through another lotos flower, in a lively shower, on the head of the king. This shower represents celestial blessings.

A Buddhist priest then advances and pours a goblet of water over the royal person. He is imitated, first by the Brahmin priests, next by the princes and princesses royal, The vessels used for this purpose are of the chank or conch shell, richly ornamented. Then come the nobles of highest rank, bearing cups of gold, silver, earthen-ware, pinchbeck, samil, and tankwah (metallic compositions peculiar to Siam). The materials of which the vessels for this royal bath are composed must be of not less than seven kinds. Last of all, the prime minister of the realm advances with a cup of iron ; and the sacred bath is finished.

Now the king descends into the golden basin, " Mangala Baghavat-thong," where he is anointed with nine varieties of perfumed oil, and dipped in fine dust brought from the bed of the Ganges.   He is then arrayed in regal robes.

On the throne, which is in the south end of the hall, and octagonal, having eight seats corresponding to eight points of the compass, the king first seats himself facing the north, and so on, moving eastward, facing each point in its order.   On the top step of each seat crouch two priests, Buddhist and Brahmin, who present to him another bowl of water, which he drinks and sprinkles on his face, each time repeating, by responses with the priests, the following prayer : —

Priests. Be thou learned in the laws of nature and of the universe.

King. Inspire me, O Thou who wert a Law unto thyself !

P. Be thou endowed with all wisdom, and all acts of industry !

K. Inspire me with all knowledge, O Thou the Enlightened !

P. Let Mercy and Truth be thy right and left arms of life !

K. Inspire me, O Thou who hast proved all Truth and all Mercy !

P. Let the Sun, Moon, and Stars bless thee !

K. All praise to Thee, through whom all forms are conquered !

P. Let the earth, air, and waters bless thee !

K. Through the merit of Thee, O thou conqueror of Death ! *

These prayers ended, the priests conduct the king to another throne, facing the east, and still more magnificent. Here the insignia of his sovereignty are presented to

---

* For these translations I am indebted to his Majesty, Maha Mongkut ; as well as for the interpretation of the several symbols used in this and other solemn rites of the Buddhists.

him, — first the sword, then the sceptre; two massive chains are suspended from his neck; and lastly the crown is set upon his head, when instantly he is saluted by roar of cannon without and music within.

Then he is presented with the golden slippers, the fan, and the umbrella of royalty, rings set with huge diamonds for each of his forefingers, and the various Siamese weapons of war: these he merely accepts, and returns to his attendants.

The ceremony concludes with an address from the priests, exhorting him to be pure in his sovereign and sacred office; and a reply from himself, wherein he solemnly vows to be a just, upright, and faithful ruler of his people. Last of all, a golden tray is handed to him, from which, as he descends from the throne, he scatters gold and silver flowers among the audience.

The following day is devoted to a more public enthronement. His Majesty, attired more sumptuously than before, is presented to all his court, and to a more general audience. After the customary salutations by prostration and salutes of cannon and music, the premier and other principal ministers read short addresses, in delivering over to the king the control of their respective departments. His Majesty replies briefly; there is a general salute from all forts, war vessels, and merchant shipping; and the remainder of the day is devoted to feasting and various enjoyment.

Immediately after the crowning of Maha Mongkut, his Majesty repaired to the palace of the Second King, where the ceremony of subordinate coronation differed from that just described only in the circumstance that the consecrated waters were poured over the person of the Second King, and the insignia presented to him, by the supreme sovereign.

Five days later a public procession made the circuit of

the palace and city walls in a peculiar circumambulatory march of mystic significance, with feasting, dramatic entertainments, and fireworks.   The concourse assembled to take part in those brilliant demonstrations has never since been equalled in any public display in Siam.

XVIII.

THE QUEEN CONSORT.

WHEN a king of Siam would take unto himself a wife, he chooses a maiden from a family of the highest rank, and of royal pedigree, and, inviting her into the guarded circle of his women, entertains her there in that peculiar state of probation which is his prerogative and her opportunity. Should she prove so fortunate as to engage his preference, it may be his pleasure to exalt her to the throne; in which event he appoints a day for the formal consummation of his gracious purpose, when the principal officers, male and female, of the court, with the priests, Brahmin as well as Buddhist, and the royal astrologers, attend to play their several parts in the important drama.

The princess, robed in pure white, is seated on a throne elevated on a high platform. Over this throne is spread a canopy of white muslin, decorated with white and fragrant flowers, and through this canopy are gently showered the typical waters of consecration, in which have been previously infused certain leaves and shrubs emblematic of purity, usefulness, and sweetness. While the princess is thus delicately sprinkled with compliments, the priests enumerate, with nice discrimination, the various graces of mind and person which henceforth she must study to acquire; and pray that she may prove a blessing to her lord, and herself be richly blessed. Then she is hailed queen, with a burst of exultant music.

Now the sisters of the king conduct her by a screened passage to a chamber regally appointed, where she is divested of her dripping apparel, and arrayed in robes becoming her queenly state, — robes of silk, heavy with gold, and sparkling with diamonds and rubies. Then the king is ushered into her presence by the ladies of the court; and at the moment of his entrance she rises to throw herself at his feet, according to the universal custom. But he prevents her; and taking her right hand, and embracing her, seats her beside him, on his right. There she receives the formal congratulations of the court, with which the ceremonies of the day terminate. The evening is devoted to feasting and merriment.

A Siamese king may have two queens at the same time; in which case the more favored lady is styled the "right hand," and the other the "left hand," of the throne. His late Majesty, Maha Mongkut, had two queens, but not "in conjunction." The first was of the right hand; the second, though chosen in the lifetime of the first, was not elevated to the throne until after the death of her predecessor.

When the bride is a foreign princess, the ceremonies are more public, being conducted in the Hall of Audience, instead of the Ladies' Temple, or private chapel.

The royal nuptial couch is consecrated with peculiar forms. The mystic thread of unspun cotton is wound around the bed seventy-seven times, and the ends held in the hands of priests, who, bowing over the sacred symbol, invoke blessings on the bridal pair. Then the nearest relatives of the bride are admitted, accompanied by a couple who, to use the obstetrical figure of the indispensable Mrs. Gamp, have their parental quiver "full of sich." These salute the bed, sprinkle it with the consecrated waters, festoon the crimson curtains with flowery garlands, and prepare the silken sheets, the pillows and cushions ; which done, they lead in the bride, who has not presided at the entertainments, but waited with her ladies in a screened apartment.

On entering the awful chamber, she first falls on her knees, and thrice salutes the royal couch with folded hands, and then invokes protection for herself, that she may be preserved from every deadly sin. Finally, she is disrobed, and left praying on the floor before the bed, while the king is conducted to her by his courtiers, who immediately retire.

The same ceremony is observed in nearly all Siamese families of respectability, with, of course, certain omissions and variations adapted to the rank of the parties.

After three days the bride visits her parents, bearing presents to them from the various members of her husband's family. Then she visits the parents of her husband, who greet her with costly gifts. In her next excursion of this kind her husband (unless a king) accompanies her, and valuable presents are mutually bestowed. A large sum of money, with jewels and other finery, is deposited with the father and mother of the bride. This is denominated *Zoon*, and at the birth of her first child it is restored to the young mother by the grandparents.

The king visits his youthful queen just one month after the birth of a prince or princess. She presents the babe to him, and he, in turn, places a costly ring on the third finger of her left hand. In like manner, most of the relatives, of both families, bring to the babe gifts of money, jewels, gold and silver ornaments, etc., which is termed *Tam Kwaan*. Even so early the infant's hair is shaved off, except the top-knot, which is permitted to grow until the child has arrived at the age of puberty.

7 *

XIX.

THE HEIR–APPARENT. — ROYAL HAIR–CUTTING.

THE Prince Somdetch Chowfa Chulalonkorn * was about ten years old when I was appointed to teach him. Being the eldest son of the queen consort, he held the first rank among the children of the king, as heir-apparent to the throne. For a Siamese, he was a handsome lad ; of stature neither noticeably tall nor short; figure symmetrical and compact, and dark complexion. He was, moreover, modest and affectionate, eager to learn, and easy to influence.

His mother dying when he was about nine years old, he, with his younger brothers, the Princes Chowfa Chaturont Rasmi and Chowfa Bhanurangsi Swang Wongse, and their lovely young sister, the Princess Somdetch Chowfa Chandrmondol (" Fà-ying "), were left to the care of a grand-aunt, Somdetch Ying Noie, a princess by the father's side. This was a tranquil, cheerful old soul, attracted toward everything that was bright and pretty, and ever busy among flowers, poetry, and those darlings of her loving life, her niece's children. Of these the little Fà-ying (whose sudden death by cholera I have described) was her favorite ; and after her death the faithful creature turned her dimmed eyes and chastened pride to the young prince Chulalonkorn. Many an earnest talk had the venerable duchess and I, in which she did not hesitate to implore me to instil into the minds of her youth-

* The present Supreme King.

THE HEIR-APPARENT.

ful wards — and especially this king that was to be — the purest principles of Christian faith and precept.   Yet with all the freshness of the religious habit of her childhood she was most scrupulous in her attendance and devotions at the temple.   Her grief for the death of her darling was deep and lasting, and by the simple force of her love she exerted a potent influence over the mind of the royal lad.

A very stern thing is life to the children of royalty in Siam.   To watch and be silent, when it has most need of confidence and freedom, — a horrible necessity for a child !   The very babe in the cradle is taught mysterious and terrible things by the mother that bore it, — infantile experiences of distrust and terror, out of which a few come up noble, the many infamous.   Here are baby heroes and heroines who do great deeds before our happier Western children have begun to think.   There were actual, though unnoticed and unconscious, intrepidity and fortitude in the manœuvres and the stands with which those little ones, on their own ground, flanked or checked that fatal enemy, their father.   Angelic indeed were the spiritual triumphs that no eye noted, nor any smile rewarded, save the anxious eye and the prayerful smile of that sleepless maternity that misery had bound with them.   But even misery becomes tolerable by first becoming familiar, and out of the depths these royal children laughed and prattled and frolicked and were glad. As for the old duchess, she loved too well and too wisely not to be timid and troubled all her life long, first for the mother, then for the children.

Such was the early training of the young prince, and for a time it availed to direct his thoughts to noble aspirations.   From his studies, both in English and Pali, he derived an exalted ideal of life, and precocious and inexpressible yearnings.   Once he said to me he envied the death of the venerable priest, his uncle ; he would rather be poor, he said, and have to earn his living, than be a king.

" 'T is true, a poor man must work hard for his daily bread ; but then he is free. And his food is all he has to lose or win. He can possess all things in possessing Him who pervades all things, — earth, and sky, and stars, and flowers, and children. I can understand that I am great in that I am a part of the Infinite, and in that alone ; and that all I see is mine, and I am in it and of it. How much of content and happiness should I not gain if I could but be a poor boy ! "

He was attentive to his studies, serene, and gentle, invariably affectionate to his old aunt and his younger brothers, and for the poor ever sympathetic, with a warm, generous heart. He pursued his studies assiduously, and seemed to overcome the difficulties and obstacles he encountered in the course of them with a resolution that gained strength as his mind gained ideas. As often as he effectually accomplished something, he indulged in ecstasies of rejoicing over the new thought, that was an inspiring discovery to him of his actual poverty of knowledge, his possibilities of intellectual opulence. But it was clear to me — and I saw it with sorrow — that for his ardent nature this was but a transitory condition, and that soon the shock must come, against the inevitable destiny in store for him, that would either confirm or crush all that seemed so fair in the promise of the royal boy.

When the time came for the ceremony of hair-cutting, customary for young Siamese princes, the lad was gradually withdrawn, more and more, from my influence. The king had determined to celebrate the heir's majority with displays of unusual magnificence. To this end he explored the annals and records of Siam and Cambodia, and compiled from them a detailed description of a very curious procession that attended a certain prince of Siam centuries ago, on the occasion of his hair-cutting; and forthwith projected a similar show for his son, but on a more elaborate and costly scale. The programme, including the procession, provided for the representation of a sort of drama, borrowed partly from the Ramayana, and partly from the ancient observances of the kings of Cambodia.

The whole royal establishment was set in motion. About nine thousand young women, among them the most beautiful of the concubines, were cast for parts in the mammoth play. Boys and girls were invited or hired from all quarters of the kingdom to "assist" in the performance. Every nation under the sun was represented in the grand procession. In our school the regular studies were abandoned, and in their place we had rehearsals of singing, dancing, recitation, and pantomime.

An artificial hill, of great height, called Khoa-Kra-Lâât, was raised in the centre of the palace gardens. On its summit was erected a golden temple or pagoda of exquisite beauty, richly hung with tapestries, displaying on the east the rising sun, on the west a moon of silver. The cardinal points of the hill were guarded by the white elephant, the sacred ox, the horse, and the lion. These figures were so contrived that they could be brought close together and turned on a pivot; and thus the sacred waters, brought for that purpose from the Brahmapootra, were to be showered on the prince, after the solemn hair-cutting, and received in a noble basin of marble.

The name given to the ceremony of hair-cutting varies according to the rank of the child. For commoners it is called " Khone Chook "; for the nobility and royalty, " Soh-Khan," probably from the Sanskrit *Sôh Sâhtha Kam,* " finding safe and sound." The custom is said to be extremely ancient, and to have originated with a certain Brahmin, whose only child, being sick unto death, was given over by the physicians as in the power of evil spirits.   In his heart's trouble the father consulted a holy man, who had been among the earliest converts to Buddhism, if aught might yet be done to save his darling from torment and perdition.   The venerable saint directed him to pray, and to have prayers offered, for the lad, and to cause that part of his hair which had never been touched with razor or shears since his birth to be shaved quite off.   The result was a joyful rescue for the child ; others pursued the same treatment in like cases with the same effect, and hence the custom of hair-cutting. The children of princes are forbidden to have the top-knot cut at all, until the time when they are about to pass into manhood or womanhood.   Then valuable presents are made to them by all who are related to their families by blood, marriage, or friendship.

When all the preparations necessary to the successful presentation of the dramatic entertainment were completed, the king, having taken counsel of his astrologers, sent heralds to the governors of all the provinces of Siam, to notify those dignitaries of the time appointed for the jubilee, and request their presence and co-operation.   A similar summons was sent to all the priests of the kingdom, who, in bands or companies, were to serve alternately, on the several days of the festival.

Early in the forenoon of the auspicious day the prince was borne in state, in a gorgeous chair of gold, to the Maha Phrasat, the order of the procession being as follows : —

First came the bearers of the gold umbrellas, fans, and great golden sunshades.

Next, twelve gentlemen, superbly attired, selected from the first rank of the nobility, six on either side of the golden chair, as a body-guard to the prince.

Then, four hundred Amazons arrayed in green and gold, and gleaming armor.

These were followed by twelve maidens, attired in cloth of gold, with fantastic head-gear adorned with precious stones, who danced before the prince to the gentle monotonous movement of the *bandos*. In the centre of this group moved three lovely girls, of whom one held a superb peacock's tail, and the two others branches of gold and silver, sparkling with leaves and rare flowers. These damsels were guarded by two duennas on either side.

After these stalked a stately body of Brahmins, bearing golden vases filled with *Khoa tôk*, or roasted rice, which they scattered on either side, as an emblem of plenty.

Another troop of Brahmins with bandos, which they rattled as they moved along.

Two young nobles, splendidly robed, who also bore gold vases, lotos-shaped, in which nestled the bird of paradise called Nok Kurraweèk, the sweetness of whose song is supposed to entrance even beasts of prey.

A troop of lads, the rising nobility of Siam, fairly covered with gold collars and necklaces.

The king's Japanese body-guard.

Another line of boys, representing natives of Hindostan in costume.

Malayan lads in costume.

Chinese lads in costume.

Siamese boys in English costume.

The king's infantry, headed by pioneers, in European costume.

Outside of this line marched about five thousand men in long rose-colored robes, with tall tapering caps. These represented guardian-angels attending on the different nations.

Then came bands of musicians dressed in scarlet, imitating the cries of birds, the sound of falling fruit, and the murmur of distant waters, in the imaginary forest they were supposed to traverse on their way to the Sacred Mount.

The order of the procession behind the golden sedan in which the prince was borne, was nearly as follows : —

Next after the chair of state came four young damsels of the highest rank, bearing the prince's betel-box, spittoon, fan, and swords.   Then followed seventy other maidens, carrying reverently in both hands the vessels of pure gold, and all the insignia of rank and office proper to a prince of the blood royal; and yet more, holding over their right shoulders golden fans.

In the train of these tripped troops of children, daughters of the nobility, dressed and decorated with fantastic splendor.

Then the maids of honor, personal attendants, and concubines of the king, chastely dressed, though crowned with gold, and decorated with massive gold chains and rings of great price and beauty.

A crowd of Siamese women, painted and rouged, in European costume.

Troops of children in corresponding attire.

Ladies in Chinese costume.

Japanese ladies in rich robes.

Malay women in their national dress.

Women of Hindostan.

Then the Kariens.

And, last of all, the female slaves and dependants of the prince.

At the foot of the hill a most extraordinary spectacle was presented.

On the east appeared a number of hideous monsters, riding on gigantic eagles.   These nondescripts, whose heads reached almost to their knees, and whose hands grasped indescribable weapons, are called Yâks.   They are appointed to guard the Sacred Mount from all vulgar approach.

A little farther on, around a pair of stuffed peacocks, were a number of youthful warriors, representing kings, governors, and chiefs of the several dependencies of Siam.

Desirous of witnessing the sublime ceremony of hair-cutting, they cautiously approach the Yâks, performing a sort of war dance, and chanting in chorus : —

Orah Pho, cha pai Kra Lâât.

" Let us go to the Sacred Mount ! "

Whereupon the Yâks, or evil angels, point their wonderful weapons at them, chanting in the same strain : —

Orah Pho, salope thâng pooang.

" Let us slay them all ! "

They then make a show of striking and thrusting, and princes, rajahs, and governors drop as if wounded.

The principal parts in the drama were assumed by his Majesty, and their excellencies the Prime Minister and the Minister of Foreign Affairs. The king was dressed for the character of P'hra Inn Suen, the Hindoo Indra, or Lord of the Sky, who has also the attributes of the Roman Genius ; but most of his epithets in Sanskrit are identical with those of the Olympian Jove. He was attended by the Prime Minister, personating the Sanskrit Saché, but called in Siamese " Vis Summo Kâm," and the Minister of Foreign Affairs as his charioteer, Ma Talee. His imperial elephant, called Aisarat, caparisoned in velvet and gold, and bearing the supernatural weapons, — *Vagra*, the thunderbolts, — was led by allegorical personages, representing winds and showers, lightning and thunder. The hill, Khoa Kra Lâât, is the Sanskrit Meru, described as a mountain of gold and gems.

His Majesty received the prince from the hands of his nobles, set him on his right hand, and presented him to the people, who offered homage. Afterward, two ladies

K

of the court led him down the flight of marble steps, where two maidens washed his feet with pure water in a gold basin, and wiped them with fine linen.

On his way to the Maha Phrasat he was met by a group of girls in charming attire, who held before him tufts of palm and branches of gold and silver. Thus he was conducted to an inner chamber of the temple, and seated on a costly carpet heavily fringed with gold, before an altar on which were lighted tapers and offerings of all descriptions. In his hand was placed a strip of palmyra leaf, on which were inscribed these mystic words : " Even I was, even from the first, and not any other thing : that which existed unperceived, supreme. Afterwards, I am that which is, and He that was, and He who must remain am I."

" Know that except Me, who am the First Cause, nothing that appears or does not appear in the mind can be trusted ; it is the mind's Maya or delusion, — as Light is to Darkness."

On the reverse was inscribed this sentence : —

" Keep me still meditating on Thy infinite greatness and my own nothingness, so that all the questions of my life may be answered and my mind abundantly instructed in the path of Niphan ! "

In his hands was placed a ball of unspun thread, the ends of which were carried round the sacred hill, and thence round the temple, and into the inner chamber, where it was bound round the head of the young prince. Thence again nine threads were taken, which, after encircling the altar, were passed into the hands of the officiating priests. These latter threads, forming circles within circles, symbolize the mystic word *Om*, which may not escape the lips even of the purest, but must be meditated upon in silence.

Early on the third day all the princes, nobles, and

officers of government, together with the third company of priests, assembled to witness the ceremony of shaving the royal top-knot. The royal sire handed first the golden shears and then a gilded razor to the happy hair-cutter, who immediately addressed himself to his honorable function. Meanwhile the musicians, with the trumpeters and conch-blowers, exerted all their noisy faculties to beguile the patient heir.

The tonsorial operation concluded, the prince was robed in white, and conducted to the marble basin at the foot of the Sacred Mount, where the white elephant, the ox, the horse, and the lion, guarding the cardinal points, were brought together, and from their mouths baptized him in the sacred waters. He was then arrayed in silk, still white, by women of rank, and escorted to a golden pagoda on the summit of the hill, where the king, in the character of P'hra Inn Suen, waited to bestow his blessing on the heir. With one hand raised to heaven, and the other on the bowed head of his son, he solemnly uttered words of Pali, which may be translated thus : —

"Thou who art come out of the pure waters, be thy offences washed away ! Be thou relieved from other births ! Bear thou in thy bosom the brightness of that light which shall lead thee, even as it led the sublime Buddha, to Niphan, at once and forever ! "

These rites ended, the priests were served with a princely banquet ; and then the nobility and common people were also feasted. About midday, two standards, called *baisêe*, were set up within a circle of people. These are not unlike the *sawekra chât*, or royal umbrella, one of the five insignia of royalty in Siam. They are about five cubits high, and have from three to five canopies. The staff is fixed in a wooden pedestal. Each circle or canopy has a flat bottom, and within the receptacle thus formed custom requires that a little cooked rice, called *k'ow k'wan,* shall be placed, together with a few cakes, a little sweet-scented oil, a handful of fragrant flour, and some young cocoanuts and plantains.   Other edibles of many kinds are brought and arranged about the *baisée,* and a beautiful bouquet adorns the top of each of the umbrella-like canopies.

Then a procession was formed, of princes, noblemen, and others, who marched around the standards nine times. As they went, seven golden candlesticks, with the candles lighted, were carried by princes, and passed from one to another; and as often as they came in front of the prince, who sat between the standards, they waved the light before him.   This procession is but another form of the *Om* symbol.

Afterwards the eldest priest or brahmin took a portion of the rice from the *baisée,* and, sprinkling it with cocoanut water, gave the lad a spoonful of it.   Then dipping his finger, first in the scented oil and then in the fragrant flour, he touched the right foot of the prince, at the same time exhorting him to be manly and strong, and to bear himself bravely in " the conflict of feeling."

Now presents of silver and gold were laid at the feet of the lad, — every prince not of the royal family, and every nobleman and high officer in the kingdom, being expected to appear with gifts.   A chowfa might receive, in the aggregate, from five hundred thousand to a million ticals.*   It should be remarked in this connection, that the late king commanded that careful note be kept of all sums of money presented by officers of his government to his children at the time of Soh-Khan, that the full amount might be refunded with the next semi-annual payment of salary.   But this decree does not relieve the more distinguished princes and endowed noblemen, who have acquired

---

* A tical is equivalent to sixty cents.

a sort of complimentary relationship to his Majesty through their daughters and nieces accepted as concubines.

The children of plain citizens, who cannot afford the luxury of a public hair-cutting, are taken to a temple, where a priest shaves the tuft, with a brief religious ceremony.

Hardly had the prince recovered his wonted frame of mind, after an event so pregnant with significance and agitation to him, when the time arrived for his induction into the priesthood. For this the rites, though simpler, were more solemn. The hair, which had been suffered to grow on the top of his young pate like an inverted brush, was now shorn close, and his eyebrows were shaven also. Arrayed in costly robes and ornaments, similar to those worn at a coronation, he was taken in charge by a body of priests at his father's palace, and by them conducted to the temple Watt P'hra Këau, his yellow-robed and barefooted escort chanting, on the way, hymns from the Buddhist liturgy. At the threshold of the temple another band of priests divested him of his fine robes and clad him in simple white, all the while still chanting. The circle being characteristic of a Buddhist ceremonial, as the cross is of their religious architecture, these priests formed a circle, standing, and holding lighted tapers in their folded palms, the high-priest in the centre. Then the prince advanced meekly, timidly, bowing low, to enter the holy ring. Here he was received by the high-priest, and with their hands mutually interfolded, one upon the other, he vowed to renounce, then and there, the world with all its cares and temptations, and to observe with obedience the doctrines of Buddha. This done, he was clad afresh in sackcloth, and led from the temple to the royal monastery, Watt Brahmanee Waid ; with bare feet and eyes downcast he went, still chanting those weird hymns

Here he remained recluse for six months. When he

returned to the world, and to the residence assigned him, he seemed no longer the impressible, ardent boy who was once my bright, ambitious scholar. Though still anxious to prosecute his English studies, he was pronounced too old to unite with his brothers and sisters in the school. For a year I taught him, from seven to ten in the evening, at his " Rose-planting House "; and even from this distant place and time I look back with comfort to those hours.

XX.

AMUSEMENTS OF THE COURT.

O F all the diversions of the court the most polite, and at the same time the most engrossing, is the drama.

In a great sala, or hall, which serves as a theatre, the actors and actresses assemble, their faces and bodies anointed with a creamy, maize-colored cosmetic. Fantastic extravagance of attire constitutes the great gun in their arsenal of attractions. Hence ear-rings, bracelets, massive chains and collars, tapering crowns with wings, spangled robes, curious finger-rings, and, strangest of all, long tapering nails of gold, are joined to complete their elaborate adornment. The play, in which are invariably enacted the adventures of gods, kings, heroes, genii, demons, and a multitude of characters mythical and fabulous, is often performed in lively pantomime, the interludes being filled by a strong chorus, with songs and instrumental accompaniment. At other times the players, in grotesque masks, give burlesque versions of the graver epics, to the great amusement of the audience.

Chinese comedies, termed Ngiu, attract the Siamese in crowds; but the foreign is decidedly inferior to the native talent. "Nang," so called, is a sort of tableau, masked, representing characters from the Hindoo mythology. Parts of the popular epic, Ramayana, are admirably rendered in this style. In front of the royal palace an immense transparent screen, mounted on great poles, is drawn across the esplanade, and behind this, at a moderate distance, great fires are lighted. Between the screen and the fire masked figures, grotesquely costumed, enact the story of Rama and Sita and the giant Rawuna, with Hanuman and his army of apes bridging the Gulf of Manaar and piling up the Himalayas, while the bards, in measured story, describe the several exploits.

A great variety of puppet-shows are contrived for the delectation of the children; and the Siamese are marvellously ingenious in the manufacture of toys and dolls, of porcelain, stone, wood, bark, and paper. They make pagodas, temples, boats, and floating houses, with miniature families to occupy them, and all true to the life in every apartment and occupation; watts, with idols and priests; palaces, with kings, queens, concubines, royal children, courtiers, and slaves, all complete in costume and attitude.

The royal children observe with grave formalities the eventful custom of "hair-cutting" for their favorite dolls; and dramas, improvised for the occasion by ingenious slaves, are the crowning glory of those high holidays of toddling princes and princesses.

The ladies of the harem amuse themselves in the early and late hours of the day by gathering flowers in the palace gardens, feeding the birds in the aviaries and the gold-fishes in the ponds, twining garlands to adorn the heads of their children, arranging bouquets, singing songs of love or glory, dancing to the music of the guitar, listening to their slaves' reading, strolling with their little ones through the parks and *parterres*, and especially in bathing. When the heat is least oppressive they plunge into the waters of the pretty retired lakes, swimming and diving like flocks of brown water-fowl.

Chess and backgammon, Chinese cards and dice, afford a continual diversion to both sexes at the court, and there are many skilful players among them.

The Chinese have established a sort of "lottery," of which they have the monopoly. It is little better than a "sweat-cloth," with thirteen figures, on which money is staked at the option of the gambler. The winning figure pays its stake thirty-fold, the rest is lost.

Kite-flying, which in Europe and America is the amusement of children exclusively, is here, as in China and Birmah, the pastime of both sexes, and all ages and conditions of people. At the season when the south-wind prevails steadily, innumerable kites of diverse forms, many of them representing gigantic butterflies, may be seen sailing and darting over every quarter of the city, and most thickly over the palace and its appendages. Parties of young noblemen devote themselves with ardor to the sport, betting bravely on results of skill or luck; and it is most entertaining to observe how cleverly they manage the huge paper toys, entangling and capturing each other's kites, and dragging them disabled to the earth.

Combats of bulls and elephants, though very popular, are not commonly exhibited at court. At certain seasons fairs are held, where exhibitions of wrestling, boxing, fencing, and dancing are given by professional competitors.

The Siamese, naturally imaginative and gay, cultivate music with great zest. Every village has its orchestra, every prince and noble his band of musicians, and in every part of Bangkok the sound of strange instruments is heard continually. Their music is not in parts like ours, but there is always harmony with good expression, and an agreeable variety of movement and volume is derived from the diversity of instruments and the taste of the players.

The principal instrument, the *khong-vong*, is composed of a series of hemispherical metallic bells or cups in-

8

verted and suspended by cords to a wooden frame. The performer strikes the bells with two little hammers covered with soft leather, producing an agreeable harmony. The hautboy player (who is usually a professional juggler and snake-charmer also) commonly leads the band. Kneeling and swaying his body forward and backward, and from side to side, he keeps time to the movement of the music. His instrument has six holes, but no keys, and may be either rough or smoothly finished.

The *ranat*, or harmonicon, is a wooden instrument, with keys made of wood from the bashoo-nut tree. These, varying in size from six inches by one to fifteen by two, are connected by pieces of twine, and so fastened to a hollow case of wood about three feet in length and a foot high. The music is "conjured" by the aid of two small hammers corked with leather, like those of the khong-vong. The notes are clear and fine, and the instrument admits of much delicacy of touch.

Beside these the Siamese have the guitar, the violin, the flute, the cymbals, the trumpet, and the conch-shell. There is the *luptima* also, another very curious instrument, formed of a dozen long perforated reeds joined with bands and cemented at the joints with wax. The orifice at one end is applied to the lips, and a very moderate degree of skill produces notes so strong and sweet as to remind one of the swell of a church organ.

The Laos people have organs and tambourines of different forms ; their guitar is almost as agreeable as that of Europe ; and of their flutes of several kinds, one is played with the nostril instead of the lips.

Another instrument, resembling the banjo of the American negroes, is made from a large long-necked gourd, cut in halves while green, cleaned, dried in the sun, covered with parchment, and strung with from four to six strings. Its notes are pleasing.

The *takhè*, a long guitar with metallic strings, is laid on the floor, and high-born ladies, with fingers armed with shields or nails of gold, draw from it the softest and sweetest sounds.

In their funeral ceremonies the chanting of the priests is usually accompanied by the lugubrious wailing music of a sort of clarionet.

The songs of Siam are either heroic or amatory; the former celebrating the martial exploits, the latter the more tender adventures, of heroes.

Athletic games and the contests of the arena and the course form so conspicuous a feature in all ceremonies, solemn or festal, of this people, that a description of them may not with advantage be wholly omitted here. The Siamese are by nature warlike, and their government has thoughtfully and liberally fostered those manly sports and exercises which constitute the natural preparation for the profession of arms. Of these the most popular are wrestling, boxing (in which both sexes take part), throwing the discus or quoit, foot-shuttlecock, and racing on foot or horseback or in chariots; to which may be added vaulting and tumbling, throwing the dart, and leaping through wheels or circles of fire.

The professional athletes and gymnasts are exercised at a tender age under male or female trainers, who employ the most approved methods of limbering and quickening and strengthening and toughening their incipient champions, to whom, though well fed, sleep is jealously allowanced and intoxicating drinks absolutely forbidden. Their bodies are rubbed with oils and unguents to render them supple; and a short langoutee with a belt forms the sum of their clothing. None but the children of Siamese or Laotians are admitted to the gymnasia. The code of laws for the government of the several classes is strictly

enforced, and nothing is permitted contrary to the established order and regulations of the games. Excessive
violence is mercifully forbidden, and those who enter to
wrestle or box, race or leap, for the prize, draw lots for
precedence and position.

The Siamese practise wrestling in its rude simplicity,
the advantage being with weight and strength, rather
than skill and address. The wrestlers, before engaging, are
rubbed and shampooed, the joints bent backward and all
the muscles relaxed, and the body and limbs freely oiled ;
but after the latter operation they roll in the dust, or are
sprinkled with earth, ground and sifted, that they may be
grappled the more firmly. They are matched in pairs,
and several couples contend at the same time. Their
struggles afford superb displays of the anatomy of action,
and the perfection of strength and skill and fierce grace
in the trained animal. Though one be seized by the heel
and thrown, — which the Siamese applaud as the climax
of the wrestler's adroitness, — they still struggle grandly
on the ground, a double Antæus of arms and legs, till one
be turned upon his back and slapped upon the breast.
That is the accepted signal of the victor.

In boxing, the Siamese cover their hands with a kind
of glove of ribbed leather, sometimes lined with brass.
On their heads they wear a leather turban, to protect the
temples and ears, the assault being directed mainly at
the head and face. Besides the usual "getting away"
of the British bruiser, blows are caught with surprising
address and strength in the gloved hand. The boxer
who by overreaching, or missing a blow he has put his
weight into, throws himself, is beaten ; or he may surrender by simply lowering his arms.

The Siamese discus, or quoit, is round, and of wood,
stone, or iron. Their manner of hurling it does not differ materially from that which all mighty players have

practised since Cæsar's soldiers pitched quoits for rations.

Quite otherwise, in its curious novelty, is their spirited and picturesque sport of foot-shuttlecock, — a game which may be witnessed only in Asia, and in the perfection of its skill and agility only in Birmah and Siam.

The shuttlecock is like our own, but the battledore is the sole of the foot. A number of young men form a circle on a clear plot of ground. One of them opens the game by throwing the feathered toy to the player opposite him, who, turning quickly and raising his leg, receives it on the sole of his foot, and sends it like a shot to another, and he to another ; and so it is kept flying for an hour or more, without once falling to the ground.

Speed, whether of two legs or four, is in high estimation among the Siamese. Their public festivals, however solemn, are usually begun with races, which they cultivate with ardor and enjoy with enthusiasm. They have the foot-race, the horse-race, and the chariot-race. In the first, the runners, having drawn lots for places, range themselves across the course, and, while waiting for the starting signal, excite themselves by leaping. At the word " Go," they make play with astonishing speed and spirit.

The race of a single horse, "against time," with or without saddle, is a favorite sport. The rider, scorning stirrup or bridle, grips the sides of his steed with his knees, and, with his right arm and forefinger stretched eagerly toward the goal, flies alone, — an inspiring picture. Sometimes two horsemen ride abreast, and at full speed change horses by vaulting from one to the other.

In the chariot-races from two to four horses are driven abreast, and the art consists in winning and keeping the advantage of ground without collision. This kind of racing is not so common as the others.

The favorite pastime of the late Second King, who greatly delighted in equestrian exercises and feats, was Croquet on Horseback, — a sport in which he distinguished himself by his brilliant skill and style, as he did in racing and hunting. This unique equestrian game is played exclusively by princes and noblemen. There are a number of small balls which must be croqueted into two deep holes, with the aid of long slender mallets. The limits of the ground are marked by a line drawn around it ; and the only conditions necessary to render the sport exciting and the skill remarkable are narrow bounds and restive steeds.

The Siamese, like other Orientals, ride with loose rein and short stirrups. Their saddles are high and hard, and have two large circular flaps, gilded and otherwise adorned, according to the rank of the rider. Cavaliers of distinction usually dress expensively, in imported stuffs, elaborately embroidered with silk and gold thread. They wear a small cap, and sometimes a strip of red, like the fillet of the Greeks and Romans, bound round the brows.

Prizes for the victors in the games and combats are of several kinds, — purses of gold and silver, suits of apparel, umbrellas, and, more rarely, a gold or silver cup.

In concluding this imperfect sketch, I feel that a word of praise is due to the spirit of moderation and humanity which seems to govern such exhibitions in Siam. Even in their gravest festivals there is an element of cheerfulness and kindness, which tends to promote genial fellowship and foster friendships, and by bringing together all sorts of people, otherwise separated by diversity of custom, prejudice, and interest, unquestionably avails to weld the several small states and dependencies of Siam into one compact and stable nation.

XXI.

SIAMESE LITERATURE AND ART.

AT the head of the Siamese writers of profane history stands, I think, P'hra Alack, or rather Cheing Meing, — P'hra Alack being the generic term for all writers. In early life he was a priest, but was appointed historian to the court, and in that capacity wrote a history of the reign of his patron and king, P'hra Narai, — (contemporary with Louis XIV.) — and left a very curious though unfinished autobiography.

Seri Manthara, celebrated as a military leader, wrote nine books of essays, on subjects relating to agriculture and the arts and sciences. Some of these, translated into the languages of Birmah and Pegu, are still extant.

Among a host of dramatic writers, Phya Doong, better known as P'hra Khein Lakonlen, is entitled to the first rank. He composed about forty-nine books in lyric and dramatic verse, besides epigrams and elegies. Of his many poems, the few that remain afford passages of much elegance and sweetness, and even of sublimity, — almost sufficient to atone for the taint of grossness he derived from the licentious imagination of his land and time.

While yet hardly out of his infancy, he was laid at the feet of the monarch, and reared in the palace at Lophaburee. Some dramatic pieces composed by the lad for his playmates to act attracted the notice of the king, who engaged teachers to instruct him thoroughly in the ancient literature of India and Persia. But he seems to

have boldly opened a way for himself, instead of following (as modern Orientals, timid or servile, are so prone to
do) the well-worn path of the old Hindoo writers.   In his
tragedy (which I saw acted) of *Manda-thi-Nung*, "The
First Mother," there are passages of noble thought and
true passion, expressed with a power and beauty peculiarly his own.

The entertainments of the theatre are devoured by the
Siamese with insatiable appetite, and the popular preference is awarded to those intellectual contests in which
the tragic and comic poets compete for the prize.   The
laughter or the tears of the sympathetic groundlings are
accepted as the expression of an infallible criticism, and
by their verdict the play is crowned or damned.   The
common people, such is their passion for the drama, get
whole tragedies or comedies " by heart."   Every day in
the year, and in every street of Bangkok, and all along
the river, booths and floating salas may be seen, in which
tragedy, comedy, and satirical burlesques, are enacted for
the entertainment of great audiences, who are thrilled, delighted, or amused.   In compositions strictly dramatic the
characters, as with us, speak and act for themselves; but
in the epic the poet recites the adventures of his heroes.

Judges are appointed by the king to determine the
merits of new plays before they are performed at court;
and on the grand occasion of the hair-cutting of the
heir-apparent (now king) his late Majesty caused the poem
" Kraelasah " to be modernized and adapted to grace the
ceremonies.

P'hra Ramawsha, a writer highly esteemed, did wonders
for the Siamese drama.   He translated the Ramayana, the
Mahabharata, and portions of the Cambodian lyrics into
Siamese; introduced masks, with magnificence of costume
and ornament; substituted theatres, or rather salas, for
the temporary booth or the open plain; and elevated the

SIAMESE ACTOR AND ACTRESS.

matter and the style of dramatic compositions from the burlesque and buffoonery to the sentimental and majestic. He was also the first to impart spirit and variety to the dialogue, and to teach actors to express like artists, and not like mere animals, the strong *human* passions of anger, love, and pity. The plays of P'hra Ramawsha are highly esteemed at court. In his management of amorous incidents and intrigues, he is, if not positively refined, at least less gross than other Siamese dramatists.

The dress of the players is always rich, and in the fashion of that worn at court. The actors and actresses attached to the royal establishment make a splendid display in this respect, large sums being expended annually on their costumes, jewels, and other adornings.

The development of native genius and skill, in the direction of the fine arts, has greatly declined, if it has not been absolutely arrested, since the reign of P'hra Narai, the enlightened founder of Lophaburee; and almost all the vestiges of art, purely national, to be found in the country now, may be traced to that golden age of Siam. The Siamese, though intelligent, clever, facile, and in a notable degree susceptible to the influences of the beautiful in nature or in art, by no means slow or awkward in imitating the graceful products of European taste and industry, are yet fettered by a peculiar oppression in their efforts to express in visible forms their artistic inspirations. No Siamese subject is to be congratulated, who by his talent or his skill has won popular applause in any branch of industry. No such man, having extraordinary cleverness or taste, dare display it to the public in works of novel utility or beauty; because he and his inventions may alike be appropriated, without reward or thanks, — the former to serve the king, the latter to adorn the palace. Many ply in secret their dangerously graceful callings, and destroy their work when it is done, rather than see it wrested from them, and with it all that is left to them of freedom, to serve the whim of a covetous and cruel master. All that P'hra Narai did to foster the sciences and arts in his land has been undone by the ruinous selfishness of his successors; and of the few suicides recorded in the annals of Siam since his time, one of the most remarkable is that of a famous painter, who poisoned himself the day after his installation at court. Thus all natural ambition has been stupidly extinguished in the breasts of the artists of a land whose remaining monuments attest her ancient excellence in architecture, sculpture, and painting.

The most remarkable examples of Siamese painting are presented in the cartoons to be found on the walls of the ancient temples, decorated with the brush before the introduction of wall-paper from Birmah. One that is still to be seen in the Watt Kheim Mah, or Mai, is especially noticeable. This temple was built by the grandmother of the late Maha Mongkut. The plant *kheim mai* (indigenous to Siam), which bears a lovely little blossom, was one of her favorite flowers, and she called her temple by its name. Being a liberal patron of the arts, she employed a promising young painter named Nai Dang to decorate the Watt. The man would hardly be remembered now but for a poem he wrote and dedicated to the queen mother, in which her beauty and goodness are extolled. I could learn of him no more than that he was self-educated, and by unaided perseverance attained a respectable proficiency in drawing and design. He had also a fair knowledge of chemistry as it is practised in the East; but, aspiring to fame and fortune, he abandoned that study and devoted himself exclusively to painting. For years he struggled desperately against the discouragements of poverty in himself and ignorance in his neighbors, but found his reward at last in this engagement to embellish the walls of the Watt Kheim Mai.

Nai Dang's must have been an original and independent mind, for his conceptions in this cartoon are as bold as his handling is vigorous and effective, while his colors are more true to nature than any that I have seen in Chinese or Japanese art.

He has grandly chosen for his subject the Birth of Buddha. The mother of the divine teacher being on a journey, is overtaken with the pangs of childbirth. Her attendants and slaves have gathered about her; but she, as if conscious of the august nature of the babe she is about to bestow upon the world, retires alone to the shade of an orange grove, where, clinging to the friendly boughs, with a look of blended rapture and pain, she gives birth to the great reformer. A few steps farther on, a circle of light is seen glowing round the feet of the infant, as it attempts to rise and walk alone. Next we find the child in a rustic cradle; a branch of the tree under which he is sleeping bends low, to shield him from the fierce rays of the sun, and his royal parents, beholding the miracle, kneel and adore him. Now he is a youthful prince, beautiful and gentle, troubled with pity for the poor, the afflicted, and the aged, as they rest by the roadside. And finally, as a hermit, he sits in the shade of a boh-tree, rapt in divine contemplation.

It is a great work, full of imagination, truth, and power, if justly contemplated by the light of a semi-barbaric age. Every figure is instinct with character and action, and the whole is rendered with infinite *naïveté*, as though it represented undisputed and familiar facts.

On the opposite wall another great cartoon represents the Hell of the Buddhists, with demons whose hideous heads are those of fabulous beasts and creeping things. As a work of imagination and force this is worthy to be the companion of the Birth of Buddha.

The roof is painted as a firmament, — stars in a blue ground; and here it is that the charm of pure feeling and noble treatment is most apparent. With five colors the artist has produced all the variety we see. No cast shadows are shown, the forms themselves are but partially shaded, yet wonderful harmony and beauty pervade the whole. All honor to Nai Dang! who alone, amid the national decay of art and culture, preserved this germ of glorious life and strength, wrapped in his own obscure, neglected life!

The practice of decorating walls and ceilings with paintings may be traced to a remote period in the history of Siamese art. In an ancient temple at Lophaburee is a curious picture, of less merit than those of Nai Dang, representing the marriage of Buddha with the princess Thiwadi, beside many of the transmigrations of the Buddhas; and there are elsewhere one or two pictures well worthy of notice, by masters whose names have not been kept in remembrance. Thus art in Siam has degenerated for want of kind, fostering patrons, and faithful, sympathetic chroniclers, till it has become a thing of mere tools and technics.

Nevertheless, they still paint with some cleverness on wood, cloth, parchment, ivory, and plastic material, as well as on gold and silver, — a sort of enamelling. They also retain a fair knowledge of effect in fresco, tracing the outline on the wet ground, and laying on the color in a thin glue; in some of their later work of this kind that I have seen, the idea of the designer is expressed with much vigor.

Their mosaics, executed in colored porcelain of several varieties, glass of all kinds, mother-of-pearl, and colored marbles, represent chiefly flowers and sprays on a brilliant ground. The most remarkable work of this kind is, I imagine, that which is lavished on the temple Watt P'hra

SPIRE OF THE TEMPLE WATT-POH.

Këau,—the walls, pillars, windows, roofs, towers, and gates being everywhere overlaid with mother-of-pearl and ivory, and profusely gilded. The several façades are likewise inlaid with ivory, glass, and mother-of-pearl, fixed with cement in the mortar, which serves as a base. In all cases these works are characterized by a touching simplicity, which seems to struggle through much that is obscure and illegible to get nearer to nature and truth. Most of the tiles employed in the roofing of temples and palaces are colored and gilt.

Among the older pictures, one in the Royal bedchamber of the abandoned palace deserves a parting glance. It is a cartoon (much defaced, and here and there retouched by clumsy Chinese hands) of The First Sin. In the foreground a newly created world is rudely represented, and here are several illuminated figures, human but gigantic. One of these, discontented with his spiritual food, is seen tasting something, which we are told is "fragrant earth"; after which, in another figure, he appears to be electrified, and here his monstrous anatomy is depicted with ludicrous attempts at detail. No one could tell me by whom or when this cartoon was painted, and the painting itself is so little appreciated that I might never have seen or heard of it but for a happy chance.

A characteristic effect in the few great works by Siamese painters appears in their management of shade. They impart to darkness a pervading inner light or clearness, and heighten the effect of the deeper shadows by permitting objects to be seen through them. In addition to the pictures I have described, one or two of some merit are to be found in the Watt Brahmanee Waid.

The florid style of architecture seems to have been familiar to the Siamese from a very early period. Their palaces, temples, and pagodas afford innumerable examples of it, many of them not unworthy of European art.

They build generally in brick, using a cement composed of sand, chalk, and molasses, in which the skin of the buffalo has been steeped. Their structures are the most solid and durable imaginable. When the masons building a wall round the new palace at Ayuthia found their bricks falling short, they tried in vain to detach a supply from the ruined temples and walls of that ancient city.

In the art of sculpture the Siamese are in advance of their civilization. Not only in their palaces, temples, and pagodas, but in their shops and dwellings likewise, and even in their ships and boats, all sorts of figures are to be seen, modelled and finished with more or less delicacy.

XXII.

BUDDHIST DOCTRINE, PRIESTS, AND WORSHIP.

"THE world is old, and all things old within it." We plod a trodden path. No truth is new to-day, save only that *one* which as a mantle covers the face of God, lest we be blinded by the unveiled glory. How many of earth's departed great, buried out of remembrance, might have lived to-day in the love of the wise and just, had theirs but been that perfect quickening which is the breath of his Spirit upon the heart, the gift that "passeth understanding !" The world's helpers must first become borrowers of God. The world's teachers must first learn of him that only wisdom, which cometh not of books nor jealous cloister cells, but out of the heart of man as it opens yearningly to the cry of humanity, — the Wisdom of Love. This alone may challenge a superior mind, prizing truths not merely for their facts, but for their motives, — motives for which individuals or great communities either act or suffer, — to explore with a calm and kindly judgment the spirit of the religion of the Buddhists ; and not its spirit only, but its every look and tone and motion as well, being so many complex expressions of the religious character in all its peculiar thoughts and feelings.

"Who, of himself, can interpret the symbol expressed by the wings of the air-sylph forming within the case of the caterpillar ? Only he who feels in his own soul the same instinct which impels the horned fly to leave room in its involucrum for antennæ yet to come." Such a man knows and feels that the potential works in him even as the actual works on him.   As all the organs of sense are framed for a correspondent world of sense, so all the organs of the spirit are framed for a correspondent world of spirit; and though these latter be not equally developed in us all, yet they surely exist in all; else how is it that even the ignorant, the depraved, and the cruel will contemplate the man of unselfish and exalted goodness with contradictory emotions of pity and respect?

We are prone to ignore or to condemn that which we do not clearly understand; and thus it is, and on no better ground, that we deny that there are influences in the religions of the East to render their followers wiser, nobler, purer.   And yet no one of respectable intelligence will question that there have been, in all ages, individual pagans who, by the simplicity of their doctrine and the purity of their practice, have approached very nearly to the perfection of the Christian graces; and that they were, if not so much the better for the religion they had, at least far, far better than if they had had no religion at all.

It is not, however, in human nature to approve and admire any course of life without inquiring into the spirit of the law that regulates it.   Nor may it suffice that the spirit is there, if not likewise the letter, — that is to say, the practice.   The best doctrine may become the worst, if imperfectly understood, erroneously interpreted, or superstitiously followed.

In Egypt, Palestine, Greece, and India, the metaphysical analysis of Mind had attained its noontide splendor, while as yet experimental research had hardly dawned.   Those ancient mystics did much to promote intellectual emancipation, by insisting that Thought should not be imprisoned within the mere outlines of any single dogmatic system ; and they likewise availed, in no feeble measure, to keep alive the heart in the head, by demanding an impartial reverence for every attribute of the mind, till, by converting these into symbols to impress the ignorant and stupid, they came at last to deify them. Thus, with the uninitiated, their system degenerated into an ignoble pantheism.

The renascence of Buddhism sought to eliminate from the arrogant and impious pantheisms of Egypt, India, and Greece a simple and pure philosophy, upholding virtue as man's greatest good and highest reward. It taught that the only object worthy of his noblest aspirations was to render the soul (itself an emanation from God) fit to be absorbed back again into the Divine essence from which it sprang. The single aim, therefore, of pure Buddhism seems to have been to rouse men to an inward contemplation of the divinity of their own nature ; to fix their thoughts on the spiritual life within as the only real and true life ; to teach them to disregard all earthly distinctions, conditions, privileges, enjoyments, privations, sorrows, sufferings ; and thus to incite them to continual efforts in the direction of the highest ideals of patience, purity, self-denial.

Buddhism cannot be clearly defined by its visible results to-day. There are more things in that subtile, mystical enigma called in the Pali *Nirwana*, in the Birmese *Niban*, in the Siamese *Niphan*, than are dreamed of in our philosophy. With the idea of Niphan in his theology, it were absurdly false to say the Buddhist has no God. His Decalogue * is as plain and imperative as the Christian's : —

I. From the meanest insect up to man thou shalt kill no animal whatsoever.

II. Thou shalt not steal.

* Translated from the Pali.

III. Thou shalt not violate the wife of another, nor his concubine.

IV. Thou shalt speak no word that is false.

V. Thou shalt not drink wine, nor anything that may intoxicate.

VI. Thou shalt avoid all anger, hatred, and bitter language.

VII. Thou shalt not indulge in idle and vain talk.

VIII. Thou shalt not covet thy neighbor's goods.

IX. Thou shalt not harbor envy, nor pride, nor revenge, nor malice, nor the desire of thy neighbor's death or misfortune.

X. Thou shalt not follow the doctrines of false gods.

Whosoever abstains from these forbidden things is said to " observe Silah " ; and whosoever shall faithfully observe Silah, in all his successive metempsychoses, shall continually increase in virtue and purity, until at length he shall become worthy to behold God, and hear his voice ; and so he shall obtain Niphan. " Be assiduous in bestowing alms, in practising virtue, in observing Silah, in performing Bavana, prayer ; and above all in adoring Guadama, the true God. Reverence likewise his laws and his priests."

Many have missed seeing what is true and wise in the doctrine of Buddha because they preferred to observe it from the standpoint and in the attitude of an antagonist, rather than of an inquirer. To understand aright the earnest creed and hope of any man, one must be at least sympathetically *en rapport* with him, — must be willing to feel, and to confess within one's self, the germs of those errors whose growth seems so rank in him. In the humble spirit of this fellowship of fallibility let us draw as near as we may to the hearts of these devotees and the heart of their mystery.

My interesting pupil, the Lady Tâlâp, had invited me

to accompany her to the royal private temple, Watt P'hra Këau, to witness the services held there on the Buddhist Sabâto, or One-thu-sin. Accordingly we repaired together to the temple on the day appointed. The day was young, and the air was cool and fresh; and as we approached the place of worship, the clustered bells of the pagodas made breezy gushes of music aloft. One of the court pages, meeting us, inquired our destination. "The Watt P'hra Këau," I replied. "To see or to hear?" "Both." And we entered.

On a floor diamonded with polished brass sat a throng of women, the *élite* of Siam. All were robed in pure white, with white silk scarfs drawn from the left shoulder in careful folds across the bust and back, and thrown gracefully over the right. A little apart sat their female slaves, of whom many were inferior to their mistresses only in social consideration and worldly gear, being their half-sisters, — children of the same father by a slave mother.

The women sat in circles, and each displayed her vase of flowers and her lighted taper before her. In front of all were a number of my younger pupils, the royal children, in circles also. Close by the altar, on a low square stool, overlaid with a thin cushion of silk, sat the high-priest, Chow Khoon Sâh. In his hand he held a concave fan, lined with pale green silk, the back richly embroidered, jewelled, and gilt.* He was draped in a yellow robe, not unlike the Roman toga, a loose and flowing habit, closed below the waist, but open from the throat to the girdle, which was simply a band of yellow cloth, bound tightly. From the shoulders hung two narrow strips, also yellow, descending over the robe to the feet, and resembling the scapular worn by certain orders of the Roman

---

* The fan is used to cover the face. Jewelled fans are marks of distinction among the priesthood.

Catholic clergy. At his side was an open watch of gold, the gift of his sovereign. At his feet sat seventeen disciples, shading their faces with fans less richly adorned.

We put off our shoes, — my child and I, — having respect for the ancient prejudice against them;* feeling not so much reverence for the place as for the hearts that worshipped there, caring to display not so much the love of wisdom as the wisdom of love; and well were we repaid by the grateful smile of recognition that greeted us as we entered.

We sat down cross-legged. No need to hush my boy, — the silence there, so subduing, checked with its mysterious awe even his inquisitive young mind. The venerable high-priest sat with his face jealously covered, lest his eyes should tempt his thoughts to stray. I changed my position to catch a glimpse of his countenance; he drew his fan-veil more closely, giving me a quick but gentle half-glance of remonstrance. Then raising his eyes, with lids nearly closed, he chanted in an infantile, wailing tone.

That was the opening prayer. At once the whole congregation raised themselves on their knees and, all together, prostrated themselves thrice profoundly, thrice touching the polished brass floor with their foreheads; and then, with heads bowed and palms folded and eyes closed, they delivered the responses after the priest, much in the manner of the English liturgy, first the priest, then the people, and finally all together. There was no singing, no standing up and sitting down, no changing of robes or places, no turning the face to the altar, nor north, nor south, nor east, nor west. All knelt *still*, with hands folded straight before them, and eyes strictly, tightly

---

* "Put off thy shoes from off thy feet, for the place whereon thou standest is holy ground."

closed. Indeed, there were faces there that expressed devotion and piety, the humblest and the purest, as the lips murmured : " O Thou Eternal One, Thou perfection of Time, Thou truest Truth, Thou immutable essence of all Change, Thou most excellent radiance of Mercy, Thou infinite Compassion, Thou Pity, Thou Charity ! "

I lost some of the responses in the simultaneous repetition, and did but imperfectly comprehend the exhortation that followed, in which was inculcated the strictest practice of charity in a manner so pathetic and so gentle as might be wisely imitated by the most orthodox of Christian priests.

There was majesty in the humility of those pagan worshippers, and in their shame of self they were sublime. I leave both the truth and the error to Him who alone can soar to the bright heights of the one and sound the dark depths of the other, and take to myself the lesson, to be read in the shrinking forms and hidden faces of those patient waiters for a far-off glimmering *Light*, — the lesson wherefrom I learn, in thanking God for the light of Christianity, to thank him for its shadow too, which is Buddhism.

Around the porches and vestibules of the temple lounged the Amazonian guard, intent only on irreverent amusement, even in the form of a grotesque and grim flirtation here and there with the custodians of the temple, who have charge of the sacred fire that burns before the altar. About eighty-five years ago this fire went out. It was a calamity of direful presage, and thereupon all Siam went into a consternation of mourning. All public spectacles were forbidden until the crime could be expiated by the appropriate punishment of the wretch to whose sacrilegious carelessness it was due ; nor was the sacred flame rekindled until the reign of P'hra-Pooti-Yaut-Fa, grandfather of his late Majesty, when the royal Hall of Audience was destroyed by lightning. From that fire of heaven it was relighted with joyful thanksgiving, and so has burned on to this day.

The lofty throne, on which the priceless P'hra Këau (the Emerald Idol) blazed in its glory of gold and gems, shone resplendent in the forenoon light. Everything above, around it, — even the vases of flowers and the perfumed tapers on the floor, — was reflected as if by magic in its kaleidoscopic surface, now pensive, pale, and silvery as with moonlight, now flashing, fantastic, with the party-colored splendors of a thousand lamps.

The ceiling was wholly covered with hieroglyphic devices, — luminous circles and triangles, globes, rings, stars, flowers, figures of animals, even parts of the human body, — mystic symbols, to be deciphered only by the initiated. Ah! could I but have read them as in a book, construing all their allegorical significance, how near might I not have come to the distracting secret of this people! Gazing upon them, my thought flew back a thousand years, and my feeble, foolish conjectures, like butterflies at sea, were lost in mists of old myth.

Not that Buddhism has escaped the guessing and conceits of a multitude of writers, most trustworthy of whom are the early Christian Fathers, who, to the end that they might arouse the attention of the sleeping nations, yielded a reluctant, but impartial and graceful, tribute to the long-forgotten creeds of Chaldea, Phenicia, Assyria, and Egypt. Nevertheless, they would never have appealed to the doctrine of Buddha as being most like to Christianity in its rejection of the claims of race, had they not found in its simple ritual another and a stronger bond of brotherhood. Like Christianity, too, it was a religion catholic and apostolic, for the truth of which many faithful witnesses had laid down their lives. It was, besides, the creed of an ancient race; and the mystery that shrouded it had a charm to pique the vanity even of self-sufficient Greeks, and stir up curiosity even in Roman arrogance and indifference. The doctrines of Buddha were eminently fitted to elucidate the doctrines of Christ, and therefore worthy to engage the interest of Christian writers; accordingly, among the earliest of these mention is made of the Buddha or Phthah, though there were as yet few or none to appreciate all the religious significance of his teachings. Terebinthus declared there was "nothing in the pagan world to be compared with his (Buddha's) *P'hra-ti-moksha*, or Code of Discipline, which in some respects resembled the rules that governed the lives of the monks of Christendom; Marco Polo says of Buddha, " Si fuisset Christianus, fuisset apud Deum maximus factus"; and later, Malcolm, the devoted missionary, said of his doctrine, " In almost every respect it seems to be the best religion which man has ever invented." Mark the " invented" of the wary Christian!

But errors, that in time crept in, corrupted the pure doctrine, and disciples, ignorant or stupid, perverted its meaning and intent, and blind or treacherous guides led the simple astray, till at last the true and plain philosophy of Buddha became entangled with the Egyptian mythology.

Over the portal on the eastern façade of the Watt P'hra Këau is a bass-relief representing the Last Judgment, in which are figures of a devil with a pig's head dragging the wicked to hell, and an angel weighing mankind in a pair of scales. Now we know that in the mythology of ancient Egypt the Pig was the emblem of the Evil Spirit, and this bass-relief of the Siamese watt could hardly fail to remind the Egyptologist of kindred compositions in old sculptures wherein the good and bad deeds of the dead are weighed by Anubis (the Siamese Anuman or Hanuman), and the souls of the wicked carried off by a pig.

In the city of Arsinoe in Upper Egypt (formerly Croco-dilopolis, now Medinet-el-Fayum), the crocodile is wor-shipped; and a sacred crocodile, kept in a pond, is perfectly tame and familiar with the priests. He is called Suchus, and they feed him with meat and corn and wine, the contributions of strangers. One of the Egyptian divinities, apparently that to whom the beast was con-secrated, is invariably pictured with the head of a croco-dile; and in hieroglyphic inscriptions is represented by that animal with the tail turned under the body. A similar figure is common in the temples of Siam; and a sacred crocodile, kept in a pond in the manner of the ancient Egyptians, is fed by Siamese priests, at whose call it comes to the surface to receive the rice, fruit, and wine that are brought to it daily.

The Beetle, an insect peculiarly sacred to the Buddhists, was the Egyptian sign of Phthah, the Father of Gods; and in the hieroglyphics it stands for the name of that deity, whose head is either surmounted by a beetle, or is itself in the form of a beetle. Elsewhere in the hiero-glyphics, where it does not represent Buddha, it evidently appears as the symbol of generation or reproduction, the meaning most anciently attached to it; whence Dr. Young, in his "Hieroglyphical Researches," inferred its relation to Buddha. Mrs. Hamilton Gray, in her work on the Sepulchres of Etruria, observes: "As scarabæi existed long before we had any account of idols, I do not doubt that they were originally the invention of some really devout mind; and they speak to us in strong language of the dan-ger of making material symbols of immaterial things. First, the symbol came to be trusted in, instead of the being of whom it was the sign. Then came the bodily concep-tion and manifestation of that being, or his attributes, in the

form of idols.   Next, the representation of all that be-
longs to spirits, good and bad.   And finally, the deification
of every imagination of the heart of man, — a written and
accredited system of polytheism, and a monstrous and
hydra-headed idolatry."

Such is the religious history of the scarabæus, a creature that so early attracted the notice of man by its
ingenious and industrious habits, that it was selected
by him to symbolize the Creator; and cutting stones to
represent it,* he wore them in token of his belief in a
creator of all things, and in recognition of the Divine
Presence, probably attaching to them at first no more
mysterious import or virtue.   There is sound reason for
believing that in this form the symbol existed before
Abraham, and that its fundamental signification of creation or generation was gradually overbuilt with arbitrary
speculations and fantastic notions.   In theory it degenerated into a crude egoism, a vaunting and hyper-stoic
hostility to nature, which, though intellectually godless,
was not without that universal instinct for divinity which,
by countless ways, seeks with an ever-present and im-
portunate longing for the one sublimated and eternal
source from which it sprang.

Through twenty-five million six hundred thousand
Asongkhies, or metempsychoses, — according to the overpowering computation of his priests, — did Buddha struggle to attain the divine omniscience of Niphan, by virtue
of which he remembers every form he ever entered, and
beholds with the clear eyes of a god the endless diversi-
ties of transmigration in the animal, human, and angelic
worlds, throughout the spaceless, timeless, numberless
universe of visible and invisible life.   According to He-
raclides, Pythagoras used to say of himself, that he re-

---

* Six rubies, exquisitely cut in the form of beetles, are worn as studs
by the present King of Siam.

9   M

membered " not only all the men, but all the animals and all the plants, his soul had passed through." That Pythagoras believed and taught the doctrine of transmigration may hardly be doubted, but that he originated it is very questionable. Herodotus intimates that both Orpheus and Pythagoras derived it from the Egyptians, but propounded it as their own, without acknowledgment.

Nearly every male inhabitant of Siam enters the priesthood at least once in his lifetime. Instead of the more vexatious and scandalous forms of divorce, the party aggrieved may become a priest or a nun, and thus the matrimonial bond is at once dissolved ; and with this advantage, that after three or four months of probation they may be reconciled and reunited, to live together in the world again.

Chow Khoon Sâh, or " His Lordship the Lake," whose functions in the Watt P'hra Këau I have described, was the High-Priest of Siam, and in high favor with his Majesty. He had taken holy orders with the double motive of devoting himself to the study of Sanskrit literature, and of escaping the fate, that otherwise awaited him, of becoming the mere thrall of his more fortunate cousin, the king. In the palace it was whispered that he and the late queen consort had been tenderly attached to each other, but that the lady's parents, for prudential considerations, discountenanced the match; "and so," on the eve of her betrothal to his Majesty, her lover had sought seclusion and consolation in a Buddhist monastery. However that may be, it is certain that the king and the high-priest were now fast friends. The latter entertained great respect for his reverend cousin, whose title (" The Lake ") described justly, as well as poetically, the graceful serenity and repose of his demeanor.

Chow Khoon Sâh lived at some distance from the palace, at the Watt Brahmanee Waid. As the friendship between the cousins ripened, his Majesty considered that it would be well for him to have the contemplative student, prudent adviser, and able reasoner nearer to him. With this idea, and for a surprise to one to whom all surprises had long since become but vanities and vexations of spirit, he caused to be erected, about forty yards from the Grand Palace, on the eastern side of the Meinam, a temple which he named *Rajah-Bah-dit-Sang*, or " The King caused me to be built "; and at the same time, as an appendage to the temple, a monastery in mediæval style, — the workmanship in both structures being most substantial and elaborate.

The sculptures and carvings on the pillars and façades — half-fabulous, half-historical figures, conveying ingenious allegories of the triumph of virtue over the passions — constituted a singular tribute to the exemplary fame of the high-priest. The grounds were planted with trees and shrubs, and the walks gravelled, thus inviting the contemplative recluse to tranquil, soothing strolls. These grounds were accessible by four gates, the principal one facing the east, and a private portal opening on the canal.

The laying of the foundation of the temple and monastery of Rajah-Bah-dit-Sang was the occasion of extraordinary festivities, consisting of theatrical spectacles and performances, a carnival of dancing, mass around every corner-stone, banquets to priests, and distributions of clothing, food, and money to the poor. The king presided every morning and evening under a silken canopy ; and even those favorites of the harem who were admitted to the royal confidence were provided with tents, whence they could witness the shows, and participate in the rejoicings in the midst of which the good work went on.

After the several services of mass had been performed, and the corner-stones consecrated by the pouring on of oil and water,* seven tall lamps were lighted to burn above them seven days and nights, and seventy priests in groups of seven, forming a perfect circle, prayed continually, holding in their hands the mystic web of seven threads, that weird circlet of life and death.

Then the youngest and fairest virgins of the land brought offerings of corn and wine, milk, honey, and flowers, and poured them on the consecrated stones. And after that, they brought pottery of all kinds, — vases, urns, ewers, goglets, bowls, cups, and dishes, — and, flinging them into the foundations, united with zeal and rejoicing in the "meritorious" work of pounding them into fine dust ; and while the instruments of music and the voices of the male and female singers of the court kept time to the measured crash and thud of the wooden clubs in those young and tender hands, the king cast into the foundation coins and ingots of gold and silver.

"Do you understand the word 'charity,' or *maitrî*, as your apostle St. Paul explains it in the thirteenth chapter of his First Epistle to the Corinthians?" said his Majesty to me one morning, when he had been discussing the religion of Sakyamuni, the Buddha.

"I believe I do, your Majesty," was my reply.

"Then, tell me, what does St. Paul really mean, to what custom does he allude, when he says, 'Even if I give my body to be burned, and have not charity, it profiteth me nothing'?"

"Custom!" said I. "I do not know of any *custom*. The giving of the body to be burned is by him esteemed the highest act of devotion, the purest sacrifice man can make for man."

* Oil is the emblem of life and love ; water, of purity.

" You have said well. It is the highest act of devotion that can be made, or performed, by man for man, — that giving of his body to be burned. But if it is done from a spirit of opposition, for the sake of fame, or popular applause, or for any other such motive, is it still to be regarded as the highest act of sacrifice ? "

" That is just what St. Paul means : the motive consecrates the deed."

" But all men are not fortified with the self-control which should fit them to be great exemplars ; and of the many who have appeared in that character, if strict inquiry were made, their virtue would be found to proceed from any other than the true and pure spirit.   Sometimes it is indolence, sometimes restlessness, sometimes vanity impatient for its gratification, and rushing to assume the part of humility for the purpose of self-delusion."

" Now," said the King, taking several of his long strides in the vestibule of his library, and declaiming with his habitual emphasis, " St Paul, in this chapter, evidently and strongly applies the Buddhist's word *maitrî*, or *maikree*, as pronounced by some Sanskrit scholars ; and explains it through the Buddhist's custom of giving the body to be burned, which was practised centuries before the Christian era, and is found unchanged in parts of China, Ceylon, and Siam to this day.   The giving of the body to be burned has ever been considered by devout Buddhists the most exalted act of self-abnegation.

" To give all one's goods to feed the poor is common in this country, with princes and people, — who often keep back nothing (not even one *cowree*, the thousandth part of a cent) to provide for themselves a handful of rice. But then they stand in no fear of starvation ; for death by hunger is unknown where Buddhism is preached and *practised*.

" I know a man, of royal parentage, and once possessed

of untold riches. In his youth he felt such pity for the poor, the old, the sick, and such as were troubled and sorrowful, that he became melancholy, and after spending several years in the continual relief of the needy and helpless, he, in a moment, gave all his goods, — in a word, ALL, — ' to feed the poor.' This man has never heard of St. Paul or his writings ; but he knows, and tries to comprehend in its fulness, the Buddhist word *maitrî*.

" At thirty he became a priest. For five years he had toiled as a gardener ; for that was the occupation he preferred, because in the pursuit of it he acquired much useful knowledge of the medicinal properties of plants, and so became a ready physician to those who could not pay for their healing. But he could not rest content with so imperfect a life, while the way to perfect knowledge of excellence, truth, and charity remained open to him; so he became a priest.

" This happened sixty-five years ago. Now he is ninety-five years old ; and, I fear, has not yet found the truth and excellence he has been in search of so long. But I know no greater man than he. He is great in the Christian sense, — loving, pitiful, forbearing, pure.

" Once, when he was a gardener, he was robbed of his few poor tools by one whom he had befriended in many ways. Some time after that, the king met him, and inquired of his necessities. He said he needed tools for his gardening. A great abundance of such implements was sent to him ; and immediately he shared them with his neighbors, taking care to send the most and best to the man who had robbed him.

" Of the little that remained to him, he gave freely to all who lacked. Not his own, but another's wants, were his sole argument in asking or bestowing. Now, he is great in the Buddhist sense also, — not loving life nor fearing death, desiring nothing the world can give, beyond

the peace of a beatified spirit. This man — who is now
the High-Priest of Siam — would, without so much as a
thought of shrinking, give his body, alive or dead, to be
burned, if so he might obtain one glimpse of eternal
truth, or save one soul from death or sorrow."

More than eighteen months after the First King of Siam
had entertained me with this essentially Buddhistic argument, and its simple and impressive illustration, a party
of pages hurried me away with them, just as the setting
sun was trailing his last long, lingering shadows through
the porches of the palace. His Majesty required my
presence; and his Majesty's commands were absolute
and instant. "Find and fetch!" No delay was to be
thought of, no question answered, no explanation afforded,
no excuse entertained. So with resignation I followed
my guides, who led the way to the monastery of Watt
Rajah-Bah-dit-Sang. But having some experience of the
moods and humors of his Majesty, my mind was not
wholly free from uneasiness. Generally, such impetu-
ous summoning foreboded an interview the reverse of
agreeable.

The sun had set in glory below the red horizon when I
entered the extensive range of monastic buildings that
adjoin the temple. Wide tracts of waving corn and
avenues of oleanders screened from view the distant city,
with its pagodas and palaces. The air was fresh and
balmy, and seemed to sigh plaintively among the betel
and cocoa palms that skirt the monastery.

The pages left me seated on a stone step, and ran to
announce my presence to the king. Long after the moon
had come out clear and cool, and I had begun to wonder
where all this would end, a young man, robed in pure
white, and bearing in one hand a small lighted taper and
a lily in the other, beckoned me to enter, and follow him;

and as we traversed the long, low passages that separate the cells of the priests, the weird sound of voices, chanting the hymns of the Buddhist liturgy, fell upon my ear. The darkness, the loneliness, the measured monotone, distant and dreamy, all was most romantic and exciting, even to a matter-of-fact English woman like myself.

As the page approached the threshold of one of the cells, he whispered to me, in a voice full of entreaty, to put off my shoes ; at the same time prostrating himself with a movement and expression of the most abject humility before the door, where he remained, without changing his posture. I stooped involuntarily, and scanned curiously, anxiously, the scene within the cell. There sat the king ; and at a sign from him I presently entered, and sat down beside him.

On a rude pallet, about six and a half feet long, and not more than three feet wide, and with a bare block of wood for a pillow, lay a dying priest. A simple garment of faded yellow covered his person ; his hands were folded on his breast ; his head was bald, and the few blanched hairs that might have remained to fringe his sunken temples had been carefully shorn, — his eyebrows, too, were closely shaven ; his feet were bare and exposed ; his eyes were fixed, not in the vacant stare of death, but with solemn contemplation or scrutiny, upward. No sign of disquiet was there, no external suggestion of pain or trouble ; I was at once startled and puzzled. Was he dying, or acting ?

In the attitude of his person, in the expression of his countenance, I beheld sublime reverence, repose, absorption. He seemed to be communing with some spiritual presence.

My entrance and approach made no change in him. At his right side was a dim taper in a gold candlestick ; on the left a dainty golden vase, filled with white lilies,

freshly gathered : these were offerings from the king.
One of the lilies had been laid on his breast, and contrasted touchingly with the dingy, faded yellow of his
robe.   Just over the region of the heart lay a coil of unspun cotton thread, which, being divided into seventy-
seven filaments, was distributed to the hands of the
priests, who, closely seated, quite filled the cell, so that
none could have moved without difficulty.   Before each
priest were a lighted taper and a lily, symbols of faith and
purity.   From time to time one or other of that solemn
company raised his voice, and chanted strangely ; and all
the choir responded in unison.   These were the words, as
they were afterward translated for me by the king.

First Voice.   Sâng-Khâng sârâ nang gâch' châ mi !
(Thou Excellence, or Perfection ! I take refuge in thee.)

All. Nama Poothô sâng-Khâng sârâ nang gâch' châ
mi ! (Thou who art named Poot-tho ! — either God,
Buddha, or Mercy, — I take refuge in thee.)

First Voice. Tuti âmpi sâng-Khâng sârâ nang gâch'
châ mi !   (Thou Holy One ! I take refuge in thee.)

All. Tè sâtiyâ sâng-Khâng sârâ nang gâch' châ mi !
(Thou Truth, I take refuge in thee.)

As the sound of the prayer fell on his ear, a flickering
smile lit up the pale, sallow countenance of the dying
man with a visible mild radiance, as though the charity
and humility of his nature, in departing, left the light of
their loveliness there.   The absorbing rapture of that
look, which seemed to overtake the invisible, was almost
too holy to gaze upon.   Riches, station, honors, kindred,
he had resigned them all, more than half a century since,
in his love for the poor and his longing after truth.
Here was none of the wavering or vagueness or incohe-
rence of a wandering, delirious death.   He was going to
his clear, eternal calm.   With a smile of perfect peace he
said : "To your Majesty I commend the poor ; and this
9 *

that remains of me I give to be burned." And that, his last gift, was indeed his all.

I can imagine no spectacle more worthy to excite a compassionate emotion, to impart an abiding impression of reverence, than the tranquil dying of that good old " pagan." Gradually his breathing became more laborious , and presently, turning with a great effort toward the king, he said, *Chan cha pi dauni !* — "I will go now !" Instantly the priests joined in a loud psalm and chant, " P'hra Arahang sâng-Khâng sârâ nang gâch' châ mi !" (Thou Sacred One, I take refuge in thee.) A few minutes more, and the spirit of the High-Priest of Siam had calmly breathed itself away. The eyes were open and fixed ; the hands still clasped ; the expression sweetly content. My heart and eyes were full of tears, yet I was comforted. By what hope ? I know not, for I dared not question it.

On the afternoon of the next day I was again summoned by his Majesty to witness the burning of that body.

It was carried to the cemetery Watt Sah Kâte ; and there men, hired to do such dreadful offices upon the dead, cut off all the flesh and flung it to the hungry dogs that haunt that monstrous garbage-field of Buddhism. The bones, and all that remained upon them, were thoroughly burned ; and the ashes, carefully gathered in an earthen pot, were scattered in the little gardens of wretches too poor to buy manure. All that was left now of the venerable devotee was the remembrance of a look.

" This," said the King, as I turned away sickened and sorrowful, " is to give one's body to be burned. This is what your St. Paul had in his mind, — this custom of our Buddhist ancestors, this complete self-abnegation in life and in death, — when he said, 'Even if I give my body to be burned, and have not charity [*maitrî*], it profiteth me nothing.'"

PRIESTS AT BREAKFAST.

COMMON MAXIMS OF THE PRIESTS OF SIAM.

Glory not in thyself, but rather in thy neighbor.

Dig not the earth, which is the source of life and the mother of all.

Cause no tree to die.

Kill no beast, nor insect, not even the smallest ant or fly.

Eat nothing between meals.

Regard not singers, dancers, nor players on instruments.

Use no perfume but sweetness of thoughts.

Neither sit nor sleep in high places.

Be lowly in thy heart, that thou mayst be lowly in thy act.

Hoard neither silver nor gold.

Entertain not thy thoughts with worldly things.

Do no work but the work of charity and truth.

Give not flowers unto women, but rather prayers.

Contract no friendship with the hope of gain.

Borrow nothing, but rather deny thy want.

Lend not unto usury.

Keep neither lance, nor sword, nor any deadly weapon.

Judge not thy neighbor.

Bake not, nor burn.

Wink not.   Be not familiar nor contemptuous.

Labor not for hire, but for charity.

Look not upon women unchastely.

Make no incisions that may draw blood or sap, which is the life of man and nature.

Give no medicines which contain poison, but study to acquire the true art of healing, which is the highest of all arts, and pertains to the wise and benevolent.

Love all men equally.

Perform not thy meditations in public places.

Make no idols of any kind.

XXIII.

CREMATION.

A S soon as his Majesty had recovered from his genuine convulsion of grief for the death of his sweet little princess, Somdetch Chow Fâ-ying, he proceeded, habited in white, with all his family, to visit the chamber of mourning. The grand-aunt of the dead child, who seemed the most profoundly afflicted of all that numerous household, still lay prostrate at the feet of her pale cold darling, and would not be comforted. As his Majesty entered, silently ushered, she moved, and mutely laid her head upon his feet, moaning, *Poot-tho! Poot-tho!* There were tears and sighs and heart-wrung sobs around. Speechless, but with trembling lips, the royal father took gently in his arms the little corpse, and bathed it in the Siamese manner, by pouring cold water upon it. In this he was followed by other members of the royal family, the more distant relatives, and such ladies of the harem as chanced to be in waiting, — each advancing in the order of rank, and pouring pure cold water from a silver bowl over the slender body. Two sisters of the king then shrouded the corpse in a sitting posture, overlaid it with perfumes and odoriferous gums, frankincense and myrrh, and, lastly, swaddled it in a fine winding-sheet. Finally it was deposited in a golden urn, and this again in another of finer gold, richly adorned with precious stones. The inner urn has an iron grating in the bottom, and the outer an orifice at its most pendent point, through which, by means of a tap or stop-cock, the fluids are drawn off daily, until the *cadavre* has become quite dry.

This double urn was borne on a gilt sedan, under a royal gilt umbrella, to the temple of the Maha Phrasat, where it was mounted on a graduated platform about six feet high. During this part of the ceremony, and while the trumpeters and the blowers of conch-shells performed their lugubrious parts, his Majesty sat apart, his face buried in his hands, confessing a keener anguish than had ever before cut his selfish heart.

The urn being thus elevated, all the insignia pertaining to the rank of the little princess were disposed in formal order below it, as though at her feet. Then the musicians struck up a passionate passage, ending in a plaintive and truly solemn dirge; after which his Majesty and all the princely company retired, leaving the poor clod to await, in its pagan gauds and mockery, the last offices of friendship. But not always alone; for thrice daily — at early dawn, and noon, and gloaming — the musicians came to perform a requiem for the soul of the dead, — "that it may soar on high, from the flaming, fragrant pyre for which it is reserved, and return to its foster parents, Ocean, Earth, Air, Sky." With these is joined a concert of mourning women, who bewail the early dead, extolling her beauty, graces, virtues; while in the intervals, four priests (who are relieved every fourth hour) chant the praises of Buddha, bidding the gentle spirit "Pass on! Pass on!" and boldly speed through the labyrinth before it, "through high, deep, and famous things, through good and evil things, through truth and error, through wisdom and folly, through sorrow, suffering, hope, life, joy, love, death, through endless mutability, into immutability!"

These services are performed with religious care daily

for six months; * that is, until the time appointed for cremation. Meanwhile, in the obsequies of the Princess Fâ-ying, arrangements were made for the erection of the customary *P'hra-mène,* — a temporary structure of great splendor, where the body lies in state for several days, on a throne dazzling with gold and silver ornaments and precious stones.

For the funeral honors of royalty it is imperative that the P'hra-mène be constructed of virgin timber. Trunks of teak, from two hundred to two hundred and fifty feet in length, and of proportionate girth, are felled in the forests of Myolonghee, and brought down the Meinam in rafts. These trunks, planted thirty feet deep, one at each corner of a square, serve as pillars, not less than a hundred and seventy feet high, to support a sixty-foot spire, an octagonal pyramid, covered with gold leaf. Attached to this pyramid are four wings, forty feet long, with handsome porches looking to the cardinal points of the compass; here also are four colossal figures of heroic myths, each with a lion couchant at its feet.

On one side of the square reserved for the P'hra-mène, á vast hall is erected to accommodate the Supreme King and his family while attending the funeral ceremonies. The several roofs of this temporary edifice have peculiar horn-like projections at the ends, and are covered with crimson cloth, while golden draperies are suspended from the ceiling. The entire space around the P'hra-mène is matted with bamboo wicker-work, and decorated with innumerable standards peculiar to Siam. Here and there may be seen grotesque cartoons of the wars of gods and giants, and rude landscapes supposed to represent the Buddhist's heaven, with lakes and groves and gardens. Beyond these are playhouses for theatrical displays, puppet-shows, masquerades, posturing, somersaulting, leap-

---

* Twelve months for a king.

ing, wrestling, balancing on ropes and wires, and the tricks of professional buffoons. Here also are restaurants, or cook-shops, for all classes of people above the degree of boors ; and these are open day and night during the period devoted to the funeral rites.

The grand lodge erected for the Second King and his household, at the cremation of his little niece, resembled that of his brother, the Supreme King, in the regal style of its decorations.

The centre of the P'hra-mène is a lofty octagon ; and directly under the great spire is a gorgeous eight-sided pyramid, diminishing by right-angled gradations to a truncated top, its base being fifty or sixty feet in circumference, and higher by twenty feet than the surrounding buildings. On this pyramid stood the urn of gold containing the remains of the royal child. Above the urn a golden canopy hung from the lofty ceiling, and far above this again a circular white awning was spread, representing the firmament studded with silver stars. Under the canopy, and just over little Fâ-ying's urn, the whitest and most fragrant flowers, gathered and arranged by those who loved her best in life, formed a bright odoriferous bower. The pyramid itself was decorated with rare and beautiful gifts, of glass, porcelain, alabaster, silver, gold, and artificial flowers, with images of birds, beasts, men, women, children, and angels. Splendid chandeliers suspended from the ceiling, and lesser lights on the angles of the pyramid, illuminated the funeral hall.

These showy preparations completed, the royal mourners only waited for the appointed time when the remains must be laid in state upon the consecrated pyre. At dawn of that day, all the princes, nobles, governors, and superior priests of the kingdom, with throngs of baser men, women, and children, in their holiday attire, came to grace the "fiery consummation" of little Fâ-ying. A

royal barge conveyed me, with my boy, to the palace,
whence we followed on foot.

The gold urn, in an ivory chariot of antique fashion,
richly gilt, was drawn by a pair of milk-white horses, and
followed and attended by hundreds of men clad in pure
white.   It was preceded by two other chariots ; in the
first sat the high-priest, reading short, pithy aphorisms
and precepts from the sacred books ; in the other followed the full brothers of the deceased. A strip of
silver cloth, six inches wide, attached to the urn, was
loosely extended to the seats of the royal mourners in this
second chariot, and thence to the chariot of the high-
priest, on whose lap the ends were laid, symbolizing the
mystic union between death, life, and the Buddha.

Next after the urn came a chariot laden with the sacred sandal-wood, the aromatic gums, and the wax tapers.
The wood was profusely carved with emblems of the indestructibility of matter ; for though the fire apparently
consumes the pile, and with it the body, the priests are
careful to interpret the process as that by which both are
endued with new vitality ; thus everything consecrated
to the religious observances of Buddhism is made to
typify some latent truth.

Then came a long procession of mythological figures,
nondescripts drawn on small wooden wheels, and covered
with offerings for the priests.   These were followed by
crowds of both sexes and all ages, bearing in their hands
the mystic triform flower, emblematic of the sacred circle,
Om, or Aum.   To hold this mystic flower above the head,
and describe with it endless circles in the air, is regarded
as a performance of peculiar virtue and " merit," and one
of the most signal acts of devotion possible to a Buddhist.
And yet, as the symbol of One great Central Spirit,
whose name it is profanation to utter, the symbol is
strangely at variance with the doctrines of Buddhism.

The moment the strange concourse, human and mythological, began to move, the conch-shells, horns, trumpets, sackbuts, pipes, dulcimers, flutes, and harps rent the air with wild wailing; but above the din rose the deep, booming, measured beat of the death-drums. Very subtile, and indescribably stirring is this ancient music, with its various weird and prolonged cadences, and that solemn thundering boom enhancing the peculiar sweetness of the dirge as it rises and falls.

Under the spell of such sounds as these the procession moved slowly to the P'hra-mène. Here the urn was lifted by means of pulleys, and enthroned on the splendid pedestal prepared for it. The silver cloth from the chariot of the high-priest was laid upon it, the ends drooping on the eastern and western sides to the rich carpet of the floor. A hundred priests, fifty on either hand, rehearsed in concert, seated on the floor, long hymns in Pali from the sacred books, principally embodying melancholy reflections on the brevity and uncertainty of human life. After which, holding the silver cloth between the thumb and forefinger, they joined in silent prayer, thereby, as they suppose, communicating a saving virtue to the cloth, which conveys it to the dead within the urn. They continued thus engaged for about an hour, and then withdrew to give place to another hundred, and so on, until thousands of priests had taken part in the solemn exercises. Meanwhile the four already mentioned still prayed, day and night, at the Maha Phrasat. A service was likewise performed for the royal family twice a day, in an adjacent temporary chapel, where all the court attended, — including the noble ladies of the harem, who occupy private oratories, hung with golden draperies, behind which they can see and hear without being seen. As long as these funeral ceremonies last, the numerous concourse of priests is sumptuously entertained.

N

At nightfall the P'hra-mène is brilliantly illuminated, within and without, and the people are entertained with dramatic spectacles derived from the Chinese, Hindoo, Malayan, and Persian classics. Effigies of the fabulous Hydra, or dragon with seven heads, illuminated, and animated by men concealed within, are seen endeavoring to swallow the moon, represented by a globe of fire. Another monster, probably the Chimæra, with the head and breast of a lion and the body of a goat, vomits flame and smoke. There are also figures of Echidna and Cerberus, the former represented as a beautiful nymph, but terminating below the waist in the coils of a dragon or python; and the latter as a triple-headed dog, evidently the canine bugaboo that is supposed to have guarded Pluto's dreadful gates.

About nine o'clock fireworks were ignited by the king's own hand, — a very beautiful display, representing, among other graceful forms, a variety of shrubbery, which gradually blossomed with roses, dahlias, oleanders, and other flowers.

The flinging of money and trinkets to the rabble is usually the most exciting of the pranks which diversify the funeral ceremonies of Siamese royalty; in this *mal à propos* pastime his Majesty took a lively part. The personal effects of the deceased are divided into two or more equal portions, one of which is bestowed on the poor, another on the priests; memorials and complimentary tokens are presented to the princes and nobles, and the friends of the royal family. The more costly articles are ticketed and distributed by lottery; and smaller objects, such as rings and gold and silver coins, are put into lemons, which his Majesty, standing on the piazza of his temporary palace, flings among the sea of heads below. There is also at each of the four corners of the P'hramène, an artificial tree, bearing gold and silver fruit, which is plucked by officers of the court, and tossed to the poor on every side. Each throw is hailed by a wild shout from the multitude, and followed by a mad scramble.

In this connection the following "notification" from the king's hand will be intelligible to the reader.

"THE NOTIFICATION

"In regard to the mourning distribution and donation in funeral service or ceremony of cremation of the remains of Her late Royal Highness celestial Princess Somdetch Chowfa Chandrmondol Sobhon Bhagiawati,* whose death took place on the 12th May, Anno Christi 1863.

"This Part consisting of a glasscoverbox enclosing a idol of Chinese fabulousquadruped called 'sai' or Lion, covered with goldleaf ornamented with coined pieces of silver & rings a black bag of funeral balls enclosing some pieces of gold and silver coins &c., in funeral service of Her late Royal Highness the forenamed princess, the ninth daughter or sixteenth offspring of His Majesty the reigning Supreme King of Siam, which took place in ceremony continued from 16th to 21st day of February Anno Christi 1864. prepared ex-property of Her late lamented Royal Highness the deceased. and assistant funds from certain members of the Royal Family. designed from his Gracious Majesty Somdetch P'hra Paramendr Maha Mongkut, Her late Royal Highness' bereaved Royal father. Their Royal Highnesses celestial princes Somdetch Chowfa Chulalonkorn the full elder brother, Chowfa Chaturont Rasmi, and Chowfa Bhangurangsi Swang-wongse, the two younger full brothers, and His Royal Highness Prince Nobhawongs Krommun Maha-suarsivivalas the eldest half brother. Their Royal Highnesses twenty-five princes, Krita-bhinihar, Gaganang Yugol &c. the younger half-

* Fâ-ying.

brothers, and their Royal Highnesses seven princesses, Yingyawlacks, Dacksinja, and Somawati, &c., the elder sisters, 18 princesses, Srinagswasti, &c., the younger half-sisters of Her late Royal Highness the deceased, for friendly acceptance of —— —— —— who is one of His present Siamese Majesty's friends who either have ever been acquainted in person or through means of correspondence &c. certain of whom have ever seen Her late Royal Highness, and some have been acquainted with certain of her late Royal Highness the deceased's elder or younger brothers and sisters.

"His Siamese Majesty, with his 29 sons, and 25 daughters above partly named, trusts that this part will be acceptable to every one of His Gracious Majesty's and their Royal Highnesses' friends who ever have been acquainted with his present Majesty, and certain of Their Royal Highnesses or Her late Royal Highness the deceased, either in person or by correspondence, or only by name through cards &c. for a token of remembrance of Her late Royal Highness the deceased and for feeling of Emotion that this path ought to be followed by every one of human beings after long or short time, as the lights of lives of all living beings are like flames of candles lighted in opening air without covering and Protecting on every side, so it shall be considered with great emotion by the readers.

"Dated ROYAL FUNERAL PLACE.
BANGKOK, 20th February, Anno Christi 1864."

Thus twelve days were passed in feasting, drinking, praying, preaching, sporting, gambling and scrambling. On the thirteenth, the double urn, with its melancholy moral, was removed from the pyramid, and the inner one, with the grating, was laid on a bed of fragrant sandal-wood, and aromatic gums, connected with a train of gun-

powder, which the king ignited with a match from the
sacred fire that burns continually in the temple Watt
P'hra Këau. The Second King then lighted his candles
from the same torch, and laid them on the pyre; and so
on, in the order of rank, down to the meanest slave,
until many hundreds of wax candles and boxes of precious spices and fragrant gums were cast into the flames.
The funeral orchestra then played a wailing dirge, and
the mourning women broke into a concerted and prolonged keen, of the most ear-piercing and heart-rending
description.

When the fire had quite burned itself out, all that remained of the bones, charred and blackened, was carefully gathered, deposited in a third and smaller urn of
gold, and again conveyed in great state to the Maha Phrasat. The ashes were also collected with scrupulous pains
in a pure cloth of white muslin, and laid in a gold dish;
afterward, attended by all the mourning women and musicians, and escorted by a procession of barges, it was
floated some miles down the river, and there committed
to the waters.

Nothing left of our lovely darling but a few charred
bits of rubbish! But in memory I still catch glimpses of
the sylph-like form, half veiled in the shroud of flame
that wrapped her last, but with the innocent, questioning
eyes still turned to me; and as I look back into their
depths of purity and love, again and again I mourn, as at
first, for that which made me feel, more and more by its
sympathy, the peculiar desolation of my life in the palace.

Immediately on the death of a Supreme King an order
is issued for the universal shaving of the bristly tuft
from the heads of all male subjects. Only those princes
who are older than their deceased sovereign are exempt
from the operation of this law.

Upon his successor devolves the duty of providing for the erection of the royal P'hra-mene — as to the proportions and adornment of which he is supposed to be guided by regard for the august rank of the deceased, and the public estimation in which his name and fame are held. Royal despatches are forthwith sent to the governors of four different provinces in the extreme north, ·where the noblest timber abounds, commanding each of them to furnish one of the great pillars for the P'hra-mène. These must be of the finest wood, perfectly straight, from two hundred to two hundred and fifty feet long, and not less than twelve feet in circumference.

At the same time twelve pillars, somewhat smaller, are required from the governors of twelve other provinces; besides much timber in other forms necessary to the construction of the grand funeral hall and its numerous supplementary buildings. As sacred custom will not tolerate the presence of pillars that have already been used for any purpose whatever, it is indispensable that fresh ones, "virgin trunks," be procured for every new occasion of the obsequies of royalty. These four great trunks are hard to find, and can be floated down the Meinam to the capital only at the seasons when that stream and its tributaries are high. This is perhaps the natural cause of the long interval that elapses — twelve months — between the death and the cremation of a Siamese king.

The "giant boles" are dragged in primitive fashion to the banks of the stream by elephants and buffaloes, and shipped in rafts. Arrived at Bangkok, they are hauled on rollers inch by inch, by men working with a rude windlass and levers, to the site of the P'hra-mène.

The following description of the cremation, at Bejre-puri, of a man "in the middle walks of life," is taken from the *Bangkok Recorder* of May 24, 1866: —

" The corpse was first to be offered to the vultures, a
hundred or more. Before the coffin was opened the filthy
and horrible gang had assembled, 'for wheresoever the
carcass is, there will the eagles (vultures) be gathered
together.' They were perched on the ridges of the temple, and even on small trees and bushes, within a few feet
of the body ; and so greedy were they that the sexton
and his assistants had to beat them off many times before
the coffin could be opened. They seemed to know that
there would be but a mouthful for each, if divided among
them all, and the pack of greedy dogs besides, that waited
for their share. The body was taken from the coffin and
laid on a pile of wood that had been prepared on a small
temporary altar. Then the birds were allowed to descend
upon the corpse and tear it as they liked. For a while it
was quite hidden in the rush. But each bird, grabbing its
part with bill and claws, spread its wings and mounted to
some quiet place to eat. The sexton seemed to think
that he too was ' making merit ' by cutting off parts of the
body and throwing them to the hungry dogs, as the dying
man had done in bequeathing his body to those carrion-
feeders. The birds, not satisfied with what they got from
the altar, came down and quarrelled with the curs for
their share.

" While this was going on, the mourners stood waiting,
with wax candles and incense sticks, to pay their last
tribute of respect to the deceased by assisting in the burning of the bones after the vultures and dogs had stripped
them. The sexton, with the assistance of another, gathered up the skeleton and put it back into the coffin, which
was lifted by four men and carried around the funeral
pile three times. It was then laid on the pile of wood,
and a few sticks were put into the coffin to aid in burning the bones. Then a lighted torch was applied to the
pile, and the relatives and other mourners advanced, and

laid each a wax candle by the torch.   Others brought incense and cast it on the pile.

"The vultures, having had but a scanty breakfast, lingered around the place until the fire had left nothing more for them, when they shook their ugly heads, and hopping a few steps, to get up a momentum, flapped their harpy wings and flew away."

XXIV.

CERTAIN SUPERSTITIONS.

MY friend Maha Mongkut used to maintain, with the doctors and sophists of his sect, that the Buddhist priesthood have no superstitions; that though they do not accept the Christian's "Providence," they do believe in a Creator (*P'hra-Tham*), at whose will all crude matter sprang into existence, but who exercises no further control over it; that man is but one of the endless mutations of matter, — was not created, but has existed from the beginning, and will continue to exist to all eternity; that though he was not born in sin, he is held by the secondary law of retribution accountable for offences committed in his person, and these he must expiate through subsequent transmigrations, until, by sublimation, he is absorbed again into the primal source of his being; and that mutability is an essential and absolute law of the universe.

In like manner they protest that they are not idolaters, any more than the Roman Catholics are pagans; that the image of Buddha, their Teacher and High-Priest, is to them what the crucifix is to the Jesuit; neither more nor less. They scout the idea that they worship the white elephant, but acknowledge that they hold the beast sacred, as one of the incarnations of their great reformer.

Nevertheless, no nation or tribe of all the human race has ever been more profoundly inoculated with a su-

10

perstition the most depraving and malignant than the Siamese. They have peopled their spiritual world with grotesques, conceived in hallucination and brought forth in nightmare, the monstrous devices of mischief on the one hand and misery on the other, — gods, demons, genii, goblins, wraiths ; and to flatter or propitiate these, especially to enlist their tutelary offices, they commit or connive at crimes of fantastic enormity.

While residing within the walls of Bangkok, I learned of the existence of a custom having all the stability and force of a Medo-Persic law. Whenever a command has gone forth from the throne for the erection of a new fort or a new gate, or the reconstruction of an old one, this ancient custom demands, as the first step in the procedure, that three innocent men shall be immolated on the site selected by the court astrologers, and at their " auspicious " hour.

In 1865, his Majesty and the French Consul at Bangkok had a grave misunderstanding about a proposed modification of a treaty relating to Cambodia. The consul demanded the removal of the prime minister from the commission appointed to arrange the terms of this treaty. The king replied that it was beyond his power to remove the Kralahome. Afterward, the consul, always irritable and insolent, having nursed his wrath to keep it warm, waylaid the king as he was returning from a temple, and threatened him with war, and what not, if he did not accede to his demands. Whereupon, the poor king, effectually intimidated, took refuge in his palace behind barred gates ; and forthwith sent messengers to his astrologers, magicians, and soothsayers, to inquire what the situation prognosticated.

The magi and the augurs, and all the seventh sons of seventh sons, having shrewdly pumped the officers, and made a solemn show of consulting their oracles, replied :

" The times are full of omen. Danger approaches from afar. Let his Majesty erect a third gate, on the east and on the west."

Next morning, betimes, pick and spade were busy, digging deep trenches outside the pair of gates that, on the east and west alike, already protected the palace.

Meanwhile, the consul either quite forgot his threats, or cooled in the cuddling of them ; yet day and night the king's people plied pick and spade and basket in the new foundations.   When all was ready, the *San Luang*, or secret council of Royal Judges, met at midnight in the palace, and despatched twelve officers to lurk around the new gates until dawn.   Two, stationed just within the entrance, assume the character of neighbors and friends, calling loudly to this or that passenger, and continually repeating familiar names.   The peasants and market folk, who are always passing at that hour, hearing these calls, stop, and turn to see who is wanted.   Instantly the myrmidons of the san luang rush from their hiding-places, and arrest, hap-hazard, six of them — three for each gate. From that moment the doom of these astonished, trembling wretches is sealed. No petitions, payments, prayers, can save them.

In the centre of the gateway a deep fosse or ditch is dug, and over it is suspended by two cords an enormous beam.   On the " auspicious " day for the sacrifice, the innocent, unresisting victims — " hinds and churls " perhaps, of the lowest degree in Bangkok — are mocked with a dainty and elaborate banquet, and then conducted in state to their fatal post of honor.   The king and all the court make profound obeisance before them, his Majesty adjuring them earnestly " to guard with devotion the gate, now about to be intrusted to their keeping, from all dangers and calamities ; and to come in season to forewarn him, if either traitors within or enemies without should conspire against the peace of his people or the safety of his throne.' Even as the last word of this exhortation falls from the royal lips, the cords are cut, the ponderous engine crushes the heads of the distinguished wretches, and three Bangkok ragamuffins are metempsychosed into three guardian-angels (*Thevedah*).

Siamese citizens of wealth and influence often bury treasure in the earth, to save it from arbitrary confiscation. In such cases a slave is generally immolated on the spot, to make a guardian genius. Among certain classes, not always the lowest, we find a greedy passion that expends itself in indefatigable digging for such precious *caches*, in the environs of abandoned temples, or among the ruins of the ancient capital, Ayudia. These treasure-seekers first pass a night near the supposed place of concealment, having offered at sunset to the genius of the spot oblations of candles, perfumed tapers, and roasted rice. They then betake themselves to slumber; and in their dreams the genie is expected to appear, and indicate precisely the hiding-place of his golden charge, at the same time offering to wink at its sacking in consideration of the regular perquisite, — "one pig's head and two bottles of arrack." On the other hand, the genie may appear in an angry aspect, flourishing the conventional club in a style that means business, and demanding by what right the intruders would tamper with his charge ; whereat sudden waking and dishevelled flight.

Another and more barbarous superstition relates to premature delivery. In such a case the embarrassed mother calls in a female magician, who declares that an evil spirit has practised a spiteful joke upon the married pair, with a design upon the life of the mother. So saying, she pops the still-born into an earthen pot, and with that in her left hand and a sword in her right, makes for the margin of a deep stream, where, with an approved imprecation upon the fiend and a savage slash at the manikin, she tosses the pot and its untimely contents into the flood.

By such witches as this, sorceries of all kinds are practised for fee. They are likewise supposed to be skilled in the art of healing, and are notable compounders of love-philters and potions.

The king supports a certain number of astrologers, whose duties consist in the prediction of events, whether great or small, from war or peace to rain or drought, and in indicating or determining future possibilities by the aspect and position of the stars. The people universally wear charms and talismans, to which they ascribe supernatural virtues. A patient in fever with delirium is said to be possessed of a devil; and should he grow frantic and unmanageable in the paroxysms, the one becomes a legion. At the close of each year, a thread of unspun cotton, of seven fibres, consecrated by priests, is reeled round all the walls of the palace; and from sunset until dawn a continuous cannonading is kept up from all the forts within hearing, to rout the evil spirits that have infested the departing year.

XXV.

THE SUBORDINATE KING.

A SECOND or subordinate kingship is an anomalous device or provision of sovereignty peculiar to Siam, Cambodia, and Laos. Inferior in station to the Supreme King only, and apparently deriving from the throne of the Phra-batts, to which he may approach so near, a reflected majesty and prestige not clearly understood by his subjects nor easily defined by foreigners, the Second King seems to be, nevertheless, belittled by the very significance of the one exclusive privilege that should distinguish him, — that of exemption from the customary prostrations before the First King, whom he may salute by simply raising his hands and joining them above his head. Here his proper right of royalty begins and ends. The part that he may play in the drama of government is cast to him in the necessity, discretion, or caprice of his absolute chief next, and yet so far, above him; it may be important, insignificant, or wholly omitted. Like any lesser *ducus* of the realm, he must appear before his lord twice a year to renew his oath of allegiance. In law, he is as mere a subject as the slave who bears his betel-box; or that other slave who, on his knees, and with averted face, presents his spittoon. In history, he shall be what circumstance or his own mind may make him: the shadow or the soul of sovereignty, even as the intellectual and moral weakness or strength may have been apportioned between him and his colleague. From his rank he derives no advantage but the *chance*.

THE PRINCESS OF CHIENGMAI.

Somdetch P'hra Pawarendr Ramesr Mahiswarer, the subordinate king of Siam, who died on the 29th of December, 1865, was the legitimate son of the supreme king, second of his dynasty, who reigned from 1809 to 1824. His father had been second king to his grandfather, "grand supreme" of Siam, and first of the reigning line. His mother was "lawful first queen consort"; and the late first or major king, Somdetch-P'hra Paramendr Maha Mongkut, was his elder full brother. Being alike legitimate offspring of the first queen, these two lads were styled *Somdetch Chowfas*, "Celestial Royal Princes"; and during the second and third reigns they were distinguished by the titles of courtesy pertaining to their royal status and relation, the elder as Chowfa Mongkut, the younger as Chowfa Chudha-Mani : *Mongkut* signifying "Royal Crown," and *Chudha-Mani* "Royal Hair-pin."

On the death of their father (in 1824), and the accession, by intrigue, of their elder half-brother, the Chowfa Mongkut entered the Buddhist priesthood; but his brother, more ardent, inquisitive, and restless, took active service with the king, in the military as well as in the diplomatic department of government. He was appointed Superintendent of Artillery and Malayan Infantry on the one hand; and on the other, Translator of English Documents and Secretary for English Correspondence.

In a cautious and verbose sketch of his character and services, written after his death by his jealous brother, the priest-king, wherein he is by turns meanly disparaged and damned with faint praise, we find this curious statement : —

"After that time (1821) he became acquainted with certain parties of English and East Indian merchants, who made their appearance or first commenced trading on late of second reign, after the former trade with Siam which had been stopped or postponed several years in consequence of some misunderstanding before. He became acquainted with certain parts of English language and literature, and certain parts of Hindoo or Bengali language, as sufficient for some unimportant conversation with English and Indian strangers who were visitors of Siam, upon the latter part of the reign of his royal father; but his royal father did not know that he possessed such knowledge of foreign language, which had been concealed to the native persons in republic affairs, whose jealousy seemed to be strong against strangers, so he was not employed in any terms with those strangers foreign affairs," — that is, during the life of his father, at whose death he was just sixteen years old.

Early in the third reign he was sent to Meeklong to superintend the construction of important works of defence near the mouth of the Meeklong River. He pushed this work with vigor, and completed it in 1835. In 1842 he commanded successfully an expedition against the Cochin-Chinese, and, in returning, brought with him to Siam many families of refugees from the eastern coast. Then he was commissioned by the king to reconstruct, "after Western models," the ancient fortifications at Paknam; and having to this end engaged a corps of European engineers and artisans, he eagerly seized the advantage the situation afforded him, by free and intelligent intercourse with his foreign assistants, to master the English language, — so that, at his death, he notably excelled the first king in the facility with which he spoke, read, and wrote it, — and to improve his acquaintance with the Western sciences and arts of navigation, naval construction and armament, coast and inland defence, engineering, transportation, and telegraphy, the working and casting of iron, etc.

On the 26th of May, 1851, twelve days after the coronation of his elder brother, the student and priest Maha

Mongkut, he was called by the unanimous voice of "the king and council" to be Second King; and throughout his subordinate reign his sagacious and alert inquiry, his quick apprehension, his energetic and liberal spirit of improvement, engaged the admiration of foreigners; whilst his handsome person, his generous temper, his gallant preference for the skilful and the brave, his enthusiasm and princely profusion in sports and shows, endeared him more and more to his people. Maha Mongkut — at no time inclined to praise him beyond his deserts, and least of all in the latter years of his life, imbittered to both by mutual jealousy and distrust — wrote almost handsomely of him under the pressure of this public opinion.

"He made everything new and beautiful, and of curious appearance, and of a good style of architecture, and much stronger than they had formerly been constructed by his three predecessors, the second kings of the last three reigns, for the space of time that he was second king. He had introduced and collected many and many things, being articles of great curiosity, and things useful for various purposes of military acts and affairs, from Europe and America, China, and other states, and placed them in various departments and rooms or buildings suitable for those articles, and placed officers for maintaining and preserving the various things neatly and carefully. He has constructed several buildings in European fashion and Chinese fashion, and ornamented them with various useful ornaments for his pleasure, and has constructed two steamers in manner of men-of-war, and two steam-yachts, and several rowing state-boats in Siamese and Cochin-Chinese fashion, for his pleasure at sea and rivers of Siam; and caused several articles of gold and silver being vessels and various wares and weapons to be made up by the Siamese and Malayan goldsmiths, for employ and dress of himself and his family, by his direction and

skilful contrivance and ability. He became celebrated
and spread out more and more to various regions of the
Siamese kingdom, adjacent States around, and far-famed
to foreign countries, even at far distance, as he became acquainted with many and many foreigners, who came from
various quarters of the world where his name became
known to most as a very clever and bravest Prince of
Siam. . . . .

" As he pleased mostly with firing of cannon and acts of
Marine power and seamen, which he has imitated to his
steamers which were made in manner of the man-of-war,
after he has seen various things curious and useful, and
learned Marine customs on board the foreign vessels of
war, his steamers conveyed him to sea, where he has enjoyed playing of firing in cannon very often. . . . .

" He pleased very much in and was playful of almost
everything, some important and some unimportant, as
riding on Elephants and Horses and Ponies, racing of
them and racing of rowing boats, firing on birds and
beasts of prey, dancing and singing in various ways pleasantly, and various curiosity of almost everything, and
music of every description, and in taming of dogs, monkeys, &c., &c., that is to say briefly that he has tested
almost everything eatable except entirely testing of Opium
and play.

" Also he has visited regions of Northeastern Province
of Sarapury and Gorath very often for enjoyment of
pleasant riding on Elephants and Horses, at forests in
chasing animals of prey, fowling, and playing music and
singing with Laos people of that region and obtaining
young wives from there."

What follows is not more curious as to its form of ex-
pression than suspicious as to its meaning and motive.
To all who know with what pusillanimity at times the
First King shrank from the approach of Christian foreign-

ers, — especially the French priests, — with what servility in his moody way he courted their favor, it will appear of very doubtful sincerity.   To those who are familiar with the circumstances under which it was written, and to whom the attitude of jealous reserve that the brothers occupied toward each other at the time of the Second King's death was no secret, it may seem (even after due allowance is made for the prejudices or the obligations of the priest) to cover an insidious, though scarcely adroit, design to undermine the honorable reputation the younger enjoyed among the missionaries, and the cordial friendship with which he had been regarded by several of the purest of them.   Certainly it is suspiciously " of a piece " with other passages, quoted further on, in which the king's purpose to disparage the merits of his brother, and damage the influence of his name abroad, is sufficiently transparent.   In this connection the reader may derive a ray of light from the fact that on the birth of the Second King's first son, an American missionary, who was on terms of intimacy with the father, named the child " George Washington "; and that child, the Prince George Washington Krom Mu'n Pawarwijagan, is the present Second King of Siam.   But to Maha Mongkut, and his " art of putting things " : —

"He was rumored to be baptized or near to be baptized in Christianity, but the fact it is false.   He was a Buddhist, but his faith and belief changed very often in favor of various sects of Buddhism by the association of his wives and various families and of persons who were believers in various sects of the established religion of the Siamese and Laos, Peguan and Burmese countries.   Why should he become a Christian ? when his pleasures consisted in polygamy and enjoyment, and with young women who were practised in pleasant dancing and singing, and who could not be easily given up at any time.

He was very desirous of having his sons to be English scholars and to be learned the art of speaking, reading and writing in English well like himself, but he said he cannot allow his sons to enter the Christian Missionary-School, as he feared his descendants might be induced to the Christianity in which he did not please to believe."

Pawarendr Ramesr had ever been the favorite and darling of his mother, and it was in his infancy that the seeds of that ignoble jealousy were sown between the royal brothers, which flourished so rankly and bore such noxious fruit in their manhood. From his tenderest years the younger prince was remarkable for his personal beauty and his bright intelligence, and before his thirteenth birthday had already learned all that his several masters could teach him. From an old priest, named P'hra Naitt, I gathered many pleasant anecdotes of his childhood.

For example, he related with peculiar pride how the young prince, then but twelve years old, being borne one day in state through the eastern gate of the city to visit his mother's lotos-gardens, observed an old man, half blind, resting by the roadside. Commanding his bearers to halt, he alighted from his sedan and kindly accosted the poor creature. Finding him destitute and helpless, a stranger and a wayfarer in the land, he caused him to be seated in his own sedan, and borne to the gardens, while he followed on foot. Here he had the old man bathed, clad in fresh linen, and entertained with a substantial meal; and afterward he took his astonished client into his service, as keeper of his cattle.

Later in life the generous and romantic prince diverted himself with the adventurous beneficence of Haroun al Raschid, visiting the poor in disguise, listening to the recital of their sufferings and wrongs, and relieving them with ready largesse of charity and justice; and nothing

so pleased and flattered him as to be called, in his assumed name of Nak Pratt, "the wise," to take part in
their sports and fêtes. The affectionate enthusiasm with
which the venerable poonghee remembered his royal pupil
was inspiring; and to see his eyes sparkle and his face
glow with sympathetic triumph, as he described the lad's
exploits of strength or skill in riding, fencing, boxing,
was a fine sight. But it was with saddened look and
tone that he whispered to me, that, at the prince's birth,
the astrologer who cast his horoscope had foretold for him
an unnatural death. This, he said, was the secret of the
watchful devotion and imprudent partiality his mother
had always manifested for him.

For such a prince to come into even the empty name
of power was to become subject to the evil eye of his
fraternal lord and rival, for whose favor officious friends
and superserviceable lackeys contended in scandalous and
treacherous spyings of the Second King's every action.
Yet, meanly beset as he was, he contrived to find means
and opportunity to enlarge his understanding and multi-
ply his attainments; and in the end his proficiency in
languages, European and Oriental, became as remarkable
as it was laudable. It was by Mr. Hunter, secretary to
the prime minister, that he was introduced to the study
of the English language and literature, and by this gentleman's intelligent aid he procured the text-books which
constituted the foundation of his educational course.

In person he was handsome, for a Siamese; of medium
stature, compact and symmetrical figure, and rather dark
complexion. His conversation and deportment denoted
the cultivation, delicacy, and graceful poise of an accomplished gentleman; and he delivered his English with a
correctness and fluency very noticeably free from the
peculiar spasmodic effort that marked his royal brother's
exploits in the language of Shakespeare.

In his palace, which he had rebuilt after the model of an English nobleman's residence, he led the life of a healthy, practical, and systematic student. His library, more judiciously selected than that of his brother, abounded in works of science, embracing the latest discoveries. Here he passed many hours, cultivating a sound acquaintance with the results of investigation and experiment in the Western world. His partiality for English literature in all its branches was extreme. The freshest publications of London found their way to his tables, and he heartily enjoyed the creations of Dickens.

For robust and exhilarating enjoyment, however, he had recourse to hunting expeditions, and martial exercises in the drilling of his private troops. Punctually at day-break every morning he appeared on the parade-ground, and proceeded to review his little army with scrupulous precision, according to European tactics; after which he led his well-trained files to their barracks within the palace walls, where the soldiers exchanged their uniform for a working-dress. Then he marched them to the armory, where muskets, bayonets, and sabres were brought out and severely scoured. That done, the men were dismissed till the morrow.

Among his courtiers were several gentlemen of Siam and Laos, who had acquired such a smattering of English as qualified them to assist the prince in his scientific diversions. Opposite the armory stood a pretty little cottage, quite English-looking, lighted with glass windows, and equipped with European furniture. Over the entrance to this quaint tenement hung a painted sign, in triumphant English, "WATCHES AND CLOCKS MADE AND REPAIRED HERE"; and hither came frequently the Second King and his favorites, to pursue assiduously their harmless occupation of *horlogerie*. Sometimes this eccentric entertainment was diversified with music, in which his

Majesty took a leading part, playing with taste and skill on the flute, and several instruments of the Laos people.

Such a prince should have been happy, in the innocence of his pastimes and the dignity of his pursuits. But the same accident of birth and station to which he owed his privileges and his opportunities imposed its peculiar disabilities and hindrances. His troubles were the troubles of a second king, who chanced to be also an ardent and aspiring man. Weary with disappointment, disheartened in his honorable longing for just appreciation, vexed with the caprice and suspicions of his elder brother; oppressed by the ever-present tyranny of the thought — so hard for such a man to bear — that the woman he loved best in the land he was inexorably forbidden to marry, because, being a princess of the first rank, she might be offered and accepted to grace the harem of his brother; a mere prisoner of state, watched by the baleful eye of jealousy, and traduced by the venal tongues of courtiers; dwelling in a torment of uncertainty as to the fate to which his brother's explosive temper and irresponsible power might devote him, hoping for no repose or safety but in his funeral-urn, — he began to grow hard and defiant, and that which, in the native freedom of his soul, should have been his noble steadfastness degenerated into ignoble obstinacy.

Among the innumerable mean torments with which his pride was persecuted was the continual presence of a certain doctor, who, by the king's command, attended him at all times and places, compelling him to use remedies that were most distasteful to him.

He was gallantly kind and courteous toward women; no act of cruelty to any woman was ever attributed to him. His children he ruled wisely, though somewhat sternly, rendering his occasional tenderness and indulgence so much the more precious and delightful to them.

Never had Siam a more popular prince. He was the embodiment of the most hopeful qualities, moral and intellectual, of his nation; especially was he the exponent and promise of its most progressive tendencies; and his people regarded him with love and reverence, as their trusty stay and support. His talents as a statesman commanded the unqualified admiration of foreigners; and it was simply the jealous and tyrannical temper of Maha Mongkut that forced him to retire from all participation in the affairs of government.

At last the mutual reserve and distrust of the royal brothers broke out in open quarrel, provoked by the refusal of the First King to permit the Second to borrow from the royal treasury a considerable sum of money. On the day after his order was dishonored, the prince set out with his congenial and confidential courtiers on a hunting expedition to the Laos province of Chiengmai, scornfully threatening to entrap one of the royal white elephants, and sell it to his Supreme Majesty for the sum he would not loan.

At Chiengmai he was regally entertained by the tributary prince of that province; and no sooner was his grievance known, than the money he required was laid at his feet. Too manly to accept the entire sum, he borrowed but a portion of it; and instead of taking it out of the country, decided to sojourn there for a time, that he might spend it to the advantage of the people. To this end he selected a lovely spot in the vicinity of Chiengmai, called Saraburee, itself a city of some consideration, where bamboo houses line the banks of a beautiful river, that traverses teak forests alive with large game. On an elevation near at hand the Second King erected a palace substantially fortified, which he named Ban Sitha (the Home of the Goddess Sitha), and caused a canal to be cut to the eastern slope.

Here he indulged freely, and on an imposing scale, in his favorite pastime of hunting, and privately took to wife the daughter of the king of Chiengmai, the Princess Sunartha Vismita. And here he was happy, only returning to Bangkok when called thither by affairs of state, or to take the semi-annual oath of allegiance.

Among the prince's concubines at this time was a woman named Kliep, envious, intriguing, and ambitious, who by consummate arts had obtained control of his Majesty's *cuisine*, — an appointment of peculiar importance and trust in the household of an Oriental prince. Finding that by no feminine devices could she procure the influence she coveted over her master's mind and affections, she finally had recourse to an old and infamous sorcerer, styled Khoon Hâte-nah ("Lord of Future Events"), an adept of the black art much consulted by women of rank from all parts of the country; and he, in consideration of an extraordinary fee, prepared for her a variety of charms, incantations, philters, to be administered to the prince, in whose food daily, for years, she mixed the abominable nostrums. The poison did its work slowly but surely, and his sturdy life was gradually undermined. His strength quite gone, and his spirit broken, his despondency became so profound that he lost all taste for the occupations and diversions that had once delighted him, and sought relief in restless changing from one palace to another, and in consulting every physician he could find.

It was during a visit to his favorite residence at Saraburee that the signs of approaching dissolution appeared, and the king's physician, fearing he might die there, took hurried steps to remove him to his palace at Bangkok. He was bound in a sedan, and lowered from his high chamber in the castle into his barge on the canal at the foot of the cliff; and so, with all his household in train, transported to the palace of Krom Hluang Wongse, physician to the

king, and one of his half-brothers.   Now miserably un-
nerved, the prince, once so patient, brave, and proud,
threw his arms round his kinsman's neck, and, weeping
bitterly, implored him to save him.   But he was presently
removed to his own palace, and laid in a chamber looking
to the east.

That night the prince expressed a wish to see his royal
brother.   The king hastened to his bedside in company
with his Excellency Chow Phya Sri Sury-wongse, the
Kralahome, or prime minister; and then and there a
silent and solemn reconciliation took place.   No words
were spoken; only the brothers embraced each other, and
the elder wept bitterly.   But from the facts brought to
light in that impressive meeting and parting, it was made
plain that the Second King died by slow poison, administered by the woman Kliep, — plain to all but the Second
King himself, who died in ignorance of the means by
which the tragic prophecy of his horoscope had been
made good.

In the very full account of his brother's death which
Maha Mongkut thought it necessary to write, he was
careful to conceal from the public the true cause of the
calamity, fearing the foreign populace, and, most of all,
the Laotians and Peguans, who were devoted to the prince,
and might attach suspicion to himself, on the ground
of his notorious jealousy of the Second King.   The
royal physicians and the Supreme Council were sworn to
secrecy; and the woman Kliep, and her accomplice Khoon
Hâte-nah, together with nine female slaves, were tortured
and publicly paraded through the environs of Bangkok,
though their crime was never openly named.   Afterward
they were thrown into an open boat, towed out on the Gulf
of Siam, and there abandoned to the mercy of winds and
waves, or death by starvation.   Among the women of the
palace the current report was, that celestial avengers had

slain the murderous crew with arrows of lightning and spears of fire.

In his Majesty's account of the last days of his royal brother, we have the characteristic queerness of his English, and a scarcely less characteristic passage of Pecksniffian cant: —

" The lamentable patient Second King ascertained himself that his approaching death was inevitable; it was great misfortune to him and his family indeed. His eldest son Prince George * Krom Mu'n Pawarwijagan, aged 27 years on that time, became very sick of painful rheumatism by which he has his body almost steady on his seat and bed, immovable to and fro, himself, since the month of October, 1865, when his father was absent from Bangkok, being at Ban Sitha as aforesaid. When his royal father returned from Ban Sitha he arrived at his palace at Bangkok on 6th December. He can only being lifted by two or three men and placed in the presence of his father who was very ill, but the eldest son forenamed prince was little better, so before death of his father as he can be raised to be stood by two men and can cribble slowly on even or level surface, by securing and supporting of two men on both sides.

" When his father became worse and approaching the point of death, upon that time his father can see him scarcely ; wherefore the Second King, on his being worse, has said to his eldest and second daughters, the half sisters of the eldest son, distempered so as he cannot be in the presence of his father without difficulty, that he (the Second King) forenamed on that time was hopeless and that he could not live more than a few days. He did not wish to do his last will regarding his family and property, particularly as he was strengthless to speak much, and consider anything deeply and accurately: he beg'd to

* George Washington.

entreat all his sons, daughters, and wives that none should be sorry for his death, which comes by natural course, and should not fear for misery of difficulty after his demise. All should throw themselves under their faithful and affectionate uncle, the Supreme King of Siam, for protection, in whom he had heartfelt confidence that he will do well to his family after his death, as such the action or good protection to several families of other princes and princesses in the royalty, who deceased before. He beg'd only to recommend his sons and daughters, that they should be always honest and faithful to his elder full brother, the Supreme King of Siam, by the same affection as to himself, and that they should have much more affection and respect toward Paternal relative persons in royalty, than toward their maternal relative persons, who are not royal descendants of his ancestors. . . . .

" On the 29th December 1865, in the afternoon, the Second King invited His Majesty the Supreme King, his elder full brother, and his Excellency Chow Phya Sri Sury-wongse Samuha P'hra-Kralahome, the Prime Minister, who is the principal head of the Government and royal cousin, to seat themselves near to his side on his bedstead where he lay, and other principals of royalty and nobility, to seat themselves in that room where he was lying, that they might be able to ascertain his speech by hearing. Then he delivered his family and followers and the whole of his property to His Majesty and His Excellency for protection and good decision, according to consequences which they would well observe."

Not a word of that royal reconcilement, of that remorseful passion of tears, of that mute mystery of humanity, the secret spell of a burdened mother's love working too late in the hearts of her headstrong boys! Not a word of that crowning embrace, which made the subordinate king supreme, by the grace of dying and forgiving!

XXVI.

THE SUPREME KING: HIS CHARACTER AND ADMINISTRATION.

OF Somdetch P'hra Paramendr Maha Mongkut, late Supreme King of Siam, it may safely be said (for all his capricious provocations of temper and his snappish greed of power) that he was, in the best sense of the epithet, the most remarkable of the Oriental princes of the present century, — unquestionably the most progressive of all the supreme rulers of Siam, of whom the native historians enumerate not less than forty, reckoning from the founding of the ancient capital (Ayudia or A-yodhya, " the abode of gods ") in A. D. 1350.

He was the legitimate son of the king P'hra Chow-P'hra Pooti-lootlah, commonly known as P'hen-din-Klang; and his mother, daughter of the youngest sister of the King Somdetch P'hra Bouromah Rajah P'hra Pooti Yout Fah, was one of the most admired princesses of her time, and is described as equally beautiful and virtuous. She devoted herself assiduously to the education of her sons, of whom the second, the subject of these notes, was born in 1804; and the youngest, her best beloved, was the late Second King of Siam.

One of the first public acts of the King P'hra Pooti-lootlah was to elevate to the highest honors of the state his eldest son (the Chowfa Mongkut), and proclaim him heir-apparent to the throne. He then selected twelve noblemen, distinguished for their attainments, prudence, and virtue, — most conspicuous among them the venerable but energetic Duke Somdetch Ong Yai, — to be tutors and guardians to the lad.   By these he was carefully taught in all the learning of his time ; Sanskrit and Pali formed his chief study, and from the first he aspired to proficiency in Latin and English, for the pursuit of which he soon found opportunities among the missionaries. His translations from the Sanskrit, Pali, and Magadthi, mark him as an authority among Oriental linguists ; and his knowledge of English, though never perfect, became at least extensive and varied ; so that he could correspond, with credit to himself, with Englishmen of distinction, such as the Earl of Clarendon and Lords Stanley and Russell.

In his eighteenth year he married a noble lady, descended from the Phya Tak Sinn, who bore him two sons.

Two years later the throne became vacant by the death of his father ; but (as the reader has already learned) his elder half-brother, who, through the intrigues of his mother, had secured a footing in the favor of the Senabawdee, was inducted by that "Royal Council" into power.   Unequal to the exploit of unseating the usurper, and fearing his unscrupulous jealousy, the Chowfa Mongkut took refuge in a monastery, and entered the priesthood, leaving his wife and two sons to mourn him as one dead to them.   In this self-imposed celibacy he lived throughout the long reign of his half-brother, which lasted twenty-seven years.

In the calm retreat of his Buddhist cloister the contemplative tastes of the royal scholar found fresh entertainment, his intellectual aspirations a new incitement.

He labored with enthusiasm for the diffusion of religion and enlightenment, and, above all, to promote a higher appreciation of the teachings of Buddha, to whose doctrines he devoted himself with exemplary zeal throughout his sacerdotal career. From the Buddhist scriptures he compiled with reverent care an impressive liturgy for his own use. His private charities amounted annually to ten thousand ticals. All the fortune he accumulated, from the time of his quitting the court until his return to it to accept the diadem offered by the Senabawdee, he expended either in charitable distributions or in the purchase of books, sacred manuscripts, and relics for his monastery.*

It was during his retirement that he wrote that notable treatise in defence of the divinity of the revelations of Buddha, in which he essays to prove that it was the single aim of the great reformer to deliver man from all selfish and carnal passions, and in which he uses these words: "These are the only obstacles in the search for Truth. The most solid wisdom is to know this, and to apply one's self to the conquest of one's self. This it is to become the *enlightened*, — the Buddha!" And he concludes with the remark of Asoka, the Indian king: "That which has been delivered unto us by Buddha, that alone is well said, and worthy of our soul's profoundest homage."

In the pursuit of his appointed ends Maha Mongkut was active and pertinacious; no labors wearied him nor pains deterred him. Before the arrival of the Protestant missionaries, in 1820, he had acquired some knowledge of Latin and the sciences from the Jesuits; but when the Protestants came he manifested a positive preference for their methods of instruction, inviting one or another of

* "On the third reign he [himself] served his eldest royal half-brother, by superintending the construction and revision of royal sacred books in royal libraries: so he was appointed the principal superintendent of clergymen's acts and works of Buddhist religion, and selector of religious learned wise men in the country, during the third reign." — *From the pen of Maha Mongkut.*

them daily to his temple, to aid him in the study of English. Finally he placed himself under the permanent tutorship of the Rev. Mr. Caswell, an American missionary ; and, in order to encourage his preceptor to visit him frequently, he fitted up a convenient resting-place for him on the route to the temple, where that excellent man might teach the poorer people who gathered to hear him. Under Mr. Caswell he made extraordinary progress in advanced and liberal ideas of government, commerce, even religion. He never hesitated to express his respect for the fundamental principles of Christianity ; but once, when pressed too closely by his reverend moonshee with what he regarded as the more pretentious and apocryphal portions of the Bible, he checked that gentleman's advance with the remark that has ever been remembered against him, " *I hate the Bible mostly !* "

As High-Priest of Siam — the mystic and potential office to which he was in the end exalted — he became the head of a new school, professing strictly the pure philosophy inculcated by Buddha : "the law of Compensation, of Many Births, and of final Niphan," * — but not Nihilism, as the word and the idea are commonly defined. It is only to the idea of God as an *ever-active* Creator that the new school of Buddhists is opposed, — not to the Deity as a primal source, from whose thought and pleasure sprang all forms of matter ; nor can they be brought to admit the need of miraculous intervention in the order of nature.

In this connection, it may not be out of place to mention a remark that the king (still speaking as a high-priest, having authority) once made to me, on the subject of the miracles recorded in the Bible : —

"You say that marriage is a holy institution ; and I believe it is esteemed a sacrament by one of the principal

* Attainment of beatitude.

branches of your sect. It is, of all the laws of the universe, the most wise and incontestable, pervading all forms of animal and vegetable life. Yet your God (meaning the Christian's God) has stigmatized it as unholy, in that he would not permit his Son to be born in the ordinary way; but must needs perform a miracle in order to give birth to one divinely inspired. Buddha was divinely inspired, but he was only *man*. Thus it seems to me he is the greater of the two, because out of his own heart he studied humanity, which is but another form of divinity; and, the carnal mind being by this contemplation subdued, he became the *Divinely Enlightened.*"

When his teacher had begun to entertain hopes that he would one day become a Christian, he came out openly against the idea, declaring that he entertained no thought of such a change. He admonished the missionaries not to deceive themselves, saying: "You must not imagine that any of my party will ever become Christians. We cannot embrace what we consider a foolish religion."

In the beginning of the year 1851 his supreme Majesty, Prabat Somdetch P'hra Nang Klou, fell ill, and gradually declined until the 3d of April, when he expired, and the throne was again vacant. The dying sovereign, forgetting or disregarding his promise to his half-brother, the true heir, had urged with all his influence that the succession should fall to his eldest son; but in the assembly of the Senabawdee, Somdetch Ong Yai (father of the present prime minister of Siam), supported by Somdetch Ong Noi, vehemently declared himself in favor of the high-priest Chowfa Mongkut.

This struck terror to the "illegitimates," and mainly availed to quell the rising storm of partisan conflict. Moreover, Ong Yai had taken the precaution to surround the persons of the princes with a formidable guard, and to distribute an overwhelming force of militia in all quar-

ters of the city, ready for instant action at a signal from
him.

Thus the two royal brothers, with views more liberal,
as to religion, education, foreign trade, and intercourse,
than the most enlightened of their predecessors had entertained, were firmly seated on the throne as " first " and
" second " kings ; and every citizen, native or foreign, began to look with confidence for the dawn of better times.

Nor did the newly crowned sovereign forget his friends
and teachers, the American missionaries. He sent for
them, and thanked them cordially for all that they had
taught him, assuring them that it was his earnest desire
to administer his government after the model of the
limited monarchy of England ; and to introduce schools,
where the Siamese youth might be well taught in the
English language and literature and the sciences of Europe.[*]

There can be no just doubt that, at the time, it was his
sincere purpose to carry these generous impulses into
practical effect ; for certainly he was, in every moral and
intellectual respect, nobly superior to his predecessor, and
to his dying hour he was conspicuous for his attachment to
a sound philosophy and the purest maxims of Buddha.
Yet we find in him a deplorable example of the degrading
influence on the human mind of the greed of possessions
and power, and of the infelicities that attend it ; for

* In this connection the Rev. Messrs. Bradley, Caswell, House, Matoon,
and Dean are entitled to special mention. To their united influence Siam
unquestionably owes much, if not all, of her present advancement and
prosperity. Nor would I be thought to detract from the high praise that
is due to their fellow-laborers in the cause of Christianity, the Roman
Catholic missionaries, who are, and ever have been, indefatigable in their
exertions for the good of the country. Especially will the name of the
excellent bishop, Monseigneur Pallegoix, be held in honor and affection by people of all creeds and tongues in Siam, as that of a pure and
devoted follower of our common Redeemer.

though he promptly set about the reforming of abuses in
the several departments of his government, and invited
the ladies of the American mission to teach in his
new harem, nevertheless he soon began to indulge his
avaricious and sensual propensities, and cast a jealous eye
upon the influence of the prime minister, the son of his
stanch old friend, the Duke Ong Yai, to whom he owed
almost the crown itself, and of his younger brother, the
Second King, and of the neighboring princes of Chiengmai
and Cochin China. He presently offended those who, by
their resolute display of loyalty in his hour of peril, had
seated him safely on the throne of his ancestors.

From this time he was continually exposed to disappointment, mortification, slights, from abroad, and conspiracy at home. Had it not been for the steadfast adherence of the Second King and the prime minister, the
sceptre would have been wrested from his grasp and bestowed upon his more popular brother.

Yet, notwithstanding all this, he appeared, to those who
observed him only on the public stage of affairs, to rule with
wisdom, to consult the welfare of his subjects, to be concerned for the integrity of justice and the purity of manners and conversation in his own court, and careful, by a
prudent administration, to confirm his power at home and
his prestige abroad. Considered apart from his domestic
relations, he was, in many respects, an able and virtuous
ruler. His foreign policy was liberal; he extended tolera-
tion to all religious sects; he expended a generous portion
of his revenues in public improvements, — monasteries,
temples, bazaars, canals, bridges, arose at his bidding on
every side ; and though he fell short of his early promise, he did much to improve the condition of his subjects.

For example, at the instance of her Britannic Majesty's Consul, the Honorable Thomas George Knox, he removed the heavy boat-tax that had so oppressed the

poorer masses of the Siamese, and constructed good roads, and improved the international chambers of judicature.

But as husband and kinsman his character assumes a most revolting aspect. Envious, revengeful, subtle, he was as fickle and petulant as he was suspicious and cruel. His brother, even the offspring of his brother, became to him objects of jealousy, if not of hatred. Their friends must, he thought, be his enemies, and applause bestowed upon them was odious to his soul. There were many horrid tragedies in his harem in which he enacted the part of a barbarian and a despot. Plainly, his conduct as the head of a great family to whom his will was a law of terror reflects abiding disgrace upon his name. Yet it had this redeeming feature, that he tenderly loved those of his children whose mothers had been agreeable to him. He never snubbed or slighted them; and for the little princess, Chow Fâ-ying, whose mother had been to him a most gentle and devoted wife, his affection was very strong and enduring.

But to turn from the contemplation of his private traits, so contradictory and offensive, to the consideration of his public acts, so liberal and beneficent. Several commercial treaties of the first importance were concluded with foreign powers during his reign. In the first place, the Siamese government voluntarily reduced the measurement duties on foreign shipping from nineteen hundred to one thousand ticals per fathom of ship's beam. This was a brave stride in the direction of a sound commercial policy, and an earnest of greater inducements to enterprising traders from abroad. In 1855 a new treaty of commerce was negotiated with his Majesty's government by H. B. M.'s plenipotentiary, Sir John Bowring, which proved of very positive advantage to both parties. On the 29th of May, 1856, a new treaty, substantially like that with Great Britain, was procured by Townsend

Harris, Esq., representing the United States ; and later in the same year still another, in favor of France, through H. I. M.'s Envoy, M. Montigny.

Before that time Portugal had been the only foreign government having a consul residing at Bangkok. Now the way was opened to admit a resident consul of each of the treaty powers ; and shortly millions of dollars flowed into Siam annually by channels through which but a few tens of thousands had been drawn before. Foreign traders and merchants flocked to Bangkok and established rice-mills, factories for the production of sugar and oil, and warehouses for the importation of European fabrics. They found a ready market for their wares, and an aspect of thrift and comfort began to enliven the once neglected and cheerless land.

A new and superb palace was erected, after the model of Windsor Castle, together with numerous royal residences in different parts of the country. The nobility began to emulate the activity and munificence of their sovereign, and to compete with each other in the grandeur of their dwellings and the splendor of their *cortéges*.

So prosperous did the country become under the benign influence of foreign trade and civilization, that other treaties were speedily concluded with almost every nation under the sun, and his Majesty found it necessary to accredit Sir John Bowring as plenipotentiary for Siam abroad.

Early in this reign the appointment of harbor-master at Bangkok was conferred upon an English gentleman, who proved so efficient in his functions that he was distinguished with the fifth title of a Siamese noble. Next came a French commander and a French band-master for the royal troops. Then a custom-house was established, and a "live Yankee" installed at the head of it, who was also glorified with a title of honor. Finally a police force

was organized, composed of trusty Malays hired from
Singapore, and commanded by one of the most energetic
Englishmen to be found in the East, — a measure which
has done more than all others to promote a comfortable
sense of "law and order" throughout the city and out-
skirts of Bangkok.   It is to be remembered, however,
in justice to the British Consul-General in Siam, Mr.
Thomas George Knox, that the sure though silent influence was his, whereby the minds of the king and the
prime minister were led to appreciate the benefits that
must accrue from these foreign innovations.

The privilege of constructing, on liberal terms, a line
of telegraph through Maulmain to Singapore, with a
branch to Bangkok, has been granted to the Singapore
Telegraph Company ; and finally a sanitarium has been
erected on the coast at Anghin, for the benefit of native
and foreign residents needing the invigoration of sea-air.*

During his retirement in the monastery the king had a
stroke of paralysis, from which he perfectly recovered ;
but it left its mark on his face, in the form of a peculiar
falling of the under lip on the right side.   In person he
was of middle stature, slightly built, of regular features
and fair complexion.   In early life he lost most of his
teeth, but he had had them replaced with a set made from
sapan-wood, — a secret that he kept very sensitively to
the day of his death.

---

* "His Excellency Chow Phya Bhibakrwongs Maha Kosa Dhipude,
the P'hraklang, Minister for Foreign Affairs, has built a sanitarium at
Anghin for the benefit of the public.   It is for benefit of the Siamese,
Europeans, or Americans, to go and occupy, when unwell, to restore their
health.   All are cordially invited to go there for a suitable length of
time and be happy ; but are requested not to remain month after month
and year after year, and regard it as a place without an owner.   To regard it in this way cannot be allowed, for it is public property, and others
should go and stop there also." —Advertisement, Siam Monitor, August
29, 1868.

Capable at times of the noblest impulses, he was equally capable of the basest actions. Extremely accessible to praise, he indiscriminately entertained every form of flattery; but his fickleness was such that no courtier could cajole him long. Among his favorite women was the beautiful Princess Tongoo Soopia, sister to the unfortunate Sultan Mahmoud, ex-rajah of Pahang. Falling fiercely in love with her on her presentation at his court, he procured her for his harem against her will, and as a hostage for the good faith of her brother; but as she, being Mohammedan, ever maintained toward him a deportment of tranquil indifference, he soon tired of her, and finally dismissed her to a wretched life of obsoleteness and neglect within the palace walls.

The only woman who ever managed him with acknowledged success was Khoon Chom Piem : hardly pretty, but well formed, and of versatile tact, totally uneducated, of barely respectable birth, — being Chinese on her father's side, — yet withal endowed with a nice intuitive appreciation of character. Once conscious of her growing influence over the king, she contrived to foster and exercise it for years, with but a slight rebuff now and then. Being modest to a fault, even at times obnoxious to the imputation of prudishness, she habitually feigned excuses for non-attendance in his Majesty's chambers, — such as delicate health, the nursing of her children, mourning for the death of this or that relative, — and voluntarily visited him only at rare intervals. In the course of six years she amassed considerable treasure, procured good places at court for members of her family, and was the means of bringing many Chinamen to the notice of the king. At the same time she lived in continual fear, was warily humble and conciliating toward her rival sisters, who pitied rather than envied her, and retained in her pay most of the female executive force in the palace.

In his daily habits his Majesty was remarkably industrious and frugal. His devotion to the study of astronomy never abated, and he calculated with respectable
accuracy the great solar eclipse of August, 1868.

The French government having sent a special commission, under command of the Baron Hugon le Tourneur,
to observe the eclipse in Siam, the king erected, at a place
called *Hua Wánn* ("The Whale's Head"), a commodious
observatory, besides numerous pavilions varying in size
and magnificence, for his Majesty and retinue, the French
commission, the Governor of Singapore (Colonel Ord) and
suite, who had been invited to Bangkok by the king, and
for ministers and nobles of Siam. Provision was made,
at the cost of government, for the regal entertainment,
in a town of booths and tabernacles, of the vast concourse
of natives and Europeans who followed his Majesty from
the capital to witness the sublime phenomenon ; and a
herd of fifty noble elephants were brought from the ancient city of Ayudia for service and display.

The prospect becoming dubious and gloomy just at
the time of first contact (ten o'clock), the prime minister
archly invited the foreigners who believed in an overruling
Providence to pray to him " that he may be pleased to
disperse the clouds long enough to afford us a good view of
the grandest of eclipses." Presently the clouds were partially withdrawn from the sun, and his Majesty observing
that one twentieth of the disk was obscured, announced
the fact to his own people by firing a cannon ; and immediately pipes screamed and trumpets blared in the royal
pavilion, — a tribute of reverence to the traditional fable
about the Angel Rahoo swallowing the sun. Both the
king and prime minister, scorning the restraints of dignity,
were fairly boisterous in their demonstrations of triumph
and delight ; the latter skipping from point to point to
squint through his long telescope. At the instant of

absolute totality, when the very last ray of the sun had become extinct, his Excellency shouted, "Hurrah, hurrah, hurrah!" and scientifically disgraced himself. Leaving his spyglass swinging, he ran through the gateway of his pavilion, and cried to his prostrate wives, "Henceforth will you not believe the foreigners?"

But that other Excellency, Chow Phya Bhudharabhay, Minister for Northern Siam, more orthodox, sat in dumfoundered faith, and gaped at the awful deglutition of the Angel Rahoo.

The government expended not less than a hundred thousand dollars on this scientific expedition, and a delegation from the foreign community of Bangkok approached his Majesty with an address of thanks for his indiscriminate hospitality.

But the extraordinary excitement, and exposure to the noxious atmosphere of the jungle, proved inimical to the constitution of the king. On his return to Bangkok he complained of general weariness and prostration, which was the prelude to fever. Foreign physicians were consulted, but at no stage of the case was any European treatment employed. He rapidly grew worse, and was soon past saving. On the day before his death he called to his bedside his nearest relatives, and parted among them such of his personal effects as were most prized by him, saying, "I have no more need of these things. I must give up my life also." Buddhist priests were constant in attendance, and he seemed to derive much comfort from their prayers and exhortations. In the evening he wrote with his own hand a tender farewell to the mothers of his many children, — eighty-one in number. On the morning of his last day (October 1, 1868) he dictated in the Pali language a farewell address to the Buddhist priesthood, the spirit of which was admirable, and clearly manifested the faith of the dying man in the doc-

11*

trines of the Reformer; for he hesitated not to say:
"Farewell, ye faithful followers of Buddha, to whom
death is nothing, even as all earthly existence is vain, all
things mutable, and death inevitable. Presently I shall
myself submit to that stern necessity. Farewell! for I
go only a little before you."

Feeling sure that he must die before midnight, he summoned his half-brother, H. R. H. Krom Hluang Wongse,
his Excellency the prime minister, Chow Phya Kralahome, and others, and solemnly imposed upon them
the care of his eldest son, the Chowfa Chulalonkorn, and
of his kingdom; at the same time expressing his last
earthly wish, that the Senabawdee, in electing his successor, would give their voices for one who should conciliate
all parties, that the country might not be distracted by
dissensions on that question. He then told them he was
about to finish his course, and implored them not to give
way to grief, "nor to any sudden surprise," that he should
leave them thus; "'t is an event that must befall all
creatures that come into this world, and may not be
avoided." Then turning his gaze upon a small image of
his adored teacher, he seemed for some time absorbed in
awful contemplation. "Such is life!" Those were actually the last words of this most remarkable Buddhist king.
He died like a philosopher, calmly and sententiously so-
liloquizing on death and its inevitability. At the final
moment, no one being near save his adopted son, Phya
Buroot, he raised his hands before his face, as in his accustomed posture of devotion; then suddenly his head
dropped backward, and he was gone.

That very night, without disorder or debate, the Senabawdee elected his eldest son, Somdetch Chowfa Chulalonkorn, to succeed him; and the Prince George Washington, eldest son of the late Second King, to succeed to
his father's subordinate throne, under the title of **Krom**

P'hra Raja Bowawn Shathan Mongkoon. The title of the present supreme king (my amiable and very promising scholar) is Prabat Somdetch P'hra Paramendr Maha Chulalonkorn Kate Klou Chow-yu-Hua.

About a year after my first ill-omened interviews with Maha Mongkut, and when I had become permanently installed in my double office of teacher and scribe, I was one day busy with a letter from his Majesty to the Earl of Clarendon, and finding that any attempt at partial correction would but render his meaning more ambiguous, and impair the striking originality of his style, I had abandoned the effort, and set about copying it with literal exactness, only venturing to alter here and there a word, such as " I hasten with *wilful* pleasure to write in reply to your Lordship's *well-wishing* letter," etc. Whilst I was thus evolving from the depths of my inner consciousness a satisfactory solution to this conundrum in King's English, his Majesty's private secretary lolled in the sunniest corner of the room, stretching his dusky limbs and heavily nodding, in an ecstasy of ease-taking. Poor P'hra-Alâck ! I never knew him to be otherwise than sleepy, and his sleep was always stolen. For his Majesty was the most capricious of kings as to his working moods, — busy when the average man should be sleeping, sleeping while letters, papers, despatches, messengers, mail-boats waited. More than once had we been aroused at dead of night by noisy female slaves, and dragged in hot haste and consternation to the Hall of Audience, only to find that his Majesty was, not at his last gasp, as we had feared, but simply bothered to find in Webster's Dictionary some word that was to be found nowhere but in his own fertile brain ; or perhaps in excited chase of the classical term for some trifle he was on the point of ordering from London, — and that word was sure to be a stranger to my brain.

Before my arrival in Bangkok it had been his not uncommon practice to send for a missionary at midnight, have him beguiled or abducted from his bed, and conveyed by boat to the palace, some miles up the river, to inquire if it would not be more elegant to write *murky* instead of *obscure*, or *gloomily dark* rather than *not clearly apparent*. And if the wretched man should venture to declare his honest preference for the ordinary over the extraordinary form of expression, he was forthwith dismissed with irony, arrogance, or even insult, and without a word of apology for the rude invasion of his rest.

One night, a little after twelve o'clock, as he was on the point of going to bed like any plain citizen of regular habits, his Majesty fell to thinking how most accurately to render into English the troublesome Siamese word *phi*, which admits of a variety of interpretations.* After puzzling over it for more than an hour, getting himself possessed with the word as with the devil it stands for, and all to no purpose, he ordered one of his lesser state barges to be manned and despatched with all speed for the British Consul. That functionary, inspired with lively alarm by so startling a summons, dressed himself with unceremonious celerity, and hurried to the palace, conjecturing on the way all imaginable possibilities of politics and diplomacy, revolution or invasion. To his vexation, not less than his surprise, he found the king in dishabille, engaged with a Siamese-English vocabulary, and mentally divided between "deuce" and "devil," in the choice of an equivalent. His preposterous Majesty gravely laid the case before the consul, who, though inwardly chafing at what he termed "the confounded coolness" of the situation, had no choice but to decide with grace, and go back to bed with philosophy.

No wonder, then, that P'hra-Alâck experienced an ac-

* Ghost, spirit, soul, devil, evil angel.

cess of gratitude for the privilege of napping for two hours in a snuggery of sunshine.

"Mam-kha," * he murmured drowsily, " I hope that in the Chat-Nah † I shall be a freed man."

"I hope so sincerely, P'hra-Alâck," said I. "I hope you'll be an Englishman or an American, for then you'll be sure to be independent."

It was impossible not to pity the poor old man, — stiff with continual stooping to his task, and so subdued! — liable not only to be called at any hour of the day or night, but to be threatened, cuffed, kicked, beaten on the head, ‡ every way abused and insulted, and the next moment to be taken into favor, confidence, bosom-friendship, even as his Majesty's mood might veer.

Alack for P'hra-Alâck! though usually he bore with equal patience his greater and his lesser ills, there were occasions that sharply tried his meekness, when his weak and goaded nature revolted, and he rushed to a snug little home of his own, about forty yards from the Grand Palace, there to snatch a respite of rest and refreshment in the society of his young and lately wedded wife. Then the king would awake and send for him, whereupon he would be suddenly ill, or not at home, strategically hiding himself under a mountain of bedclothes, and detailing Mrs. P'hra-Alâck to reconnoitre and report. He had tried this primitive trick so often that its very staleness infuriated the king, who invariably sent officers to seize the trembling accomplice and lock her up in a dismal cell as a hostage for the scribe's appearance. At dusk the poor fellow would emerge, contrite and terrified, and prostrate himself at the gate of the palace. Then his Majesty (who, having spies posted in every quarter of the town,

* *Kha*, " your slave."
† The next state of existence.
‡ The greatest indignity a Siamese can suffer.

knew as well as P'hra-Alâck himself what the illness or the absence signified) leisurely strolled forth, and, finding the patient on the threshold, flew always into a genuine rage, and prescribed "decapitation on the spot," and "sixty lashes on the bare back," both in the same breath. And while the attendants flew right and left, — one for the blade, another for the thong, — the king, still raging, seized whatever came most handy, and belabored his bosom-friend on the head and shoulders. Having thus summarily relieved his mind, he despatched the royal secretary for his ink-horn and papyrus, and began inditing letters, orders, appointments, before scymitar or lash (which were ever tenderly slow on these occasions) had made its appearance. Perhaps in the very thick of his dictating he would remember the connubial accomplice, and order his people to " release her, and let her go."

Slavery in Siam is the lot of men of a much finer intellectual type than any who have been its victims in modern times in societies farther west. P'hra-Alâck had been his Majesty's slave when they were boys together. Together they had played, studied, and entered the priesthood. At once bondman, comrade, classmate, and confidant, he was the very man to fill the office of private secretary to his royal crony. Virgil made a slave of his a poet, and Horace was the son of an emancipated slave. The Roman leech and chirurgeon were often slaves; so, too, the preceptor and the pedagogue, the reader and the player, the clerk and the amanuensis, the singer, the dancer, the wrestler, and the buffoon, the architect, the smith, the weaver, and the shoemaker ; even the *armiger* or squire was a slave. Educated slaves exercised their talents and pursued their callings for the emolument of their masters ; and thus it is to-day in Siam. *Mutato nomine, de te fabula narratur*, P'hra-Alâck !

The king's taste for English composition had, by much

exercise, developed itself into a passion. In the pursuit
of it he was indefatigable, rambling, and petulant. He
had " Webster's Unabridged " on the brain, — an exasperating form of king's evil. The little dingy slips that
emanated freely from the palace press were as indiscriminate as they were quaint. No topic was too sublime or
too ignoble for them. All was " copy " that came to
those cases, — from the glory of the heavenly bodies to
the nuisance of the busybodies who scolded his Majesty
through the columns of the Bangkok Recorder.

I have before me, as I write, a circular from his pen,
and in the type of his private press, which, being without
caption or signature, may be supposed to be addressed
"to all whom it may concern." The American missionaries had vexed his exact scholarship by their peculiar
mode of representing in English letters the name of a
native city (*Prippri*, or in Sanskrit *Bejrepuri*). Whence
this droll circular, which begins with a dogmatic line:—

" None should write the name of city of Prippri thus
— P'et cha poory."

Then comes a pedantic demonstration of the derivation
of the name from a compound Sanskrit word, signifying
" Diamond City." And the document concludes with a
characteristic explosion of impatience, at once critical,
royal, and sacerdotal: "Ah ! what the Romanization of
American system that P'etch' abury will be ! Will whole
human learned world become the pupil of their corrupted
Siamese teachers ? It is very far from correctness. Why
they did not look in journal of Royal Asiatic Society,
where several words of Sanskrit and Pali were published
continually ? Their Siamese priestly teachers considered
all Europeans as very heathen; to them far from sacred
tongue, and were glad to have American heathens to become their scholars or pupils ; they thought they have
taught sacred language to the part of heathen ; in fact,

they themselves are very far from sacred language, being sunk deeply in corruption of sacred and learned language, for tongue of their former Laos and Cambodian teachers, and very far from knowledge of Hindoostanee, Cinghalese, and Royal Asiatic Society's knowledge in Sanskrit, as they are considered by such the Siamese teachers as heathen; called by them Mit ch'a thi-thi, &c., &c., i. e. wrongly seer or spectator, &c., &c."

In another slip, which is manifestly an outburst of the royal petulance, his Majesty demands, in a "displayed" paragraph : —

" Why name of Mr. Knox [Thomas George Knox, Esq., British Consul] was not published thus : Missa Nok or Nawk. If name of Chow Phya Bhudharabhay is to be thus : P'raya P'oo t'a ra P'ie. And why the London was not published thus : Lundun or Landan, if Bejrepuri is to be published P'etch' abury."

In the same slip with the philological protest the following remarkable paragraphs appear :—

" What has been published in No. 25 of Bangkok Recorder thus : —

" ' The king of Siam, on reading from some European paper that the Pope had lately suffered the loss of some precious jewels, in consequence of a thief having got possession of his Holiness' keys, exclaimed, " What a man ! professing to keep the keys of Heaven, and cannot even keep his own keys ! " ' "

" The king on perusal thereof denied that it is false. He knows nothing about his Holiness the Pope's sustaining loss of gems, &c., and has said nothing about religious faith."

This is curious, in that it exposes the king's unworthy fear of the French priesthood in Siam. The fact is that he did make the rather smart remark, in precisely these words : " Ah ! what a man ! professing to keep the keys of Heaven, and not able to guard those of his own bureau!" and he was quite proud of his hit. But when it appeared in the Recorder, he thought it prudent to bar it with a formal denial. Hence the politic little item which he sent to all the foreigners in Bangkok, and especially to the French priests.

His Majesty's mode of dealing with newspaper strictures (not always just) and suggestions (not always pertinent) aimed at his administration of public affairs, or the constitution and discipline of his household, was characteristic. He snubbed them with sententious arrogance, leavened with sarcasm.

When the Recorder recommended to the king the expediency of dispersing his Solomonic harem, and abolishing polygamy in the royal family, his Majesty retorted with a verbal message to the editor, to the purport that " when the Recorder shall have dissuaded princes and noblemen from offering their daughters to the king as concubines, the king will cease to receive contributions of women in that capacity."

In August, 1865, an angry altercation occurred in the Royal Court of Equity (sometimes styled the International Court) between a French priest and Phya Wiset, a Siamese nobleman, of venerable years, but positive spirit and energy. The priest gave Phya Wiset the lie, and Phya Wiset gave it back to the priest, whereupon the priest became noisy. Afterward he reported the affair to his consul at Bangkok, with the embellishing statement that not only himself, but his religion, had been grossly insulted. The consul, one Monsieur Aubaret, a peppery and pugnacious Frenchman, immediately made a demand upon his Majesty for the removal of Phya Wiset from office.

This despatch was sent late in the evening by the hand of Monsieur Lamarche, commanding the troops at the

Q

royal palace ; and that officer had the consul's order to present it summarily.   Lamarche managed to procure admittance to the penetralia, and presented the note at two o'clock in the morning, in violation of reason and courtesy as well as of rules, excusing himself on the ground that the despatch was important and his orders peremptory.   His Majesty then read the despatch, and remarked that the matter should be disposed of "to-morrow."   Lamarche replied, very presumptuously, that the affair required no investigation, as *he* had heard the offensive language of Phya Wiset, and that person must be deposed without ceremony.   Whereupon his Majesty ordered the offensive foreigner to leave the palace.

Lamarche repaired forthwith to the consul, and reported that the king had spoken disrespectfully, not only of his Imperial Majesty's consul, but of the Emperor himself, besides outrageously insulting a French messenger. Then the fire-eating functionary addressed another despatch to his Majesty, the purport of which was, that, in expelling Lamarche from the palace, the King of Siam had been guilty of a political misdemeanor, and had rudely disturbed the friendly relations existing between France and Siam ; that he should leave Bangkok for Paris, and in six weeks lay his grievance before the Emperor ; but should first proceed to Saigon, and engage the French admiral there to attend to any emergency that might arise in Bangkok.

His Majesty, who knew how to confront the uproar of vulgarity and folly with the repose of wisdom and dignity, sent his own cousin, the Prince Mom Rachoday, Chief Judge of the Royal Court of Equity, to M. Aubaret, to disabuse his mind, and impart to him all the truth of the case.   But the "furious Frank" seized the imposing magnate by the hair, drove him from his door, and flung his betel-box after him, — a reckless impulse

of outrage as monstrous as the most ingenious and deliberate brutality could have devised. Rudely to seize a
Siamese by the hair is an indignity as grave as to spit in
the face of a European ; and the betel-box, beside being
a royal present, was an essential part of the insignia of
the prince's judicial office.

On a later occasion this same Aubaret seized the opportunity a royal procession afforded to provoke the king to
an ill-timed discussion of politics, and to prefer an intemperate complaint against the Kralahome, or prime minister. This characteristic flourish of ill temper and bad
manners, from the representative of the politest of nations, naturally excited lively indignation and disgust
among all respectable dwellers, native or foreign, near the
court, and a serious disturbance was imminent. But a
single dose of the King's English sufficed to soothe the
spasmodic official, and reduce him to "a sense of his situation."

" To the Hon. the Monsieur Aubaret, *the Consul for H. I. M.*

" Sir :—The verbal insult or bad words without any
step more over from lower or lowest person is considered
very slight & inconsiderable.

" The person standing on the surface of the ground or
floor Cannot injure the heavenly bodies or any highly
hanging Lamp or glope by ejecting his spit from his
mouth upward it will only injure his own face without
attempting of Heavenly bodies — &c.

" The Siamese are knowing of being lower than heaven
do not endeavor to injure heavenly bodies with their spit
from mouth.

" A person who is known to be powerless by every one,
as they who have no arms or legs to move oppose or injure or deaf or blind &c. &c. cannot be considered and
said that they are our enemies even for their madness in

vain — it might be considered as easily agitation or uneasiness.

" Persons under strong desires without any limit or acting under illimited anger sometimes cannot be believed
at once without testimony or witness if they stated
against any one verbally from such the statements of the
most desirous or persons most illimitedly angry hesitation
and mild enquiry is very prudent from persons of considerable rank."

No signature.

Never were simplicity with shrewdness, and unconscious humor with pathos, and candor with irony, and
political economy with the sense of an awful bore, more
quaintly blended than in the following extraordinary hint,
written and printed by his Majesty, and freely distributed
for the snubbing of visionary or speculative adventurers :

" NOTICE.

" When the general rumor was and is spread out from
Siam, circulated among the foreigners to Siam, chiefly
Europeans, Chinese, &c, in three points : —

" 1. That Siam is under quite absolute Monarchy.
Whatever her Supreme Sovereign commanded, allowed,
&c all cannot be resisted by any one of his Subjects.

" 2. The Treasury of the Sovereign of Siam, was full
for money, like a mountain of gold and silver ; Her Sovereign most wealthy.

" 3. The present reigning Monarch of Siam is shallow
minded and admirer of almost everything of curiosity,
and most admirer of European usages, customs, sciences,
arts and literature &c, without limit. He is fond of flattering term and ambitious of honor, so that there are now
many opportunities and operations to be embraced for
drawing great money from Royal Treasury of Siam, &c.

" The most many foreigners being under belief of such

general rumour, were endeavoring to draw money from him in various operations, as aluring him with valuable curiosities and expectations of interest, and flattering him, to be glad of them, and deceiving him in various ways; almost on every opportunity of Steamer coming to Siam, various foreigners partly known to him and acquainted with him, and generally unknown to him, boldly wrote to him in such the term of various application and treatment, so that he can conclude that the chief object of all letters written to him, is generally to draw money from him, even unreasonable. Several instances and testimonies can be shown for being example on this subject — the foreigners letters addressed to him, come by every one steamer of Siam, and of foreign steamers visiting Siam; 10 and 12 at least and 40 at highest number, urging him in various ways; so he concluded that foreigners must consider him only as a mad king of a wild land!

"He now states that he cannot be so mad more, as he knows and observes the consideration of the foreigners towards him. Also he now became of old age,* and was very sorry to lose his principal members of his family namely, his two Queens, twice, and his younger brother the late Second King, and his late second son and beloved daughter, and moreover now he fear of sickness of his eldest son, he is now unhappy and must solicit his friends in correspondence and others who please to write for the foresaid purpose, that they should know suitable reason in writing to him, and shall not urge him as they would urge a madman! And the general rumours forementioned are some exaggerated and some entirely false; they shall not believe such the rumours, deeply and ascertainedly.

"ROYAL RESIDENCE GRAND PALACE
    BANGKOK 2nd July 1867."

      * He was sixty-two at this time.

And now observe with what gracious ease this most astute and discriminating prince could fit his tone to the sense of those who, familiar with his opinions, and reconciled to his temper and his ways, however peculiar, could reciprocate the catholicity of his sympathies, and appreciate his enlightened efforts to fling off that tenacious old-man-of-the-sea custom, and extricate himself from the predicament of conflicting responsibilities. To these, on the Christian New Year's day of 1867, he addressed this kindly greeting : —

" S. P. P. M. Mongkut :

    " Called in Siamese ' P'hra-Chomklau chao-yuhua,' in Magadhi or language of Pali ' Siamikanam Maha Rajah,' In Latin ' Rex Siamensium,' In French ' Le Roi de Siam,' In English ' The King of Siam,' and in Malayan ' Rajah Maha Pasah ' &c.

    " Begs to present his respectful and regardful compliments and congratulations in happy lives during immediately last year, and wishes the continuing thereof during the commencing New Year, and ensuing and succeeding many years, to his foreign friends, both now in Siam namely, the functionary and acting Consuls and consular officers of various distinguished nations in Treaty Power with Siam and certain foreign persons under our salary, in service in any manner here, and several Gentlemen and Ladies who are resident in Siam in various stations : namely, the Priests, Preachers of religion, Masters and Mistresses of Schools, Workmen and Merchants, &c, and now abroad in various foreign countries and ports, who are our noble and common friends, acquainted either by ever having had correspondences mutually with us some time, at any where and remaining in our friendly remembrance or mutual remembrance, and whosoever are in service to us as our Consuls, vice consuls and consular assistants, in various foreign ports. Let them know our remembrance and good wishes toward them all.

" Though we are not Christians, the forenamed King was glad to arrive this day in his valued life, as being the 22,720th day of his age, during which he was aged sixty-two years and three months, and being the 5,711th day of his reign, during which he reigned upon his kingdom 15 years and 8 months up to the current month.

" In like manner he was very glad to see & know and hope for all his Royal Family, kindred and friends of both native and foreign, living near and far to him had arrived to this very remarkable anniversary of the commencement of Solar Year in Anno Christi 1867.

" In their all being healthy and well living like himself, he begs to express his royal congratulation and respect and graceful regards to all his kindred friends both native and foreign, and hopes to receive such the congratulation and expression of good wishes toward him and members of his family in very like manner, as he trusts that the amity and grace to one another of every of human beings who are innocent, is a great merit, and is righteous and praiseworthy in religious system of all civil religion, and best civilized laws and morality, &c.

" Given at the Royal Audience Hall, ' Anant Samagome,' Grand Palace, Bangkok," etc., etc.

The remoter provinces of Siam constitute a source of continual anxiety and much expense to the government ; and to his Majesty (who, very conscious of power, was proud to be able to say that the Malayan territories and rajahs — Cambodia, with her marvellous cities, palaces, and temples, once the stronghold of Siam's most formidable and implacable foes; the Laos country, with its warlike princes and chiefs — were alike dependencies and tribu-

taries of his crown) it was intolerably irritating to find
Cambodia rebellious. So long as his government could
successfully maintain its supremacy there, that country
formed a sort of neutral ground between his people and
the Cochin-Chinese; a geographical condition which was
not without its political advantages. But now the unscrupulous French had strutted upon the scene, and with
a flourish of diplomacy and a stroke of the pen appropriated to themselves the fairest portion of that most fertile
province. His Majesty, though secretly longing for the
intervention and protection of England, was deterred by
his almost superstitious fear of the French from complain-
ing openly. But whenever he was more than commonly
annoyed by the pretensions and aggressive epistles of his
Imperial Majesty's consul he sent for me, — thinking,
like all Orientals, that, being English, my sympathy for
him, and my hatred of the French, were jointly a fore-
gone conclusion. When I would have assured him that
I was utterly powerless to help him, he cut me short with
a wise whisper to " consult Mr. Thomas George Knox ";
and when I protested that that gentleman was too honorable to engage in a secret intrigue against a colleague,
even for the protection of British interests in Siam, he
would rave at my indifference, the cupidity of the French,
the apathy of the English, and the fatuity of all geographers in " setting down " the form of government in Siam
as an " absolute monarchy."

" *I* an absolute monarch ! For I have no power over
French. Siam is like a mouse before an elephant ! Am
I an absolute monarch ? What shall *you* consider me ? "

Now, as I considered him a particularly absolute and
despotic king, that was a trying question ; so I discreetly
held my peace, fearing less to be classed with those obnoxious savans who compile geographies than to provoke
him afresh.

"I have no power," he scolded; "I am not absolute! If I point the end of my walking-stick at a man whom, being my enemy, I wish to die, he does not die, but lives on, in spite of my 'absolute' will to the contrary. What does Geographies mean? How can I be an absolute monarchy?"

Such a conversation we were having one day as he "assisted" at the founding of a temple; and while he reproached his fate that he was powerless to "point the end of his walking-stick" with absolute power at the peppery and presumptuous Monsieur Aubaret, he vacantly flung gold and silver coins among the work-women.

In another moment he forgot all French encroachments, and the imbecility of geographers in general, as his glance chanced to fall upon a young woman of fresh and striking beauty, and delightful piquancy of ways and expression, who with a clumsy club was pounding fragments of pottery — urns, vases, and goglets — for the foundation of the *watt*. Very artless and happy she seemed, and free as she was lovely; but the instant she perceived she had attracted the notice of the king, she sank down and hid her face in the earth, forgetting or disregarding the falling vessels that threatened to crush or wound her. But the king merely diverted himself with inquiring her name and parentage; and some one answering for her, he turned away.

Almost to the latest hour of his life his Majesty suffered, in his morbid egotism, various and keen annoyance, by reason of his sensitiveness to the opinions of foreigners, the encroachments of foreign officials, and the strictures of the foreign press. He was agitated by a restless craving for their sympathy on the one hand, and by a futile resentment of their criticisms or their claims on the other.

An article in a Singapore paper had administered moral

12

correction to his Majesty on the strength of a rumor that
" the king has his eye upon another princess of the highest rank, with a view to constituting her a queen consort."
And the Bangkok Recorder had said : " Now, considering
that he is full threescore and three years of age, that he
has already scores of concubines and about fourscore sons
and daughters, with several Chowfas among them, and
hence eligible to the highest posts of honor in the kingdom, this rumor seems too monstrous to be credited.   But
the truth is, there is scarcely anything too monstrous for
the royal polygamy of Siam to bring forth."   By the light
of this explanation the meaning of the following extract
from the postscript of a letter which the king wrote in
April, 1866, will be clear to the reader, who, at the same
time, in justice to me, will remember that, by the death
of his Majesty, on the 1st of October, 1868, the seal of
secrecy was broken.

"Very Private Post Script.

" There is a newspaper of Singapore entitled Daily
News just published after last arrival of the steamer
Chowphya in Singapore, in which paper, a correspondence
from an Individual resident at Bangkok dated 16th March
1866 was shown.   but I have none of that paper in my
possession. . . . . I did not noticed its number & date to
state to you now, but I trust such the paper must be in
hand of several foreigners in Bangkok, may you have read
it perhaps — other wise you can obtain the same from
any one or by order to obtain from Singapore ; after perusal thereof you will not be able to deny my statement
forementioned more over as general people both native &
foreigners here seem to have less pleasure on me & my
descendant, than their pleasure and hope on other amiable
family to them until the present day.

" What was said there in for a princess considered by

the Speaker or Writer as proper or suitable to be head
on my *harem* (a room or part for confinement of Women
of Eastern monarch *) there is no least intention occurred
to me even once or in my dream indeed! I think if I do
so, I will die soon perhaps!

.   .   .   .   .

"This my handwriting or content hereof shall be kept
secretly.

"I beg to remain

"Your faithful & well-wisher

"S. P. P. M. MONGKUT R. S.

" on 5441th day of reign.

"the writer here of beg to place his confidence on you
alway."

As a true friend to his Majesty, I deplore the weakness
which betrayed him into so transparent a sham of virtuous indignation. The "princess of the highest rank,"
whom the writer of the article plainly meant, was the
Princess of Chiengmai; but from lack of accurate infor-
mation he was misled into confounding her with the
Princess Tui Duang Prabha, his Majesty's niece. The
king could honestly deny any such intention on his part
with regard to his niece; but, at the same time, he well
knew that the writer erred only as to the individual, and
not as to the main fact of the case. The Princess of
Chiengmai was the wife, and the Princess Tui Duang
the daughter, of his full brother, the Second King, lately
deceased.

Much more agreeable is it — to the reader, I doubt not,
not less than to the writer — to turn from the king, in
the exercise of his slavish function of training honest
words to play the hypocrite for ignoble thoughts, to the

---

* A parenthetical drollery inspired by the dictionary.

gentleman, the friend, the father, giving his heart a holiday in the relaxations of simple kindness and free affection, — as in the following note : —

" Dated RANCHAUPURY 34th February 1865.
" To LADY L—— & HER SON LUISE, *Bangkok.*

"'We having very pleasant journey . . . . to be here which is a township called as above named by men of republick affairs in Siam, & called by common people as ' Parkphrieck ' where we have our stay a few days. & will take our departure from hence at dawn of next day. We thinking of you. both regardfully & beg to send here with some wild aples & barries which are delicate for tasting & some tobacco which were and are principal product of this region for your kind acceptance hoping this wild present will be acceptable to you both.

" We will be arrived at our home Bangkok on early part of March.

" We beg to remain
" Your faithful
" S. P. P. M. MONGKUT R. S.
" in 5035th day of reign.

" And your affectionate pupils

"YING YULACKS.   MANEABHADAHORN.
SOMDETCH CHOWFA CHULALONKORN.* KRITAHINIHAR.
PRABHASSOR.   SOMAWATI."

* The present king.

XXVII.

MY RETIREMENT FROM THE PALACE.

IN 1864 I found that my labors had greatly increased;
I had often to work till ten o'clock at night to accomplish the endless translations required of me. I also began to perceive how continually and closely I was watched, but how and by whom it seemed impossible to discover. Among the inducements to me to accept the position of teacher to the royal family was his Majesty's assurance, that, if I gave satisfaction, he would increase my salary after a year's trial. Nearly three years had passed when I first ventured to remind the king of this promise. To my astonishment he bluntly informed me that I had *not* given satisfaction, that I was " difficult " and unmanageable, "more careful about what was right and what was wrong than for the obedience and submission." And as to salary, he continued: "Why you should be poor ? You come into my presence every day with some petition, some case of hardship or injustice, and you demand ' your Majesty shall most kindly investigate, and cause redress to be made '; and I have granted to you because you are important to me for translations, and so forth. And now you declare you must have increase of salary ! Must you have everything in this world ? Why you do not make *them* pay you ? If I grant you all your petition for the poor, you ought to be rich, or you have no wisdom."

At a loss what answer to make to this very unsympa-

thetic view of my conduct, I quietly returned to my
duties, which grew daily in variety and responsibility.
What with translating, correcting, copying, dictating,
reading, I had hardly a moment I could call my own;
and if at any time I rebelled, I brought down swift ven-
geance on the head of the helpless native secretary.

But it was my consolation to know that I could befriend
the women and children of the palace, who, when they saw
that I was not afraid to oppose the king in his more outrageous caprices of tyranny, imagined me endued with
supernatural powers, and secretly came to me with their
grievances, in full assurance that sooner or later I would see
them redressed.   And so, with no intention on my part,
and almost without my own consent, I suffered myself to
be set up between the oppressor and the oppressed.   From
that time I had no peace.   Day after day I was called upon
to resist the wanton cruelty of judges and magistrates,
till at last I found myself at feud with the whole " San
Luang."   In cases of torture, imprisonment, extortion, I
tried again and again to excuse myself from interfering,
but still the mothers or sisters prevailed, and I had no
choice left but to try to help them.   Sometimes I sent
Boy with my clients, sometimes I went myself ; and in no
single instance was justice granted from a sense of right,
but always through fear of my supposed influence with
the king.   My Siamese and European friends said I was
amassing a fortune.   It seemed not worth my while to
contradict them, though the inference was painful to me,
for in truth my championship was not purely disinter-
ested ; I suffered from continual contact with the sufferings of others, and came to the rescue in self-defence and
in pity for myself not less than for them.

A Chinaman had been cruelly murdered and robbed by
a favorite slave in the household of the prime minister's
brother, leaving the brother, wife, and children of the vic-

tim in helpless poverty and terror. The murderer had screened himself and his accomplices by sharing the plunder with his master. The widow cried for redress in vain. The ears of magistrates were stopped against her, and she was too poor to pay her way ; but still she went from one court to another, until her importunity irritated the judges, who, to intimidate her, seized her eldest son; on some monstrous pretext, and cast him into prison. This double cruelty completed the despair of the unhappy mother. She came to me fairly frenzied, and " commanded " me to go at once into the presence of the king and demand her stolen child ; and then, in a sudden paroxysm of grief, she embraced my knees, wailing, and praying to me to help her. It was not in human nature to reject that maternal claim. With no little trouble I procured the liberation of her son ; but to keep him out of harm's way I had to take him into my own home and change his name. I called him Timothy, which by a Chinese abbreviation became Ti.

When I went with this woman and the brother of the murdered man to the palace of the premier, we found that distinguished personage half naked and playing chess. Seeing me enter, he ordered one of his slaves to bring him a jacket, into which he thrust his arms, and went on with the game; and not until that was finished did he attend to me. When I explained my errand he seemed vexed, but sent for his brother, had a long talk with him, and concluded by warning my unhappy *protégés* that if he heard any more complaints from them they should be flogged. Then turning to me with a grim smile, he said : " Chinee too much bother. Good by, sir ! "

This surprised me exceedingly, for I had often known the premier to award justice in spite of the king. That same evening, as I sat alone in my drawing-room, making notes, as was my custom, I heard a slight noise, as of some one in the room.   Looking round, I saw, to my amazement, one of the inferior judges of the prime minister's court crouching by the piano.   I asked how he dared to enter my house unannounced.   " Mam," said he, " your servants admitted me ; they know from whom I come, and would not venture to refuse me.   And now it is for you to know that I am here from his Excellency Chow Phya Krala-home, to request you to send in your resignation at the end of this month."

" By what authority does he send me this message ? " I asked.

" I know not ; but it were best that you obey."

" Tell him," I replied, unable to control my anger at the cowardly trick to intimidate me, " I shall leave Siam when I please, and that no man shall set the time for me."

The man departed, cringing and crouching, and excusing himself.   This was the same wretch at whose instigation poor Moonshee had been so shamefully beaten.

I did not close my eyes that night.   Again and again prudence advised me to seek safety in flight, but the argument ended in my turning my back on the timid monitor, and resolving to stay.

About three weeks after this occurrence, his Majesty was going on an excursion " up country," and as he wished me to accompany my pupils, the prime minister was required to prepare a cabin for me and my boy on his steamer, the Volant.   Before we left the palace one of my anxious friends made me promise her that I would partake of no food nor taste a drop of wine on board the steamer, — an injunction in the sequel easy to fulfil, as our wants were amply provided for at the Grand Palace, where we spent the whole day.   But I cite this incident to show the state of mind which led me to prolong my stay, hateful as it had become.

After this, affairs in the royal household went smoothly

enough for some time ; but still my tasks increased, and my health began to fail. When I informed his Majesty that I needed at least a month of rest, and that I thought of making a trip to Singapore, he was so unwilling that I should rate highly the services I rendered him, that he was careful to assure me I had not "favored" him in any way, nor given him satisfaction ; and that if I must be idle for a month, he certainly should not pay me for the time ; and he kept his word. Nevertheless, while I was at Singapore he wrote to me most kindly, assuring me that his wives and children were anxious for my return.

After the sad death of the dear little princess, Chow Fâ-ying, the king had become more cordial ; but the labor he imposed upon me was in proportion to the confidence he reposed in me. At times he required of me services, in my capacity of secretary, not to be thought of by a European sovereign ; and when I declined to perform them, he would curse me, close the gates of the palace against me, and even subject me to the insults and threats of the parasites and slaves who crawled about his feet. On two occasions — first for refusing to write a false letter to Sir John Bowring, now Plenipotentiary for the Court of Siam in England ; and again for declining to address the Earl of Clarendon in relation to a certain British officer then in Siam — he threatened to have me tried at the British Consulate, and was so violent that I was in real fear for my life. For three days I waited, with doors and windows barred, for I knew not what explosion.

After the death of the Second King, his Majesty behaved very disgracefully. It was well known that the ladies of the prince's harem were of the most beautiful of the women of Laos, Pegu, and Birmah ; above all, the Princess of Chiengmai was famed for her manifold graces of person and character. Etiquette forbade the royal brothers to pry into the constitution of each other's *sérail*, but by means most unworthy of his station, and regardless of the privilege of his brother, Maha Mongkut had learned of the acquisition to the subordinate king's establishment of this celebrated and coveted beauty; and although she was now his legitimate sister-in-law, privately married to the prince, he was not restrained by any scruple of morality or delicacy from manifesting his jealousy and pique.* Moreover, this disgraceful feeling was fostered by other considerations than those of mere sensuality or ostentation. Her father, the tributary ruler of Chiengmai, had on several occasions confronted his aggressive authority with a haughty and intrepid spirit; and once, when Maha Mongkut required that he should send his eldest son to Bangkok as a hostage for the father's loyalty and good conduct, the unterrified chief replied that he would be his own hostage. On the summons being repeated in imperative terms, the young prince fled from his father's court and took refuge with the Second King in his stronghold of Ban Sitha, where he was most courteously received and entertained until he found it expedient to seek some securer or less compromising place of refuge.

The friendship thus founded between two proud and daring princes soon became strong and enduring, and resulted in the marriage of the Princess Sunartha Vismita (very willingly on her part) to the Second King, about a year before his death.

The son of the King of Chiengmai never made his appearance at the court of Siam; but the stout old chief, attended by trusty followers, boldly brought his own "hostage" thither; and Maha Mongkut, though secretly chafing, accepted the situation with a show of graciousness, and overlooked the absence of the younger vassal.

* See portrait, Chap. XXV.

With the remembrance of these floutings still galling him, the Supreme King frequently repaired to the Second King's palace on the pretext of arranging certain "family affairs" intrusted to him by his late brother, but in reality to acquaint himself with the charms of several female members of the prince's household; and, scandalous as it should have seemed even to Siamese notions of the divine right of kings, the most attractive and accomplished of those women were quietly transferred to his own harem. For some time I heard nothing more of the Princess of Chiengmai; but it was curious, even amusing, to observe the serene contempt with which the "interlopers" were received by the rival incumbents of the royal gynecium, — especially the Laotian women, who are of a finer type and much handsomer than their Siamese sisters.

Meantime his Majesty took up his abode for a fortnight at the Second King's palace, thereby provoking dangerous gossip in his own establishment; so that his "head wife," the Lady Thieng, even made bold to hint that he might come to the fate of his brother, and die by slow poison. His harem was agitated and excited throughout, — some of the women abandoning themselves to unaccustomed and unnatural gayety, while others sent their confidential slaves to consult the astrologers and soothsayers of the court; and by the aid of significant glances and shrugging of shoulders, and interchange of signs and whispers, with feminine telegraphy and secret service, most of those interested arrived at the sage conclusion that their lord had fallen under the spells of a witch or enchantress.

ᐧSuch was the domestic situation when his Majesty suddenly and without warning returned to his palace, but in a mood so perplexing as to surpass all precedent and baffle all tact. I had for some time performed with surprising success a leading part in a pretty little court play,

of which the well-meant plot had been devised by the
Lady Thieng. Whenever the king should be dangerously
enraged, and ready to let loose upon some tender culprit
of the harem the monstrous lash or chain, I — at a secret
cue from the head wife — was to enter upon his Majesty,
book in hand, to consult his infallibility in a pressing
predicament of translation into Sanskrit, Siamese, or
English. Absurdly transparent as it was, — perhaps the
happier for its very childishness, — under cover of this
naive device from time to time a hapless girl escaped the
fatal burst of his wrath. Midway in the rising storm of
curses and abuse he would turn with comical abruptness
to the attractive interruption with all the zest of a
scholar. I often trembled lest he should see through the
thinly covered trick, but he never did. On his return
from the prince's palace, however, even this innocent
stratagem failed us; and on one occasion of my having
recourse to it he peremptorily ordered me away, and forbade my coming into his presence again unless sent for.
Daily, after this, one or more of the women suffered from
his petty tyranny, cruelty, and spite. On every hand I
heard sighs and sobs from young and old; and not a
woman there but believed he was bewitched and beside
himself.

I had struggled through many exacting tasks since I
came to Siam, but never any that so taxed my powers of
endurance as my duties at this time, in my double office
of governess and private secretary to his Majesty. His
moods were so fickle and unjust, his temper so tyrannical,
that it seemed impossible to please him; from one hour
to another I never knew what to expect. And yet he
persevered in his studies, especially in his English correspondence, which was ever his solace, his pleasure, and
his pride. To an interested observer it might have afforded rare entertainment to note how fluently, though

oddly, he spoke and wrote in a foreign language, but for his caprices, which at times were so ridiculous, however, as to be scarcely disagreeable. He would indite letters, sign them, affix his seal, and despatch them in his own mail-bags to Europe, America, or elsewhere ; and, months afterward, insist on my writing to the parties addressed, to say that the instructions they contained were *my* mistake, — errors of translation, transcription, anything but his intention. In one or two instances, finding that the case really admitted of explanation or apology from his Majesty, I slyly so worded my letter, that, without compromising him, I yet managed to repair the mischief he had done. But I felt this could not continue long. Always, on foreign-mail days, I spent from eight to ten hours in this most delicate and vexatious work. At length the crash came.

The king had promised to Sir John Bowring the appointment of Plenipotentiary to the Court of France, to negotiate, on behalf of Siam, new treaties concerning the Cambodian possessions. With characteristic irresolution he changed his mind, and decided to send a Siamese Embassy, headed by his Lordship P'hra Nah Why, now known as his Excellency Chow Phya Sri Sury-wongse. No sooner had he entertained this fancy than he sent for me, and coolly directed me to write and explain the matter to Sir John, if possible attributing his new views and purpose to the advice of her Britannic Majesty's Consul ; or, if I had scruples on that head, I might say the advice was my own, — or "anything I liked," so that I justified his conduct.

At this distance of time I cannot clearly recall all the effect upon my feelings of so outrageous a proposition ; but I do remember that I found myself emphatically declining to do "anything of the kind." Then, warned by his gathering rage, I added that I would express to Sir

John his Majesty's regrets, but to attribute the blame to those who had had no part in the matter, that I could never do. At this his fury was grotesque. His talent for invective was always formidable, and he tried to overpower me with threats. But a kindred spirit of resistance was aroused in me. I withdrew from the palace, and patiently abided the issue, resolved, in any event, to be firm.

His Majesty's anger was without bounds; and in the interval so fraught with anxiety and apprehension to me, when I knew that a considerable party in the palace — judges, magistrates, and officers about the person of the king — regarded me as an eminently proper person to behead or drown, he condescended to accuse me of abstracting a book that he chanced just then to miss from his library, and also of honoring and favoring the British Consul at the expense of his American colleague, then resident at Bangkok. In support of the latter charge, he alleged that I had written the American Consul's name at the bottom of a royal circular, after carefully displaying my own and the British functionary's at the top of it.

The circular in question, which had given just umbrage to the American official, was fortunately in the keeping of the Honorable * Mr. Bush, and was written by the king's own hand, as was well known to all whom it concerned. These charges, with others of a more frivolous nature, — such as disobeying, thwarting, scolding his Majesty, treating him with disrespect, as by standing while he was seated, thinking evil of him, slandering him, and calling him wicked, — the king caused to be reduced to writing and sent to me, with an intimation that I must forthwith acknowledge my ingratitude and guilt, and make atonement by prompt compliance with his wishes. The secretary who brought the document to my house was accompanied by a number of the female slaves of the pal-

* Here the title is Siamese.

ace, who besought me, in the name of their mistresses, the wives of the " Celestial Supreme," to yield, and do all that might be required of me.

Seeing this shaft miss its mark, the secretary, being a man of resources, produced the other string to his bow. He offered to bribe me, and actually spent two hours in that respectable business ; but finally departed in despair, convinced that the amount was inadequate to the cupidity of an insatiable European, and mourning for himself that he must return discomfited to the king.

Next morning, my boy and I presented ourselves as usual at the inner gate of the palace leading to the school, and were confronted there by a party of rude fellows and soldiers, who thrust us back with threats, and even took up stones to throw at us. I dare not think what might have been our fate, but for the generous rescue of a crowd of the poorest slaves, who at that hour were waiting for the opening of the gate. These rallied round us, and guarded us back to our home. It was, indeed, a time of terror for us. I felt that my life was in great danger ; and so difficult did I find it to prevent the continual intrusion of the rabble, both men and women, into my house, that I had at length to bar my doors and windows, and have double locks and fastenings added. I became nervous and excited as I had never been before.

My first impulse was to write to the British Consul and invoke his protection ; but that looked cowardly. Nevertheless, I did prepare the letter, ready to be despatched at the first attempt upon our lives or liberty. I wrote also to Mr. Bush, asking him to find without delay the obnoxious circular, and bring it to my house. He came that very evening, the paper in his hand. With infinite difficulty I persuaded the native secretary, whom I had again and again befriended in like extremities, to procure for him an audience with the king.

On coming into the presence of his Majesty, Mr. Bush simply handed him the circular, saying, "Mam tells me you wish to see this." The moment the caption of the document met his eye, his Majesty's countenance assumed a blank, bewildered expression peculiar to it, and he seemed to look to my friend for an explanation ; but that gentleman had none to offer, for I had made none to him.

And to crown all, even as the king was pointing to his brow to signify that he had forgotten having written it, one of the little princesses came crouching and crawling into the room with the missing volume in her hand. It had been found in one of the numerous sleeping-apartments of the king, beside his pillow, just in time !

Mr. Bush soon returned, bringing me assurances of his Majesty's cordial reconciliation ; but I still doubted his sincerity, and for weeks did not offer to enter the palace. When, however, on the arrival of the Chow Phya steamer with the mail, I was formally summoned by the king to return to my duties, I quietly obeyed, making no allusion to my " bygones."

As I sat at my familiar table, copying, his Majesty approached, and addressed me in these words : —

"Mam ! you are one great difficulty. I have much pleasure and favor on you, but you are too obstinate. You are not wise. Wherefore are you so difficult ? You are only a woman. It is very bad you can be so strong-headed. Will you now have any objection to write to Sir John, and tell him I am his very good friend ?"

"None whatever," I replied, "if it is to be simply a letter of good wishes on the part of your Majesty."

I wrote the letter, and handed it to him for perusal. He was hardly satisfied, for with only a significant grunt he returned it to me, and left the apartment at once, — to vent his spite on some one who had nothing to do with the matter.

In due time the following very considerate but significant reply (addressed to his Majesty's " one great difficulty ") was received from Sir John Bowring : —

CLAREMONT, EXETER, 30 June, 1867.

DEAR MADAM : — Your letter of 12th May demands from me the attention of a courteous reply. I am quite sure the ancient friendship of the King of Siam would never allow a slight, or indeed an unkindness, to me ; and I hope to have opportunities of showing his Majesty that I feel a deep interest in his welfare.

As regards the diplomacy of European courts, it is but natural that those associated with them should be more at home, and better able to direct their course, than strangers from a distance, however personally estimable ; and though, in the case in question, the mission of a Siamese Ambassador to Paris was no doubt well intended, and could never have been meant to give me annoyance, it was not to be expected he would be placed in that position of free and confidential intercourse which my long acquaintance with public life would enable me to occupy. In remote regions, people with little knowledge of official matters in high quarters often take upon themselves to give advice in great ignorance of facts, and speak very unadvisedly on topics on which their opinions are worthless and their influence valueless.

As regards M. Aubaret's offensive proceedings, I doubt not he has received a caution * on my representation, and that he, and others of his nation, would not be very willing that the Emperor — an old acquaintance of mine — should hear from my lips what I might have to say. The will of the Emperor is supreme, and I am afraid the Cambodian question is now referred back to Siam. It

* Aubaret, French Consul at Bangkok, whose overbearing conduct has been described elsewhere.

might have been better for me to have discussed it with his Imperial Majesty. However, the past is past. Personal influence, as you are aware, is not transferable ; but when by the proper powers I am placed in a position to act, his Majesty may be assured — as I have assured himself — that his interests will not suffer in my hands.

I am obliged to you for the manner in which you have conveyed to me his Majesty's gracious expressions

And you will believe me to be

Yours very truly,

JOHN BOWRING.

No friend of mine knew at that time how hard it was for me to bear up, in the utter loneliness and forlornness of my life, under the load of cares and provocations and fears that gradually accumulated upon me.

But ah ! if any germ of love and truth fell from my heart into the heart of even the meanest of those wives and concubines and children of a king, if by any word of mine the least of them was won to look up, out of the depths of their miserable life, to a higher, clearer, brighter light than their Buddha casts upon their path, then indeed I did not labor in vain among them.

In the summer of 1866 my health suddenly broke down, and for a time, it was thought that I must die. When good Dr. Campbell gave me the solemn warning all my trouble seemed to cease, and but for one sharp pang for my children, — one in England, the other in Siam, — I should have derived pure and perfect pleasure from the prospect of eternal rest, so weary was I of my tumultuous life in the East ; and though in the end I regained my strength in a measure, I was no longer able to comply with the pitiless exactions of the king. And so, yielding to the urgent entreaties of my friends, I decided to return to England.

It took me half a year to get his Majesty's consent; and it was not without tiresome accusations of ingratitude and idleness that he granted me leave of absence for six months.

I had hardly courage to face the women and children the day I told them I was going away. It was hard to be with them; but it seemed cowardly to leave them. For some time most of them refused to believe that I was really going; but when they could doubt no longer, they displayed the most touching tenderness and thoughtfulness. Many sent me small sums of money to help me on the journey. The poorest and meanest slaves brought me rice cakes, dried beans, cocoanuts, and sugar. It was in vain that I assured them I could not carry such things away with me; still the supplies poured in.

The king himself, who had been silent and sullen until the morning of my departure, relented when the time came to say good by. He embraced Boy with cordial kindness, and gave him a silver buckle, and a bag containing a hundred dollars to buy sweetmeats on the way. Then turning to me, he said (as if forgetting himself): "Mam! you much beloved by our common people, and all inhabitants of palace and royal children. Every one is in affliction of your departure; and even that opium-eating secretary, P'hra-Alâck, is very low down in his heart because you *will* go. It shall be because you must be a good and true lady. I am often angry on you, and lose my temper, though I have large respect for you. But nevertheless you ought to know you are difficult woman, and more difficult than generality. But you will forget, and come back to my service, for I have more confidence on you every day. Good by!" I could not reply; my eyes filled with tears.

Then came the parting with my pupils, the women and the children. That was painful enough, even while the king was present; but when he abruptly withdrew, great was the uproar. What could I do, but stand still and submit to kisses, embraces, reproaches, from princesses and slaves? At last I rushed through the gate, the women screaming after me, "Come back!" and the children, "Don't go!" I hurried to the residence of the heir-apparent, to the most trying scene of all. His regret seemed too deep for words, and the few he did utter were very touching. Taking both my hands and laying his brow upon them, he said, after a long interval of silence, "*Mam cha klap ma thort!*" — "Mam dear, come back, please!" "Keep a brave and true heart, my prince!" was all that I could say; and my last "God bless *you!*" was addressed to the royal palace of Siam.

To this young prince, Chowfa Chulalonkorn, I was strongly attached. He often deplored with me the cruelty with which the slaves were treated, and, young as he was, did much to inculcate kindness toward them among his immediate attendants. He was a conscientious lad, of pensive habit and gentle temper; many of my poor clients I bequeathed to his care, particularly the Chinese lad Ti. Speaking of slavery one day, he said to me: "These are not slaves, but nobles; they know how to bear. It is we, the princes, who have yet to learn which is the more noble, the oppressor or the oppressed."

When I left the palace the king was fast failing in body and mind, and, in spite of his seeming vigor, there was no real health in his rule, while he had his own way. All the substantial success we find in his administration is due to the ability and energy of his accomplished premier, Phya Kralahome, and even his strength has been wasted. The native arts and literature have retrograded; in the mechanic arts much has been lost; and the whole nation is given up to gambling.

The capacity of the Siamese race for improvement in

any direction has been sufficiently demonstrated, and the government has made fair progress in political and moral reforms; but the condition of the slaves is such as to excite astonishment and horror. What may be the ultimate fate of Siam under this accursed system, whether she will ever emancipate herself while the world lasts, there is no guessing. The happy examples free intercourse affords, the influence of European ideas, and the compulsion of public opinion, may yet work wonders.

On the 5th of July, 1867, we left Bangkok in the steamer Chow Phya. All our European friends accompanied us to the Gulf of Siam, where we parted, with much regret on my side; and of all those whose kindness had bravely cheered us during our long (I am tempted to write) *captivity*, the last to bid us God-speed was the good Captain Orton, to whom I here tender my heartfelt thanks.

XXVIII.

THE KINGDOM OF SIAM.

WITH her despotic ruler, priest and king; her religion of contradictions, at once pure and corrupt,
lovely and cruel, ennobling and debasing; her laws,
wherein wisdom is so perversely blended with blindness,
enlightenment with barbarism, strength with weakness,
justice with oppression; her profound scrutiny into mystic forms of philosophy, her ancient culture of physics,
borrowed from the primitive speculations of Brahminism;
— Siam is, beyond a peradventure, one of the most remarkable and thought-compelling of the empires of the Orient;
a fascinating and provoking enigma, alike to the theo-
logian and the political economist. Like a troubled dream,
delirious in contrast with the coherence and stability of
Western life, the land and its people seem to be conjured
out of a secret of darkness, a wonder to the senses and a
mystery to the mind.

And yet it is a strangely beautiful reality. The enchanting variety of its scenery, joined to the inexhaustible productiveness of its soil, constitutes a challenge to
the charms of every other region, except, perhaps, the
country watered by the great river of China. Through
an immense, continuous level of unfailing fertility, the
Meinam rolls slowly, reposefully, grandly, in its course
receiving draughts from many a lesser stream, filling
many a useful canal in its turn, and, from the abundance

the generous rains bestow, distributing supplies of refreshment and fatness to innumerable acres.

In a soil at once so rich and so well watered, the sun, with its vivifying heats, engenders a mighty vegetation, delighting the eye for more than half the year with endless undulations of grain and a great golden Eden of fruit. Its staples are solid blessings: rice, the Asiatic's staff of life; sugar, most popular of dietetic luxuries; indigo, most valuable of dyes; in the drier tracts, cotton, tobacco, coffee, a variety of palms (from one species of which sugar not unlike that of the maple is extracted), the wild olive, and the fig. Then there are vast forests of teak, that enduring monarch of the vegetable kingdom, ebony, satin-wood, eagle-wood; beside ivory, beeswax and honey, raw silk, and many aromatic gums and fragrant spices. And though the scenery is less various and picturesque than that of the regions of Gangetic India, where ranges of noble mountains make the land majestic, nevertheless nature riots here in bewildering luxuriances of vegetable forms and colors. Vast tracts, shady and cool with dense dark foliage; trees, tall and strong, spreading their giant arms abroad, with prickly, shining shrubs between, while parasites and creepers, wild, bright, and beautiful, trail from the highest boughs to the ground; the bamboo, shooting to the height of sixty feet and upward, with branches gracefully drooping; the generous, kind banana; fairy forests of ferns of a thousand forms; tall grasses, with their pale and plumy blossoms; the many-trunked and many-rooted banyan; the boh, sacred to Buddha,— all combine to form a garden that Adam might have dressed and kept, and only Eve could spoil.

It is only when he approaches the borders of the land that the traveller is greeted by grand mountains, crowned with impenetrable forests, and forming an amphitheatre around the graceful plains. Along the coast the view is more diversified; islands, the most picturesque, and rich with diversified vegetation, make happy, striking contrasts, here and there, with the deep blue sea around them.

The extent and boundaries of the kingdom and its dependencies have been variously described; but according to the statement of his Majesty Maha Mongkut, the dominion of his predecessors, before the possession of Malacca by the Portuguese, extended over the whole of the Malayan peninsula, including the islands of Singapore and Pinang, which at that time formed a part of the realm of the Rajah of Quedah, who still pays tribute to the crown of Siam. It was at the instigation of English settlers that the states of Johore, Singapore, Rambo, Talangore, Pahang, and Puah became subject to British rule; so that to-day the Siamese dominion, starting from the little kingdom of Tringamu, extends from the fourth to the twenty-second degree of north latitude, giving about 1,350 miles of length, while from east to west its greatest breadth is about 450 miles. On the north it is bounded by several provinces of Laos, tributaries of Ava and China; on the east by the empire of Anam; on the west by the sea and British possessions; on the south by the petty states of Pahang and Puah. Beyond Siam proper are the kingdom of Ligor and the four small states, Quedah, Patan, Calantan, and Yeingana; on the east a part of the kingdom of Cambodia, Muang Korat, and several provinces of Laos; on the north the kingdoms of Chiengmai, Laphun, Lakhon, Muang Phiëë, Muang Naun, Muang Loan, and Luang Phrabang. The great plain of Siam is bounded on the east by a spur of the Himalayan range, which breaks off in Cambodia, and is found again in the west, extending almost to the extremity of the Malayan states on the north these two mountain ranges approach each other, and form that multitude of small hills which imparts so picturesque an aspect to the Laos country. This plain is watered by the river Meinam,* or Chow Phya, whose innumerable branches, great and small, and the many canals which, fed by it, intersect the capital in all directions, constitute it the high-road of the Empire. For many miles its banks are fringed with the graceful bamboo, the tamarind, the palm, and the peepul, the homes of myriads of birds of the land and of the water, — creatures of brilliant plumage and delightful song.

Siam has some excellent harbors, though the principal one, on the gulf, is partially obstructed by great banks of sand that have accumulated at the mouth of the Chow Phya. Ships of ordinary burden, however, can cross these banks at high tide, and in a few hours cast anchor in the heart of the capital, in from sixty to seventy feet of water. Here they are snug and safe. Besides, the gulf itself is free from the typhoons so destructive to shipping on the China seas.

In all the Malayan Islands there are numerous unimportant streams, which, though limited in their course, form excellent harbors at their debouchement on the coast. The eastern regions of Laos and Cambodia are watered by the river Meikhong, which has a course of nearly a thousand miles; but its navigation, like that of the Meinam at its mouth, is impeded by sand-banks. The smaller streams, Chantabun, Pet Rue, and Tha Chang, all run into the Meikhong, which, mingling its waters with those of the Meinam, flows through Chiengmai, receives the waters of Phitsalok, and then, diverging by many channels, inundates the great plain of Siam once every year, in the month of June. By the end of August this entire region has become one vast sheet of water, so that

* "Mother of Waters," — a common Siamese term for all large streams.

boats traverse it in every direction without injury to the young rice springing up beneath them.

The climate of Siam is more or less hot according to the latitude ; only continual bathing can render it endurable. There are but two seasons, the wet and the dry. As soon as the southwest monsoon sets in, masses of spongy *cumuli* gather on the summits of the western mountains, giving rise to furious squalls about sunset, and dispersing in peals of thunder and torrents of refreshing rain. From the beginning to the end of the rainy season, this succession of phenomena is repeated every evening. The monsoon from the north brings an excess of rain, and the thermometer falls. With the return of the dry season the air becomes comparatively cool, and most favorable to health ; this continues from October to January. The dews are extremely heavy in the months of March and April. At dawn the atmosphere is impregnated with a thick fog, which, as the sun rises, descends in dews so abundant that trees, plants, and grass drip as from a recent shower of rain.

The population of Siam is still a matter of uncertainty ; but it is officially estimated at from six to seven millions of souls, comprising Siamese or Thai-Malay, Laotians, Cambodians, Peguans, Kariens, Shans, and Loas.

Siam produces enormous quantities of excellent rice, of which there are forty distinct varieties ; and her sugar is esteemed the best in the world. Her rivers and lakes abound in fish, as well as in turtles and aquatic birds. The exports are rice, sugar, cotton, tobacco, hemp, cutch, fish (salted and dried), cocoanut oil, beeswax, dried fruits, gamboge, cardamoms, betel-nuts, pepper, various gums and barks, sapan-wood, eagle-wood, rosewood, kracheewood, ebony, ivory, raw silk, buffalo-hides, tiger-skins, armadillo-skins, elephants' tusks and bones, rhinoceros bones, turtle-shells, peacocks' tails, bird's-nests, kingfishers' feathers, &c.

The revenue arising from duties and tolls on imported and native produce being mostly collected in kind, only a small part is converted into specie; the rest is distributed in part payment of salaries to the dependants of the court, whose name is legion. Princes of the blood royal, high officers of state, provincial governors, and most of the judges, receive grants of provinces, districts, villages, and farms, to support their several dignities and reward their services; and the rents, fees, fines, bribes, and sops of these assignments are collected by them for their own behoof. Thus, to one man are given the fees, to another the fines or bribes, which custom has attached to his functions; to others are alloted offices, by virtue of which certain imposts are levied; to this man the land; to another the waters of rivers and canals; to a third the fruit-bearing trees. But money is distributed with a niggard hand, and only once a year. Every officer of revenue is permitted to pocket, and " charge to salary," a part of all that he collects in taxes, fines, extortions, bribes, gifts, and " testimonials."

The rulers of Laos pay to the crown of Siam a tribute of gold and silver " trees," rings set with gems, and chains of solid gold. The trees, which appear to be composed entirely of the precious metals, are really nothing more than cylinders and tubes of tin, substantially gilt or plated, designed to represent the graceful clove-tree indigenous to that part of the country; the leaves and blossoms, however, are of solid gold and silver. Each tree is planted in an artificial gilt mound, and is worth from five hundred to seven hundred ticals, while the chains and rings are decorated with large and pure rubies.

The raw silk, elephants' tusks, and other rare products of Siam, are highly prized by the Mohammedan traders, who compete one with another in shipping them for the Bombay markets. They are usually put up at auction;

and, strange to say, the auctioneers are women of the royal harem, the favorite concubines of the First King. The shrewd Moslem broker, turning a longing eye upon the precious stores of the royal warehouses, employs his wife, or a trusty slave, to approach this Nourmahal or that Rose-in-bloom with presents, and promises of generous premium to her whose influence shall procure for the bidder the acceptance of his proposal. By a system of secret service peculiar to these traders, the amount of the last offer is easily discovered, and the new bidder "sees that" (if I may be permitted to amuse myself with the phraseology of the Mississippi bluff-player) and "goes" a few ticals "better." There are always several enterprising Stars of the Harem ready to vary the monotony by engaging in this unromantic business; and the agitation among the "sealed" sisterhood, though by no means boisterous, is lively, though all have tact to appear indifferent in the presence of their awful lord. The meagreness of the royal allowance of pin-money is the consideration that renders the prize important in the eyes of each of the competitors; and yet it is strange, in all the feminine vanity and vexation of spirit that the occasion engenders, how little of jealous bitterness and heartburning is directed against the lucky lady. The competitors agree upon a favorable opportunity to present the tenders of their respective clients to his Majesty. Each selecting the most costly and attractive of her bribes, and displaying them to advantage on a tray of gold, lays the written bid on the top; or with a shrewd device of the maternal instinct, so fertile in pretty tricks of artfulness, places it in the hands of a pet child, who is taught to present it winningly as the king descends to his midday meal. The attention of his Majesty is attracted by the display of showy toys; he deigns to inquire as to the donors; the "sealed proposals" are respectfully, and doubtless with more or less coquetry, pressed upon him; and the matter is then and there concluded, almost invariably in favor of the highest bidder. This semi-romantic mode of traffic was gravely encouraged by his late Majesty, for the benefit of his favorites of the harem; and great store of produce, of the finer varieties, was thus disposed of in the palace.

The poll-tax on the Chinese, levied once in three years, is paid in bullion.

The annual income of the public treasury rarely exceeds the outgo; but whatever the state of the exchequer, and of the funds reserved for the service of the state, the personal resources of the monarch are always most abundant. Nor do the great sums lavished upon his favorites and children deplete, in any respect, his vast treasures, because they are all supported by grants of land, monopolies of market, special taxes, tithes, *douceurs*, and other patrimonial or tributary provisions. A certain emolument is also derived from the valuable mines of the country, though, poorly worked as they are, but small importance has as yet been ascribed to these as a source of revenue; yet the gold of Bhangtaphan is esteemed the purest and most ductile in the world. Beside mines of iron, antimony, gold, and silver, there are quarries of white marble. The extraordinary number of idols and works of art cast in metal seems to indicate that these mines were once largely worked; and it is believed that the vast quantities of gold which for centuries has been consumed in the construction of images and the adornment of temples, pagodas, and palaces, were drawn from them. The country abounds in pits, bearing marks of great age; and there are also remains of many furnaces, which are said to have been abandoned in the wars with Pegu. Mineral springs — copious and, no doubt, valuable — are numerous in some parts of the country.

The exports of Siam are various and profitable; and of the raw materials, teak timber is entitled to the first consideration. The domestic consumption of this most useful wood in the construction of dwellings, sacred edifices, ships, and boats, is enormous; yet the forests traversed by the great rivers seem inexhaustible, and the supply continues so abundant that the variations in the price are very slight. The advantage the country must derive from her extensive commerce in a commodity so valuable may hardly be overrated.

Next in importance are the native sugars, rice, cotton, and silk, which find their way in large quantities to the markets of China and Hindostan. Among other articles of crude produce may be mentioned ivory * (a single fine tusk being often valued at five thousand dollars), wax, lead, copper, tin, amber, indigo, tobacco, honey, and bird's-nests. There are also precious stones of several varieties, and the famous gold of Bhangtaphan. Forty different kinds of rice are named, but these may properly be reduced to four classes, — the Common or table, the Small-grained or mountain, the Glutinous, and the Vermilion rice. From the glutinous rice arrack is distilled. The areca, or pinang-nut, and the betel, are used almost universally, chewed with lime, the lime, — being dyed with turmeric, which imparts to it a rich vermilion tint; the areca-nut is also used in dying cotton thread.

The characteristic traits of the Siamese Court are *hauteur*, insolent indifference, and ostentation, the natural features and expression of tyranny; and every artifice that power and opulence can devise is employed to inspire the minds of the common people with trembling awe and devout veneration for their sovereign master. Though the late Supreme King wisely reformed certain of the stunning customs of the court with more modest innovations,

---

* In Siam reserved as a royal appropriation.

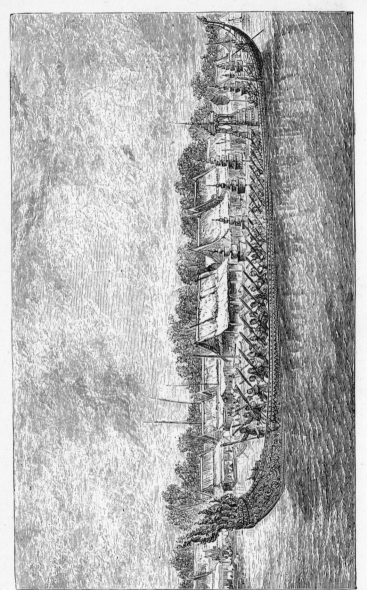

A Royal Barge.

nevertheless he rarely went abroad without extravagant display, especially in his annual visitations to the temples. These were performed in a style studiously contrived to strike the beholder with astonishment and admiration.

The royal state barge, one hundred cubits long, beside being elaborately carved, and inlaid with bits of crystal, porcelain, mother-of-pearl, and jade, is richly enamelled and gilt. The stem, which rises ten or eleven feet from the bows, represents the *nagha mustakha sapta,* the seven-headed serpent or alligator. A phrasat, or elevated throne (also termed *p'hra-the-nang*), occupies the centre, supported by four pillars. The extraordinary beauty of the inlaying of shells, mother-of-pearl, crystal, and precious stones of every color, the splendor of the gilding, and the elegance of the costly kinkob curtains with which it is hung, combine to render this one of the most striking and beautiful objects to be seen on the Meinam. The barge is usually manned by one hundred and fifty men, their paddles gilt and silver-tipped.

This government reproduces, in many of its shows of power, pride, and ostentation, a *tableau vivant* of European rule in the darker ages, when, on the decline of Roman dominance, the principles of feudal dependence were established by barbarians from the North. Under such a system, it is impossible to ascertain, or to represent by any standards of currency, the amount of the royal revenues and treasures. But it is known that the riches of the Siamese monarch are immense, and that a magnificent share of the legal plunder drawn into the royal treasury is sunk there, and never returns into circulation again. The hoarding of money seems to be the cherished practice of all Oriental rulers, and even a maxim of state policy ; and that the general diffusion of property among his subjects offers the only safe assurance of prosperity for himself and stability for his throne is the last precept of prudence an Asiatic monarch ever learns.

The armies of Siam are raised on the spur of the moment, as it were, for any pressing emergency. When troops are to be called out, a royal command, addressed to all viceroys and governors, requires them to raise their respective quotas, and report to a commander-in-chief at a general rendezvous. These recruits are clothed, equipped with arms and ammunition, and " subsisted" with daily rations of rice, oil, etc., but are not otherwise paid. The small standing army, which serves as the nucleus upon which these irregulars are gathered and formed, consists of infantry, cavalry, elephant-riders, archers, and private body-guards, paid at the rate of from five to ten dollars a month, with clothing and rations. The infantry are armed with muskets and sabres ; the cavalry, with bows and arrows as well as spears ; but the spear, which is from six to seven feet long, is the favorite weapon of this arm of the service, and they handle it with astonishing dexterity. The king's private body-guards are well paid, clothed, and quartered, having their stations and barracks within the palace walls and near the most attractive streets and avenues, while other troops are lodged outside.

It is customary to detain the families of conscripts in the districts to which they belong, as prisoners on parole, — hostages for the good conduct of their young men in the army ; and for the desertion or treachery of the soldier, his wife or children, mother or sisters, as the case may be, are tortured, or even executed, without compunction or remorse. The long and peaceful reign of the late king, however, has almost effaced from the minds of the youth of Siam the remembrance of such monstrous oppressions.

The Siamese are but indifferent sailors, their nautical

excursions being mainly confined to short coasting trips, or boating in safe and familiar channels. The more adventurous export trade is carried on almost wholly by foreigners. About one thousand war-boats constitute the bulk of the navy. These are constructed from the solid bole of the teak-tree, excavated partly with fire, partly with the adze ; and, while they are commonly from eighty to a hundred feet long, the breadth rarely exceeds eight or nine feet, though the apparent width is increased by the addition of a sort of light gallery. They are made to carry fifty or sixty rowers, with short oars working on a pivot. The prow, which is solid, has a flat terrace, on which, for the king's up-country excursions, they mount a small field-piece, a nine or a twelve pounder. There are also several men-of-war belonging to the government, built by European engineers.

The number of vessels in the merchant marine cannot be great. Dwelling so long in peace and security at home, the tastes and the energies of the Siamese people have been confirmed, by their political circumstances, in that inclination toward agricultural rather than commercial pursuits which their geographical conditions naturally engender. The extreme fertility of the soil, watered by innumerable streams, and intersected in every direction by a network of capacious canals (of which the Klong Yai, Klong Bangkok-noi, and Klong P'hra-cha-dee, are the most remarkable); the generating heats of the climate; the teeming plains of the upper provinces, bulwarked by mighty mountains; and, above all, that magnificent mother, the Meinam, winding in her beauty and bounty through a vast and lovely vale to the sea, in her course subjecting all things to the enriching and adorning influence of her touch, — all combine by their irresistible inducements to determine the native to the tilling of the ground.

13 *

Nothing can be more delightful than an excursion through the country immediately after the subsidence of the floods. Then nature is draped in hues as charming as they are various, from the palest olive to the liveliest green; broad fields wave with tall golden spires of grain, or are dotted with tufted sheaves heavy with generous crops; the refreshed air is perfumed with the fragrance of the orange, lemon, citron, and other tropical fruits and flowers; and on every side the landscape is a scene of lovely meadows, alive with flocks and herds, and busy with herdsmen, husbandmen, and gardeners.

The most considerable of the many canals by which communication is maintained with all parts of the country is Klong Yai, the Great Canal, supposed to have been begun in the reign of Phya Tâk. It is nearly a hundred cubits deep, twenty Siamese fathoms broad, and forty miles long. Bangkok has been aptly styled "the Venice of the Orient"; for not only the villages thickly studding the banks of the Meinam, but the remoter hamlets as well, even to the confines of the kingdom, have each its own canals. In fact, the lands annually inundated by the Mother of Waters are so extensive, and for the most part lie so low, and the number of water-ducts, natural and artificial, is so great, that of all the torrents that descend upon the country in the months of June, July, and August (when the whole land is as a sea, in which towns and villages show like docks connected by drawbridges, with little islets between of groves and orchards, whose tops alone are visible), not a tithe ever returns to the ocean.

The modern bridges of Siam, which are mostly of iron in the European style, are made to be drawn for the passage of the King's barge, since the royal head may not without desecration pass under anything trodden by the foot of man. The more ancient bridges, however, are of stone and brick; and here and there are strange artificial lakes, partly filled up with the *débris* of temples that once stood on their banks. Of roads there are but few that are good, and all are of comparatively recent construction.

XXIX.

THE RUINS OF CAMBODIA.* — AN EXCURSION TO THE NAGHKON WATT.

OUR journey from Bangkok to Kabin derived its memorable interest from those features and feelings which join to compose the characteristic romance of Eastern travel by unhackneyed ways, — the wild freedom of the plain, the tortuous, suspicious mountain track, the tangled jungle, the bewildering wastes and glooms of an unexplored region, with their suggestions of peril and adventure, and especially that glorious participation in the enlargement and liberty of an Eastern wanderer's life which these afford. Once you begin to feel that, you will be happy, whether on an elephant or in a buffalo-cart, — the very privations and perils including a charm of excitement all unknown to the formal European tourist.

The rainbow mists of morning still lay low on the plain, as yet unlifted by the breeze that, laden with odor and song, gently rocked the higher branches in the forest, as our elephants pressed on, heavily but almost noiselessly, over a parti-colored carpet of wild-flowers. Strange birds

---

* The Cambodian was, without doubt, in its day, one of the most powerful of the empires of the East. As to its antiquity, two opinions prevail, — one ascribing to it a duration of 1,300 years, the other of 2,400. The native historians reckon 2,400 years from the building of the Naghkon Watt, or Naghkon Ongkhoor ; but this computation, not agreeing with the mythological traditions of the country, which date from the Year of the World 205, is not accepted as authentic by the more learned Cambodians.

darted from bough to bough among the wild myrtles and limes, and great green and golden lizards gleamed through the shrubbery as we approached Siemrâp.

The more extensive and remarkable ruins of Cambodia seem concentrated in this part of the country, though they are by no means confined to it, but are found widely scattered over the neighboring territories.

From Sisuphon we diverged in a northeasterly direction, and at evening found ourselves in the quaint, antique town of Phanomsôk, half ruined and deserted, where the remains of a magnificent palace can still be traced.

The country between Cambodia and Siam is an inclined plane falling off to the sea, beginning from the Khoa Don Rèke, or highlands of Korat, which constitutes the first platform of the terraces that gradually ascend to the mountain chain of Laos, and thence to the stupendous Himalayas.

Khoa Don Rèke ("the Mountain which Bears on the Shoulders," the Cambodian Atlas) includes in its domain the Dong Phya Fai (" Forest of the Lord of Fire "), whence many tributary streams flow into the beautiful Pachim River.

At sunrise next morning we resumed our journey, and after a long day of toiling through treacherous marshes and tangled brushwood came at sunset upon an object whose presence there was a wonder, and its past a puzzle, — a ridge or embankment of ten or twelve feet elevation, which, to our astonishment, ran high and dry through the swampy lowlands. In the heart of an interminable forest it stretches along one side of the tangled trail, in some places walling it in, at others crossing it at right angles , now suddenly diving into the depths of the forest, now reappearing afar off, as if to mock our cautious progress, and invite us to follow it. The eye, wistfully pursuing its eccentric sweep, suddenly loses it in impenetrable shadows. There is not a vestige of any other ruin near it, and the long lines it here and there shows, ghostly white in the moonlight, seem like spectral strands of sand.

Our guides tell us this isolated ridge was once the great highway of ancient Cambodia, that it can be traced from the neighborhood of Nohk Burree to Naghkon Watt, and thence to the very heart of Cochin China; and one assures us that no man has ever seen the end of it.

So on we went, winding our devious way over pathless ground, now diving into shady valleys, now mounting to sunny eminences where the breeze blew free and the eye could range far and wide, but not to find aught that was human. Gradually the flowering shrubs forsook us, and dark forest trees pressed grimly around, as we traversed the noble stone bridges that those grand old Cambodians loved to build over comparatively insignificant streams. The moon, touching with fantastic light the crumbling arches and imparting a charm of illusion to the scene, the clear spangled sky, the startling voices of the night, and the influence of the unknown, the mysterious, and the weird, overcame us like a dream. Truly there is naught of the commonplace or vulgar in this land of ruins and legends, and the foretaste of the wonders we were about to behold met our view in the great bridges.

Taphan Hin (" the Stone Bridge ") and the finer and more artistic Taphan Thevadah ("the Angel's Bridge ") are both imposing works. Arches, still resting firmly on their foundations, buttressed by fifty great pillars of stone, support a structure about five hundred feet long and eighty broad. The road-bed of these bridges is formed of immense blocks or beams of stone, laid one upon another, and so adjusted that their very weight serves to keep the arches firm.

In a clearing in the forest, near a rivulet called by the

Cambodians *Sthieng Sinn* (" Sufficient to our Need "), we encamped ; and, having rested and supped, again followed our guides over the foaming stream, and recrossed the Stone Bridge on foot, marvelling at the work of a race of whose existence the Western nations know nothing, who have no name in history, yet who builded in a style surpassing in boldness of conception, grandeur of proportions, and delicacy of design, the best works of the modern world, — stupendous, beautiful, enduring !

The material is mostly freestone, but a flinty conglomerate appears wherever the work is exposed to the action of the water.

Formerly a fine balustrade crowned the bridge on both sides, but it has been broken down. The ornamental parts of these massive structures seem to have been the only portions the invading vandals of the time could destroy.

The remains of the balustrade show that it consisted of a series of long quarry stones, on the ridges of which caryatidian pillars, representing the seven-headed serpent, supported other slabs grooved along the rim to receive semi-convex stones with arabesque sculptures, affording a hint of ancient Cambodian art.

On the left bank we found the remains of a staircase leading down to the water, not far from a spot where a temple formerly stood.

Next morning we crossed the Taphan Teph, or Heavenly Bridge, — like the Taphan Hin and the Taphan Thevadah a work of almost superhuman magnitude and solidity.

Leaving the bridges, our native pilots turned off from the ancient causeway to grope through narrow miry paths in the jungle.

On the afternoon of the same day we arrived at another stone bridge, over the Paleng River.   This, according to our guides, was abandoned by the builders, because the country was invaded by the hostile hordes who destroyed Naghkon Watt. Slowly crumbling among the wild plantains and the pagan lotoses and lilies, these bridges seem to constitute the sole memorial, in the midst of that enchanting desolation, of a once proud and populous capital.

From the Paleng River, limpid and cheerful, a day's journey brought us to the town of Siemrâp; and, after an unnecessary delay of several hours, we started with lighter pockets for the ruins of Naghkon Watt.

Naghkon, or Ongkoor, is supposed to have been the royal city of the ancient kingdom of Cambodia, or Khaimain, of which the only traditions that remain describe in wild extravagances its boundless territory; its princes without number who paid tribute in gold, silver, and precious stuffs; its army of seventy thousand war elephants, two hundred thousand horsemen, and nearly six millions of foot soldiers; and its royal treasure-houses covering "three hundred miles of ground." In the heart of this lonely region, in a district still bearing the name of Ongkoor, and quite apart from the ruined temples that abound hard by, we found architectural remains of such exceeding grandeur, with ruins of temples and palaces which must have been raised at so vast a cost of labor and treasure, that we were overwhelmed with astonishment and admiration.

What manner of people were these?

Whence came their civilization and their culture?

And why and whither did they disappear from among the nations of the earth?

The site of the city is in itself unique. Chosen originally for the strength of its position, it yet presents none of the features which should mark the metropolis of a powerful people. It seems to stand aloof from the world, exempt from its passions and aspirations, and shunning even its thrift. Confronting us with its towering portal, overlaid with colossal hieroglyphics, the majestic ruin of the watt stands like a petrified dream of some Michael Angelo of the giants — more impressive in its loneliness, more elegant and animated in its grace, than aught that Greece and Rome have left us, and addressing us with a significance all the sadder and more solemn for the desolation and barbarism which surround it.

Unhappily, the shocks of war, seconding the slowly grinding mills of time, have left but few of these noble monuments ; and slowly, but ruthlessly, the work of destruction and decay goes on.

Vainly may we seek for any chronicle of the long line of monarchs who must have swayed the sceptre of the once powerful empire of Maha Naghkon. Only a vague tradition has come down, of a celestial prince to whom the fame of founding the great temple is supposed to belong; and of an Egyptian king, who, for his sacrilege, was changed into a leper. An interesting statue, representing the latter, still stands in one of the corridors, — somewhat mutilated, but sufficiently well preserved to display a marked contrast to the physical type of the present race of Cambodians.

The inscriptions with which some of the columns are covered are illegible ; and if you question the natives as to the origin of Naghkon Watt, they will tell you that it was the work of the Leper King, or of P'hra-Inn-Sûen, King of Heaven, or of giants, or that " it made itself."

These magnificent edifices seem to have been designed for places of worship rather than of royal habitation, for nearly all are Buddhist temples.

The statues and sculptures on the walls of the outer corridor are in *alto relievo*, and generally life-size. · The

T

statue of the Leper King, set up in a sort of pavilion, is moderately colossal, and is seated in a tranquil and noble attitude ; the head especially is a masterpiece, the features being classic and of manly beauty.

Approaching the temple of Ongkoor, the most beautiful and best preserved of these glorious remains, the traveller is compensated with full measure of wonder and delight for all the fatigues and hardships of his journey. Complete as is the desolation, a strange air of luxury hangs over all, as though the golden glow of sunshine and the refreshing gloom were for the glory and the ease of kings.

At each angle of the temple are two enormous lions, hewn, pedestal and all, from a single block. A flight of stone steps leads up to the first platform, of terraces. To reach the main entrance from the north staircase we traverse a noble causeway, which midway crosses a deep and wide moat.that seems to surround the building.

The main entrance is by a long gallery, having a superb central tower, with two others of less height on each side. The portico of each of the three principal towers is formed by four projecting columns, with a spacious staircase between. At either extremity are similar porticos, and beyond these is a very lofty door, or gateway, covered with gigantic hieroglyphs, where gods and warriors hang as if self-supported between earth and sky. Then come groves of columns that in girth and height might rival the noblest oaks. Every pillar and every part of the wall is so crowded with sculptures that the whole temple seems hung with petrified tapestry.

On the west side, the long gallery is flanked by two rows of almost square columns. The blank windows are cut out of the wall, and finished with stone railings or

RUINS OF THE NAGHKON WATT.

balconies of curiously twisted columns ; and the different compartments are equally covered with sculptures of subjects taken from the Ramayâna. Here are Lakshman and Hanuman leading their warriors against Rawana, — some with ten heads, others with many arms. The monkeys are building the stone bridge over the sea. Rama is seen imploring the aid of the celestial protector, who sits on high, in grand and dreamy contemplation. Rama's father is challenging the enemy, while Rawana is engaged in combat with the leader of the many-wheeled chariots. There are many other figures of eight-handed deities ; and all are represented with marvellous skill in grouping and action.

The entire structure is roofed with tiers of hewn stone, which is also sculptured ; and remains of a ceiling may still be traced. The symmetrical wings terminate in three spacious pavilions and this imposing colonnade, which, by its great length, height, and harmonious proportions, is conspicuous from a great distance, and forms an appropriate vestibule to so grand a temple.

Traversing the building, we cross another and finer causeway, formed of great blocks of stone carefully joined, and bordered with a handsome balustrade, partly in ruins, very massive, and covered with sculptures.

On either side are six great platforms, with flights of steps ; and on each we find remains of the seven-headed serpent, — in some parts mutilated, but on the whole sufficiently preserved to show distinctly the several heads, some erect as if guarding the entrance, others drawn back in a threatening attitude. A smaller specimen is nearly perfect and very beautiful.

We passed into an adytum, wardered by gigantic effigies whose mystic forms we could hardly trace ; above us that ponderous roof, tier on tier of solid stone, upheld by enormous columns, and incrusted with strange carvings.

Everywhere we found fresh objects of wonder, and each new spot, as we explored it, seemed the greatest wonder of all.

In the centre of the causeway are two elegant pavilions with porticos ; and at the foot of the terrace we come upon two artificial lakes, which in the dry season must be supplied either by means of a subterranean aqueduct or by everlasting springs.

A balustrade not unlike that of the causeway, erected upon a sculptured basement, starts from the foot of the terrace and runs quite round the temple, with arms, or branches, descending at regular intervals.

The terrace opens into a grand court, crowded with a forest of magnificent columns with capitals, each hewn from a single block of stone. The basement, like every other part of the building, is ornamented in varied and animated styles; and every slab of the vast pile is covered with exquisite carvings representing the lotos, the lily, and the rose, with arabesques wrought with the chisel with astonishing taste and skill. The porticos are supported by sculptured columns ; and the terraces, which form a cross, have three flights of steps, at each of which are four colossal lions, reclining upon pedestals.

The temple is thus seen to consist of three distinct parts, raised in terraces one above the other. The central tower of the five within the inner circle forms an octagon, with four larger and four smaller sides. On each of the four larger faces is a colossal figure of Buddha, which overlooks from its eminence the surrounding country.

This combination of four Buddhas occurs frequently among the ruins of Cambodia. The natives call it *P'hra Mook Bulu* ("Lord of Four Faces"), though not only the face, but the whole body, is fourfold.

A four-faced god of majestic proportions presides over the principal entrance to the temple, and is called

Bhrama, or, by corruption, *Phrâm,* signifying divine protection.

As the four cardinal points of the horizon naturally form a cross, called "phram," so we invariably find the cross in the plan of these religious monuments of ancient Cambodia, and even in the corridors, intersecting each other at right angles.* These corridors are roofed with great blocks of stone, projecting over each other so as to form an arch, and, though laid without cement, so accurately adjusted as to leave scarcely a trace of the joinings. The galleries of the temple also form a rectangle. The ceilings are vaulted, and the roofs supported by double rows of columns, cut from a single block.

There are five staircases on the west side, five on the east, and three on each of the remaining sides. Each of the porticos has three distinct roofs raised one above the other, thus nobly contributing to the monumental effect of the architecture.

In some of the compartments the entire space is occupied with representations of the struggle between angels and giants for possession of the snake-god, Sarpa-deva, more commonly called *Phya Naghk.* The angels are seen dragging the seven-headed monster by the tail, while the giants hold fast by the heads. In the midst is Vishnu, riding on the world-supporting turtle.

The most interesting of all the sculptures at Naghkon Watt are those that appear to represent a procession of warriors, some on foot, others mounted on horses, tigers, birds, and nondescript creatures, each chief on an elephant at the head of his followers. I counted more than a thousand figures in one compartment, and observed with admiration that the artist had succeeded in portraying the different races in all their physical characteristics,

* The cross is the distinctive character and sign for the Doctors of Reason in the primitive Buddhism of Kasyapa.

from the flat-nosed savage, and the short-haired and broad-faced Laotian, to the more classic profile of the Rajpoot, armed with sword and shield, and the bearded Moor. A panorama in life-size of the diverse nationalities, it yet displays, in the physical conformation of each race, a re-markable predominance of the Hellenic type — not in the features and profiles alone, but equally in the fine atti-tudes of the warriors and horsemen.

The bass-reliefs of another peristyle represent a combat between the king of apes and the king of angels, and if not the death, at least the defeat, of the former. On an adjoining slab is a boat filled with stalwart rowers with long beards, — a group very admirable in attitude and expression. In fact, it is in these bass-reliefs that the greatest delicacy of touch and the finest finish are mani-fest.

On the south side we found representations of an an-cient military procession. The natives interpret these as three connected allegories, symbolizing heaven, earth, and hell; but it is more probable that they record the history of the methods by which the savage tribes were reclaimed by the colonizing foreigners, and that they have an inti-mate connection with the founding of these monuments.

One compartment represents an ovation : certain person-ages are seen seated on a dais, surrounded by many women, with caskets and fans in their hands, while the men bring flowers and bear children in their arms.

In another place, those who have rejected the new religion and its priests are precipitated into a pit of perdition, in the midst of which sits the judge, with his executioners, with swords in their hands, while the guilty are dragged before him by the hair and feet. In the distance is a furnace, and another crowd of " infidels " under punishment. But the converted (the " born again ") are conducted into palaces, which are represented on the

SCULPTURES OF THE NAGHKON WATT.

upper compartments. In these happier figures the features as well as the attitudes denote profound repose, and in the faces of many of the women and children one may trace lines of beauty and tender grace.

On the east side a number of men, in groups on either hand, are in the act of dragging in contrary directions the great seven-headed dragon. One mighty angel watches the struggle with interest, while many lesser angels float overhead. Below is a great lake or ocean, in which are fishes, aquatic animals, and sea-monsters.

On another panel an angel is seated on a mountain (probably Mount Meru), and other angels, with several heads, assist or encourage those who are contending for possession of the serpent. To the right are another triumphal procession and a battle scene, with warriors mounted on elephants, unicorns, griffins, eagles with peacocks' tails, and other fabulous creatures, while winged dragons draw the chariots.

On the north side is another battle-piece, the most conspicuous figure being that of a chief mounted on the shoulders of a giant, who holds in each hand the foot of another fighting giant. Near the middle of this peristyle is a noble effigy of a royal conqueror, with long flowing beard, attended by courtiers with hands clasped on their breasts. These figures are all in *alto relievo*, and well executed.

The greater galleries are connected with two smaller ones, which in turn communicate with two colonnades in the form of a cross; the roofs of these are vaulted. Four rows of square columns, each still hewn from a single block, extend along the sides of the temple. These are covered with statues and bass-reliefs, many of the former being in a state of dilapidation which, considering the extreme hardness of the stone, indicates great age, while others are true *chefs-d'œuvre*.

The entire structure forms a square, and every part is admirable both in general effect and detail. There are twelve superb staircases, the four in the middle having from fifty to sixty steps, each step a single slab. At each angle is a tower. The central tower, larger and higher than the others, communicates with the lateral galleries by colonnades, covered, like the galleries themselves with a double roof. Opposite each of the twelve staircases is a portico with windows resembling in form and dimensions those described above.

In front of each colonnade connected with the tower is a dark, narrow chapel, to which there is an ascent of eight steps ; each of these chapels (which do not communicate with each other) contains a gigantic idol, carved in the solid wall, and at its feet another, of the same proportions, sleeping.

This mighty pile, the wondrous Naghkon Watt, is nearly three miles in circumference ; the walls are from seventy to eighty feet high, and twenty feet thick.

We wandered in astonishment, and almost with awe, through labyrinths of courts, cloisters, and chambers, encountering at every turn some new marvel, unheard of, undreamed of, until then. Even the walls of the outer courts were sculptured with whole histories of wars and conquests, in forms that seemed to live and fight again. Prodigious in size and number are the blocks of stone piled in those walls and towers. We counted five thousand and three hundred *solid* columns. What a mighty host of builders must that have been ! And what could have been their engines and their means of transport, seeing that the mountains from which the stone was quarried are nearly two days' journey from the temple ?

All the mouldings, sculptures, and bass-reliefs seem to have been executed after the walls and pillars were in their places ; and everywhere the stones are fitted together in a manner so perfect that the joinings are not easy to find. There is neither mortar nor mark of the chisel; the surfaces are as smooth as polished marble.

On a fallen column, under a lofty and most beautiful arch, we sat, and rested our weary, excited eyes on the wild but quiet landscape below; then slowly, reluctantly departed, feeling that the world contains no monument more impressive, more inspiring, than, in its desolation, and yet wondrous preservation, the temple of Maha Naghkon Watt.

Next morning our elephants bore us back to Siemrâp through an avenue of colonnades similar to that by which we had come; and as we advanced we could still descry other gates and pillars far in the distance, marking the line of some ancient avenue to this amazing temple.

XXX

THE LEGEND OF THE MAHA NAGHKON.*

MANY hundreds of thousands of years ago, when P'hra Atheitt, the Sun-god, was nearer to earth than he is now, and the city of the gods could be seen with mortal eyes, — when the celestial sovereigns, P'hra Indara and P'hra Insawara, came down from Meru, the sacred mountain, to hold high converse with mortal kings, sages, and heroes, — when the moon and the stars brought tidings of good-will to men, and wisdom flourished, love and happiness were spread abroad, and sorrow, suffering, disease, old age, and death were almost banished, — there lived in Thaisiampois a mighty monarch whose years could hardly be numbered, so many were they and so long. And yet he was not old; such were the warmth and strength and vigor imparted by the near glories of the P'hra Atheitt, that the span of human life was lengthened unto a thousand, and even fifteen hundred years. The days of the King Sudarsana had been prolonged beyond those of the oldest of his predecessors, for the sake of his exceeding wisdom and goodness. But yet this King was troubled; he had no son, and the thought of dying without leaving behind him one worthy to represent his name and race was grievous to him. So, by the advice of the wise men of his kingdom, he caused prayers and offerings to be made in all the temples, and took to wife the beautiful Princess Thawadee.

* Translated from a MS. presented to the author by the Supreme King of Siam.

At that very time P'hra Indara, ruler of the highest heaven, dreamed a dream; and behold! in his sleep a costly jewel fell from his mouth to the lower earth; whereat P'hra Indara was troubled. Assembling all the hosts of heaven, the angels, and the genii, he showed them his dream, but they could not interpret it. Last of all, he told it to his seven sons; but from them likewise its meaning was hidden. A second time P'hra Indara dreamed, and yet a third time, that a more and more costly jewel had fallen from his lips, and at last, when he awoke, the interpretation was revealed to his own thought, — that one of his sons should condescend to the form of humanity, and dwell on the earth, and be a great teacher of men.

Then the King of Heaven imparted to the celestial princes the meaning of the threefold vision, and demanded which of them would consent to become man.

The divine princes heard, and answered not a word; till the youngest and best-beloved of Heaven opened his lips and spake, saying: "Hear, O my Lord and Father! I have yearned toward the race thou hast created out of the fire and flame of thy breast and the smoke of thy nostrils. Let me go unto them, that I may teach them the wisdom of truth."

Then P'hra Indara gave him leave to depart on his mission of love; and all the hosts of heaven, knowing that he should never more gladden their hearts with his presence, accompanied him, sorrowful, to the foot of Mount Meru · and immediately a blazing star shot from the mount, and burst over the palace of Thaisiampois.

That night the gracious Princess Thawadee conceived and became with child, and the P'hra Somannass was no longer a prince of the highest heaven.

The Princess Thawadee had been the only and darling daughter of a mighty king, and still mourned her separa-

tion from her beloved sire. Her only solace was to sit in
the phrasat of the Grand Palace, and look with longing
toward her early home. Here, day after day, she sat with
her maidens, weaving flowers, and singing low the songs
of her childhood. When this became known abroad
among the multitude, they gathered from every side to
behold one so famed for her goodness and beauty.

Thus by degrees her interest was aroused. She became
thoughtful for her people, and presently found happiness
in dispensing food, raiment, and comfort to the poor who
flocked to see her.

One day, as she was reposing in the porch after her
customary benefactions, a cloud of birds, flying eastward,
fell dead as they passed over the phrasat. The sages
and soothsayers of the court were terrified. What might
the omen be ? Long and anxious were their counsels,
and grievous their perturbations one with another; until
at last an aged warrior, who had conquered many armies
and subjugated kingdoms, declaring that as faithful servants they should lay the weighty matter before their
lord, bade all the court follow him, and approached his
sovereign, saying : —

"Long live P'hra Chow P'hra Sudarsana, lord and king
of our happy land, wherefrom sorrow and suffering and
death are wellnigh banished ! Let him investigate with
a true spirit and a clear mind the matter we bring for
judgment, even though it be to the tearing out of his
own heart and casting it away from him."

" Speak," said the King, " and fear not ! Has it ever
been thought that evil is dearer unto me than good ? Even
to the tearing out of my heart and casting it to dogs
shall justice be rendered in the land."

Then the sages, soothsayers, and warriors spake as with
one voice: " It is well known unto the lord our King,
that the Queen, our lovely lady Thawadee, is with child.

But what manner of birth is this that she has conceived, in that it has already brought grief and death into the land ? For as the Queen sat in the porch of the temple, a great flight of birds that hastened, thirsty, toward the valleys of the east, when they would have passed over the phrasat were struck dead, as by an unseen spirit of mischief. Let the King search this matter, and put away the strange thing of evil out of our land, lest it make a greater sorrow."

When the King heard these words, he was sore smitten, and hung down his head, and knew not what to say; for the Queen, so gentle and beautiful, was very dear to him. But, remembering his royal word, he shook off his grief and took counsel with his astrologers, who had foretold that the unborn prince would prove either a glorious blessing or a dire curse to the land. And now, by the awful omen of the birds, they declared that the Queen had conceived the evil spirit Kala Mata, and that she must be put to death, she and the fiend with her.

Then the King in council commanded that the sweet young Thawadee should be set upon a floating raft, and given to the mercy of winds and waves.

But the brave chief who should have executed the sentence, overcome on beholding her beauty and innocence, interceded for her with the council; and it was finally decreed that, for pity's sake, and because the Queen was unconscious of any evil, she should not be slain, but "put away," after the dreadful birth. To this the stricken monarch thankfully agreed.

In due time the Queen was delivered of a male child, so beautiful that it filled all beholders with delight. His eyes were as sunshine, his forehead like the glow of the full moon, his lips like clustered roses, and his cry like the melody of many instruments; and the Queen loved him, and comforted herself with his beauty.

When the mother was strong again, the infant prince being then about a month old, the sentence of the council was carried into effect, and the poor princess and her child were banished forever from the beloved land of Thaisiampois.

Clasping her baby to her breast, she went forth, terrified and stunned. On and on, not knowing whither, she wandered, pressing her sleeping babe to her bosom, and moaning to the great gods above.

Then P'hra Indara, king of highest heaven, came down to earth, assumed the form and garb of a Bhramin, and followed her silently, shortening the miles and smoothing the rough places, until she reached the bank of a deep and rapid stream. Here, as she sat down, faint and footsore, to nurse her babe, there came to her a grave and venerable pilgrim, who gently questioned her sorrows and comforted her with thrilling words, saying her child was born to bring peace and happiness to earth, and not trouble and death.

Quickly Thawadee dried her tears, and consented to be led by the good old man, who had come to her as if from heaven. From under his garment he produced a shell filled with food from paradise, of which she partook with ecstasy; and gave her to drink water from everlasting springs, that overflowed her soul with perfect peace. Then he led her to a mountain, and prepared in the cleft of a rock a hiding-place for her and her child, and left her with a promise of quick return.

For fifty years she dwelt in the cave, knowing neither trouble nor weariness nor hunger, nor any of the ills of life. The young Somannass, as the good Bhramin had named him, grew to be a youth of wondrous beauty. The melody of his voice tamed the wild creatures of the forest, and charmed even the seven-headed dragons of the lake in which his mother bathed him every morning. Then again P'hra Indara appeared to them in the form and garb of the aged Bhramin ; and he rejoiced in the strength and beauty of the young Somannass, and his heart yearned after his beloved son. But, hiding his emotion, he held pleasant converse with the Queen, and begged to be permitted to take the boy away with him for a season. She consented ; and instantly, as in a flash of lightning, he transported the prince into the highest heaven, and Somannass found himself seated on a glorious throne by the side of P'hra Indara the Divine, before whom the hosts of heaven bowed in homage.

Here he was initiated in all the mysteries of life and death, with all wisdom and foresight. His celestial royal father showed him the stars coursing hither and thither on their errands of love and mercy ; showed him comets with tails of fire flashing and whizzing through the centuries, spreading confusion and havoc in their path ; showed him the spirits of rebellion and crime transfixed by the spears of the Omnipotent. He heard the music of the spheres, he tasted heavenly food, and drank of the river that flows from the footstool of the Most Highest.

And so he forgot the forlorn Queen, his mother, and desired to return to earth no more.

Then P'hra Indara laid his hand upon the brow of the lad, and showed him the generations yet to come, rejoicing in his prayers and precepts ; and Somannass, beholding, stretched his arms to the earth again. And P'hra Indara promised to build him a palace hardly less grand and fair than the heavenly abode, a temple which should be the wonder of the world, a stupendous and everlasting monument of his love to men.

So Somannass returned to the Queen, his mother ; and P'hra Indara sent down myriads of angels, with Phya Kralewana, chief of angels, to build a dwelling fit for the heavenly prince. In one night it was done, and the rising sun shone on domes like worlds and walls like armies. And because the seven-headed serpent, Phya Naghk, had shown the way to the mines of gold and silver and iron, and the quarries of marble and granite, the grateful builders laid the sign of the serpent on the foundations, terraces, and bridges; but on the walls they left the effigy of the Queen Thawadee, the beautiful and bountiful lady.

Then swift-winged angels flew to heaven, and, returning, brought fruits and flowers the most curious and exquisite; and immediately there bloomed a garden there, of such ravishing loveliness and perfume that the gods themselves delighted to visit it. Also they filled the great stables with white elephants and chargers. And then the angels transported Thawadee and Somannass to their new abode, the fame of which was so spread abroad that the great King Sudarsana, with all his court, and followers without number, and all his army, came to see it. And great was their astonishment to find again the fair and gentle Thawadee, who thus was reunited to her husband; and he took up his abode with her, and they lived together in love.

But the Prince Somannass built temples, and preached, and taught the people, and healed their infirmities, and led them in the paths of virtue and truth.

And the fame of his wisdom and goodness flew through all the lands, so that many kings became willing vassals unto him; but there came from a far-off country, where the heavens drop no rain, but where one great river suddenly floods the plains and then shrinks back into itself like a living thing, a king of lofty stature and exceeding craft. And the Prince Somannass was gracious toward him, and showed him many favors. But his heart was black and bad, and he would have turned the pure heart of the prince to worship the dragon and other beasts;

wherefore Somannass changed him into a leper, and cast him out of his palace, and caused a stone statue to be made of him, which stands to this day, a warning to all tempters and evil-doers.   And he caused the face of the great P'hra Indara to be carved on the north and on the south and on the east and on the west — so that all men might know the true God, who is God alone in heaven, Sevarg-Savan !

THE END.